Entrepreneurship and Economic Progress

Economic progress is often analyzed narrowly as income growth, but this volume shows that other aspects of progress – new and improved goods, and improved methods of production – are ultimately more significant. Not only have these other dimensions of progress been responsible for much of the increase in human welfare, they are also what drives income growth.

Progress is the result of entrepreneurship, and both entrepreneurship and this broader conception of progress have been neglected in contemporary economic analysis. This volume develops a framework that demonstrates how entrepreneurship produces economic progress, and contrasts that framework with the mainstream theory of economic growth. The contrast is interesting from an academic perspective, but there are also significant differences in policy implications.

The policy conclusions of mainstream economic growth theory focus on investment in physical and human capital and on technological improvements, whereas this volume's approach shows that an institutional structure that promotes entrepreneurship is the crucial factor that produces economic progress. *Entrepreneurship and Economic Progress* discusses the institutional features that promote entrepreneurship and draws on historical examples from the twentieth century to illustrate its major points.

Randall G. Holcombe is DeVoe Moore Professor of Economics at Florida State University, USA.

Routledge Foundations of the Market Economy
Edited by
Mario J. Rizzo
New York University

Lawrence H. White
University of Missouri at St. Louis

A central theme in this series is the importance of understanding and assessing the market economy from a perspective broader than the static economics of perfect competition and Pareto optimality. Such a perspective sees markets as causal processes generated by the preferences, expectations, and beliefs of Economic agents. The creative acts of entrepreneurship that uncover new information about preferences, prices, and technology are central to these processes with respect to their ability to promote the discovery and use of knowledge in society.

The market economy consists of a set of institutions that facilitate voluntary cooperation and exchange among individuals. These institutions include the legal and ethical framework as well as more narrowly "economic" patterns of social interaction. Thus the law, legal institutions, and cultural and ethical norms, as well as ordinary business practices and monetary phenomena, fall within the analytical domain of the economist.

Previous books in this series include:
The Meaning of Market Process
Essays in the development of modern Austrian economics
Israel M. Kirzner

Prices and Knowledge
A market-process perspective
Esteban F. Thomas

Keynes' General Theory of Interest
A reconsideration
Fiona C. Maclachlan

Laissez-Faire Banking
Kevin Dowd

Expectations and the Meaning of Institutions
Essays in economics by Ludwig Lachmann
Edited by Don Lavoie

Money and the Market
Essays on free banking
Kevin Dowd

Calculation and Coordination
Essays on socialism and transitional political economy
Peter J. Boettke

Keynes and Hayek
The money economy
G.R. Steele

The Constitution of Markets
Essays in political economy
Viktor J. Vanberg

Foundations of Entrepreneurship and Economic Development
David A. Harper

Markets, Information and Communication
Austrian perspectives on the internet economy
Edited by Jack Birner and Pierre Garrouste

The Constitution of Liberty in the Open Economy
Lüder Gerken

Liberalism Against Liberalism
Javier Aranzadi

Money and Markets
Essays in honor of Leland B. Yeager
Edited by Roger Koppl

Entrepreneurship and Economic Progress
Randall G. Holcombe

Entrepreneurship and Economic Progress

Randall G. Holcombe

Routledge
Taylor & Francis Group

NEW YORK AND LONDON

First published 2007
by Routledge
270 Madison Ave, New York, NY 10016

Simultaneously published in the UK
by Routledge
2 Park Square, Milton Park, Abingdon, Oxon OX14 4RN

Routledge is an imprint of the Taylor & Francis Group, an informa business

Typeset in Times New Roman by
Newgen Imaging Systems (P) Ltd, Chennai, India
Printed and bound in Great Britain by
Biddles Ltd, King's Lynn

Library of Congress Cataloging in Publication Data
Holcombe, Randall G.
　　Entrepreneurship and economic progress / Randall G. Holcombe.
　　　p. cm.
　　Includes bibliographical references and index.
　　1. Entrepreneurship. 2. Economic development. I. Title.

　HB615.H63 2006
　658.4'21–dc22　　　　　　　　　　　　　　　　　2006011539

British Library Cataloguing in Publication Data
A catalogue record for this book is available from the British Library

ISBN10: 0–415–77090–4 (hbk)
ISBN10: 0–203–96634–1 (ebk)

ISBN13: 978–0–415–77090–3 (hbk)
ISBN13: 978–0–203–96634–1 (ebk)

To Ross, Mark, and Connor

Contents

Preface

My interest in the topic of this book began with a reflection on Israel Kirzner's work on entrepreneurship, and in particular on the contrast he drew between his ideas and those of Joseph Schumpeter. Kirzner emphasized this contrast in his 1973 book, *Competition and Entrepreneurship*, arguing that Schumpeter depicted entrepreneurship as disequilibrating, whereas he argued entrepreneurship was equilibrating. Despite the contrast that Kirzner drew, it seemed to me that Kirzner's and Schumpeter's ideas complemented each other, and not only made a more complete theory of entrepreneurship but also helped illuminate the theory of economic growth in the process. I published my initial ideas on the subject in a 1998 article, "Entrepreneurship and Economic Growth," discussing the relationship between Kirzner's and Schumpeter's ideas on entrepreneurship, and that article went on to connect the ideas of entrepreneurship and economic progress. Kirzner found more in common with Schumpeter in his later work than he did in his 1973 book, but he did not link his ideas with Schumpeter's in the way that I did. As I considered the topic in more detail, a series of related articles followed up that initial article, providing the foundation for the ideas in this book. The ideas are related enough that it seemed worthwhile to present them together in a book so that rather than appearing as isolated ideas in a series of articles, they could be aggregated as a more comprehensive examination of entrepreneurship and economic progress.

At the same time, I was examining the relationship between institutions and economic growth with James Gwartney and Robert Lawson, which pointed toward more substantial connections between entrepreneurship and economic progress. That work emphasized the institutional framework that enables economic growth, which is clearly related to entrepreneurship because good institutions provide the incentive for productive entrepreneurship. This aspect of growth theory has been neglected by the mainstream theory of economic growth, although I note throughout the book that many other scholars have emphasized the importance of institutions to economic growth. This relationship is increasingly viewed as important, and is a welcome development in economics; yet for many reasons – explained in this book – the contemporary orientation of growth theory leaves out some of the most important causes and effects of growth.

The series of articles that I wrote on entrepreneurship provided the building blocks for the more comprehensive study of entrepreneurship and economic progress that appears in this book, and I am grateful to the publishers of those articles for allowing me to use portions of them here. Some material in the book is taken from "Entrepreneurship and Economic Growth," *Quarterly Journal of Austrian Economics*, 1, no. 2 (Summer 1998), pp. 45–62, "Equilibrium Versus the Invisible Hand," *Review of Austrian Economics*, 12, no. 2 (1999), pp. 227–243, "Political Entrepreneurship and the Democratic Allocation of Economic Resources," *Review of Austrian Economics*, 15, nos. 2/3 (June 2002), pp. 143–159, "Information, Entrepreneurship, and Economic Progress," in Roger Koppl, ed., *Advances in Austrian Economics: Austrian Economics and Entrepreneurial Studies*, vol. 6. Amsterdam: JAI, 2003, pp. 173–195, "The Origins of Entrepreneurial Opportunities," *Review of Austrian Economics*, 16, no. 1 (2003), pp. 25–43, "National Income Accounting and Public Policy," *Review of Austrian Economics*, 17, no. 4 (2004), pp. 387–405, and "Progress and Entrepreneurship," *Quarterly Journal of Austrian Economics*, 6, no. 3 (Fall 2003), pp. 10–28.

Many people helped me formulate my ideas on this topic over the years, and the mention of some will almost surely leave out others I have forgotten to mention. That said, helpful comments from Peter Boettke, Anthony Carilli, James Cobb, Steve Horwitz, Israel Kirzner, Peter Lewin, Edward Lopez, and anonymous reviewers of this book manuscript were all helpful. I am also grateful for the support of my family: my wife, Lora, and my children Ross, Mark, and Connor, to whom the book is dedicated.

Randall G. Holcombe
Tallahassee, Florida

1 Progress and entrepreneurship

Economists have been studying the factors that improve people's material well-being at least as far back as Adam Smith wrote his monumental treatise, *The Wealth of Nations*, in 1776, but the phenomenon of economic progress – or as it is often more narrowly studied, growth – barely predates Smith.[1] Half a century before Smith wrote, economic progress would have been nearly imperceptible over a person's lifetime. Since then, economic progress has accelerated with each generation, and has manifested itself partly in income growth, but even more in new methods of production and in new types of output. Entrepreneurship has played an indispensable role in the production of economic progress. The link between entrepreneurship and progress may seem obvious, yet the connection between the two in economic analysis is tenuous, partly because mainstream economics has not done a very good job of depicting either entrepreneurship or progress. Because neither entrepreneurship nor progress is accurately represented in the economic analysis of growth, mainstream economic analysis has overlooked the key factors that create economic progress, and the policy recommendations that have come from economic analysis regarding economic growth are often counterproductive.

Economists tend to represent economic growth as growth in the level of income, but economic progress is much broader than that. To focus on income growth is to ignore the most important elements of economic progress. Changes in the characteristics of goods and services produced, and in the methods of production, are more significant for economic well-being than growth in the level of income. Improvements in the type of output the economy produces and improvements in methods of production – the factors that create economic progress – are the result of entrepreneurship, but entrepreneurship is rarely represented in models of economic growth. In the twentieth-century-economic theory of the firm, firms are run by managers who choose the optimal levels of inputs and outputs so their firms can produce efficiently. Managers are not entrepreneurs. There are important differences between growth and progress, and between management and entrepreneurship. Chapter 2 focuses on the distinction between growth and progress, while Chapter 3 looks at the differences between management and entrepreneurship. The remaining chapters then consider how entrepreneurship in firms creates economic progress, and discuss how economic policy can be designed to foster entrepreneurship and economic progress.

If one wants to use economic analysis to understand how human welfare has improved over time and how it can continue to be improved, then the analysis must focus on progress, broadly defined, rather than narrowly on income growth. Because progress is the result of entrepreneurship, an economic analysis of progress must incorporate entrepreneurship. Yet economic analysis has largely ignored the entrepreneurial foundations of progress. An examination of the theory of economic growth can help illustrate why this has been the case.

Growth theory in economics

The full title of Adam Smith's monumental treatise, *An Inquiry Into the Nature and Causes of the Wealth of Nations*, indicates that his interest was in explaining the causes of prosperity – a topic that was of general interest to economists of Smith's day. That topic fell from the forefront of economic inquiry as Thomas Robert Malthus's *Essay on Population*[2] and David Ricardo's *Principles of Political Economy*[3] argued, early in the nineteenth century, that most people were destined to remain at a subsistence level of income because population growth would always outstrip the availability of resources to support the population. Throughout the twentieth century, the focus of economic analysis was on the properties of economic equilibrium. Elaborate mathematical models were developed to depict equilibrium in economics, and the focus of macroeconomics was on arriving at a full-employment equilibrium with low inflation, while the focus of microeconomics was on eliminating "market failures" that prevented the optimal allocation of resources. From a public policy standpoint, the ultimate goal was to arrive at the optimal equilibrium allocation of resources. Prior to the 1990s, economic growth was typically studied with economic development in the field of growth and development and the field focused primarily on less-developed economies.

The issue in growth and development was how to implement policies that could spur development in those less-developed economies so that their economies could be transformed from less-developed economies into developed economies. At the risk of some oversimplification, essentially the subdiscipline viewed economies as falling into one of the three types: less developed, developed, and those in transition from less developed to developed.[4] In keeping with the twentieth-century focus on equilibrium outcomes, "developed" was the desired outcome, and the idea was to try to move less-developed economies into that desirable condition. While the literature did consider income growth in developed economies to a limited degree, the broader conception of economic progress was considered only to the extent that transitioning from less developed to developed was progress.

In the 1990s, economic growth was elevated from a relatively obscure subfield in economics to one of the more glamorous and high-profile areas of economic inquiry. The rising profile of economic growth as an area of inquiry began with a 1988 article by Robert Lucas, "On the Mechanics of Economic Development."[5] Lucas presented a mathematical framework for examining economic development as a part of macroeconomics. The rising profile of economic growth thus came along as its subject matter moved from a focus on less-developed economies toward a more general focus on growth as a macroeconomic phenomenon.

This change in the orientation of the study of economic growth is appropriate. Since its inception in the 1930s following John Maynard Keynes's *General Theory*,[6] macroeconomics has focused on fluctuations in economic output. When problems arise in the macroeconomy, it moves away from full employment, and macroeconomics has focused on why economic fluctuations can lead to unemployment – and to inflation – and what policies can be used to bring the economy back to full employment and low inflation. The benchmark and policy goal in this type of analysis is the economy with full employment and low inflation. This is a short-run framework with no long-run analysis or policy goals. The goal of Keynesian macroeconomic policy is to maintain an equilibrium with full employment and low inflation, and the notion that the full-employment level of output could be increased over time is at best a peripheral part of the theory.

A mathematical framework for the theory of economic growth had been developed by Robert Solow in a 1956 article,[7] but until the 1990s macroeconomic fluctuations and economic growth were viewed as different issues. By building growth theory into macroeconomics, the two issues came together under the broader umbrella of the study of the trajectory of the economy. Its long-run trajectory fell more under what could be seen as growth theory while its short-run trajectory was more along the line of traditional macroeconomics as it had been developed since Keynes, but the integrating idea was that the short-run fluctuations and the long-run trends were all a part of the same underlying process.

The taxonomy of countries in growth theory prior to the 1990s was a natural outgrowth of the static equilibrium approach to economics that dominated mainstream economics in the twentieth century. In that framework, welfare is maximized when resources are allocated as efficiently as possible, which is accomplished in competitive equilibrium. Various factors, such as externalities, public goods, monopolies, and information problems, can prevent the attainment of this welfare maximization, and the challenge from the standpoint of economic policy is to design policies to overcome these problems and get as close to the optimal allocation of resources as possible.[8] Economic theory pointed toward policies that generated efficient resource allocation in a static sense, not growth in a dynamic sense. Once an economy reached that benchmark of competitive equilibrium, the policy goal was accomplished. Of course, less-developed economies were obviously worse off than developed economies, so the focus of growth and development economics was to transform less-developed economies into developed economies, not to produce growth more generally. Developed economies were already developed, so there was no growth and development issue there. The focus of growth and development in economics was on less-developed economies.

In both macroeconomics and microeconomics, growth was a peripheral issue prior to the 1990s because in both cases, the frameworks pointed toward optimality as a static equilibrium outcome. In macroeconomics it was a full-employment equilibrium with low inflation and in microeconomics it was the Pareto optimal competitive equilibrium, and from the standpoint of economic welfare, once those outcomes were reached optimality was achieved and the theoretical framework did not allow for any further improvements. Of course, there was the Solow growth framework lurking in the background and economists could talk about growth in that framework, but the framework for analyzing growth was not integrated with the mainstream models in microeconomics or macroeconomics until Lucas's 1988 article on economic development.

The idea that there is a close relationship between the processes that generate economic growth and the processes that underlie fluctuations in aggregate income was not entirely new in the 1990s, although prior to Lucas's 1988 article the idea was decidedly outside the mainstream of development theory. Joseph Schumpeter's book, *The Theory of Economic Development*, first published in German in 1912 and appearing in English in 1934[9] clearly related the two, and his 1939 book, *Business Cycles*, drew an even closer relationship.[10] As Schumpeter described it, business cycles result from the creative destruction of entrepreneurship. An economic equilibrium is disturbed by an innovation introduced into the economy. The innovation creates opportunities for people who are utilizing the innovation or who undertake activities that are complementary to its use, but it disrupts existing markets. Innovations alter or perhaps eliminate opportunities for people who make their livelihood in markets that produce substitutes for the innovation. The introduction of the automobile disrupted many industries related to horse-drawn transportation, the computer transformed the typewriter industry, the introduction of the passenger airliner had a substantial impact on firms running passenger trains, and the introduction of digital photography disrupted the film industry. These disruptions cause business cycles as resources are temporarily displaced from their old uses, but at the same time the underlying cause of the business cycles is the engine of economic growth. As Schumpeter sees it, macroeconomic fluctuations and economic growth are two manifestations of the same underlying process.

The integration of growth theory and macroeconomics in the 1990s echoes Schumpeter's insight that growth and macroeconomic fluctuations are part of the same underlying process. However, Schumpeter's most significant insights about the role of entrepreneurship in the process have not found their way into growth theory in the early twenty-first century. Schumpeter saw the creative destruction of entrepreneurial innovation as a disruptive and disequilibrating force in the economy, whereas the neoclassical growth theory built on the foundations laid by Solow and Lucas depict growth as a part of a general equilibrium process. The equilibrium nature of the growth process described in this growth theory rules out the types of entrepreneurship that Schumpeter described.[11]

Furthermore, in those general equilibrium growth models, growth is depicted as an increase in aggregate output, which ignores the crucial distinction between economic growth and economic progress. While it is true that developed economies enjoy increasing levels of income through economic growth, a more important component of economic progress is the array of new and improved goods and services that progress brings with it. When economic progress is viewed more broadly than just income growth, and when entrepreneurship is recognized as the engine of economic progress, some policy implications are substantially different from those suggested by neoclassical growth theory. In the end, the development of this idea is more than just an academic exercise. The ultimate conclusions of this study are policy implications for fostering economic progress in both developed and less-developed nations, and the policy implications depend critically on recognizing the role of entrepreneurship in generating economic progress.

Economics and entrepreneurship

In the previous section, and throughout the book, the neoclassical model of the economy that is the well-established paradigm of mainstream economics at the beginning of the twenty-first century is criticized for failing to incorporate entrepreneurship into its framework. However, there is a substantial body of analysis in economics and in other related disciplines (especially management) that explicitly recognizes the role and importance of entrepreneurship. Much of that work is cited throughout the book, and there is much more that is not cited but that makes a substantial contribution to the understanding of entrepreneurship. Thus, it is important to clarify at the outset what, exactly, is the target of the critical comments aimed at neoclassical economics.

The problem with the neoclassical framework is that by construction it does not allow any role for entrepreneurship. Despite the fact that many prominent economists have written about and recognized the crucial role for entrepreneurship in producing economic progress,[12] the neoclassical framework within which economic analysis takes place does not incorporate it into its framework. In the neoclassical model, output, Q, is a function of capital, K, and labor, L, or $Q = f(K, L)$. Within this framework, firms produce some standard output and running a firm means only choosing the optimal quantities of inputs K and L to produce the optimal level of output. While economic analysis does get more sophisticated at times when looking at entrepreneurship specifically, when looking at the economy as a whole, this formulation provides the framework for economic analysis. The general equilibrium models of growth, which came into fashion in the 1990s and were discussed in the previous section, depict firms (and whole economies) that are always in equilibrium, and in which firms do not engage in any entrepreneurial activity.[13] The problem, then, is not that no economists recognize the role of entrepreneurship, but rather that entrepreneurship remains outside the basic framework of mainstream economic analysis, and especially the mainstream economic analysis of growth.

A good reference for standard neoclassical economics is C.E. Ferguson's *Microeconomic Theory*, because it provides such a clear exposition of the neoclassical framework.[14] But while Ferguson's book is a good reference, it is several decades old, so perhaps a better illustration of contemporary microeconomics theory comes from two standard microeconomics textbooks: Hal Varian's

Intermediate Microeconomics and Besanko and Braeutigam's *Microeconomics*.[15] These books describe the microeconomic framework essentially the same way that Ferguson did decades ago, in which competitive firms are devoid of any entrepreneurial elements. This is the framework upon which the firms in general equilibrium growth models are built.

These books by Varian and Besanko and Braeutigam are interesting for present purposes because they show how the contemporary theory of the firm does not depict firms as entrepreneurial, but these specific books are also of interest because the authors have written other volumes in which firms are depicted as very entrepreneurial. Shapiro and Varian's *Information Rules: A Strategic Guide to the Network Economy*,[16] discusses entrepreneurial strategies for competitive firms and explains how firms can act to gain market power and a competitive edge, and Besanko, Dranove, Shanley, and Schaefer's, *Economics of Strategy*,[17] also discusses entrepreneurial strategies at length.

What makes these two pairs of books so interesting for present purposes is that it is apparent that both Varian and Besanko are well aware of the crucial entrepreneurial aspects of firms and that entrepreneurship is essential for firm survival. Yet when those two authors write microeconomic theory books, rather than incorporate this entrepreneurial element – that they obviously know well – into their exposition of microeconomics, they leave it out completely and depict profit-maximizing competitive firms as producers of homogeneous products who are content if they can earn "normal profits" into the indefinite future. The firms in their microeconomics textbooks are definitely not the firms in their other books, yet when economics as a discipline goes on to model the process of economic growth, it incorporates the firms that populate microeconomic theory rather than the entrepreneurial firms that strive to innovate and to differentiate their products. Despite the recognition of the importance of entrepreneurship as an activity that takes place within markets, the economic analysis of the market system takes place with a much narrower view of firm behavior and of competition that assumes entrepreneurship out of the picture altogether.

What you can see depends on where you are looking

Economists have been interested in the causes of prosperity for hundreds of years. As noted earlier, the title of Adam Smith's *The Wealth of Nations* reveals what Smith hoped to explain in his book. But in economics, as in anything else, what people can see depends on their vantage point. A person standing on a mountain peak can see more than someone in a valley, but that does not mean that the person on the mountain peak can see everything better than the person in the valley. Someone interested in understanding aquatic life in mountain streams would be better off looking in the valleys than gazing from the peaks.

The economic models used in growth theory offer a particular vantage point, which will be good for looking at some things, but which will overlook others. What follows in this volume is not intended to be a general critique of neo-classical economics, which offers considerable insight into the operation of the economy. Rather, it suggests that these neoclassical models have some clearly identifiable shortcomings when applied to the subject of economic growth. When one analyzes economic processes through the lens of neoclassical economics, the framework helps to see some things much more clearly; at the same time, it obscures other things.

No matter how complex economic models are, their whole purpose is to simplify things so that real-world processes that are difficult to understand become more easily understandable within the model. If one could understand economic reality without the model, the model would serve no purpose. The purpose it serves is to make simplifying assumptions about economic actors, such as firms and consumers, and the environment within which they act, and then to illustrate the logical implications of the interactions among the actors. Mathematical models are an excellent tool for doing this, because they reveal the inherent logic that underlies the system. The model is then used as an analogy to the real world. The model works a certain way. If we understand the model, and if the operation of the real world is analogous to the operation of the model, then we understand the real world.

Even the most complex model relies on simplifying assumptions to make it more understandable than the real world. Some aspects of the real world are assumed away. (Most economic models contain no spatial dimension, for example, because this is not crucial to understanding what the model is trying to explain.) Sometimes unrealistic assumptions are made. (Models often assume that markets are perfectly competitive, that firms in an industry produce homogeneous products, and that firms have no power to set their own prices, even though this is rarely true.) Simplifying assumptions have the virtue of making models easier to understand, and as long as they do not affect the interactions among economic actors in the real world, they can make the analogy between the model and the real world clearer, and thereby make it easier to understand the real world.

Consider a roadmap, which is a model of the geographic world. The map contains many simplifying assumptions. It assumes some things away. For example, it will probably not contain all the water towers, radio towers, bridges, and many other features of the real world, because they are not relevant to understanding how to get from one place to another using the roads. By leaving them out of the model, the map is easier to understand. The map also contains unrealistic features. Typically, roads are larger than they would be to scale, to make them easier to see, and the roads on the map are not the same color as the actual roads, again to highlight their locations. This is unrealistic, but the unrealistic features of this model (the map) make it easier to understand. The same is true of economic models. Unrealistic assumptions, and the fact that some things are not included in the model, make the model easier to understand, so such assumptions are virtues.[18]

A potential problem, however, is that a model can never explain the things that it assumes away, and sometimes unrealistic assumptions that help to understand certain phenomena can be misleading when trying to understand other phenomena. Because any model is a simplified depiction of reality, no model can be used to understand every aspect of reality. There is an art involved in choosing the right model for the purpose at hand. The person who is going to drive from New York to Chicago would use a different map from the pilot who was going to fly from New York to Chicago, because different features of the real world would be important to understanding the roadways versus understanding the airways. Similarly, the framework of neoclassical economics does an excellent job of conveying the properties of economic equilibrium and examining the equilibrating forces in the economy. However, because of its assumptions, the neoclassical framework has serious deficiencies for analyzing the underlying causes of prosperity. The neoclassical model does not provide the appropriate vantage point for looking at this issue.

Progress and entrepreneurship

The neoclassical vantage point leaves out the two central concepts of this book: progress and entrepreneurship. Neoclassical theory analyzes growth, not progress. Output is measured as a homogeneous quantity, which assumes away the possibility for developing new and improved products. Even when neoclassical models depict heterogeneous outputs by having many industries that each produce different goods, the models do not depict changes in the quality of those goods or model the introduction of new goods. In a trivial sense, an economy with n goods could add another and produce $n + 1$ goods, but where does the new good come from? Growth theory, as its name indicates, models the increase in the quantity of output in an economy, not the changes in the characteristics of the economy's output. Yet, economic progress, while it does encompass growth, mainly occurs because of new and improved goods and services, not just more of the same output it was producing before. By assuming progress out of the model and just looking at the growth of output, neoclassical theory misrepresents the entire process of growth. As Chapter 2 explains, economic growth cannot be understood independently of the progress that comes with new and changing goods and services.

While the neoclassical framework misrepresents progress as growth, it leaves entrepreneurship out of the model altogether. Entrepreneurs discover new markets, they bring new and improved goods and services to market, and they discover better ways of producing the economy's output. When the framework of the model does not allow for these types of changes, it cannot possibly depict the entrepreneurial processes that produce the changes. Chapter 3 discusses the role of entrepreneurship in an economy and contrasts it with the management activities that are a part of the neoclassical framework.

The neoclassical framework in economics provides substantial insight into economic processes, but it cannot explain those things that it assumes away, and it assumes away elements that are crucial to the understanding of economic progress. What follows is an attempt to fill that void by pointing in the direction of a more accurate framework for analyzing economic growth and economic progress.

One asset that neoclassical growth theory has is its elegant mathematical framework. It is rigorous and self-contained. The model encompasses an entire economy, albeit one much simpler than the real-world economy, and it depicts an orderly process of an economy always in equilibrium. The framework in this book is not so orderly and is not so self-contained. One reason is that the entrepreneurial process is not orderly or easily described. Entrepreneurship is an innovative activity, so entrepreneurial discoveries are necessarily unpredictable. If we could predict them, they would become a part of the economic routine and would not be innovations. Perhaps the ideas presented here could be recast in a more rigorous framework, but they have not been analyzed and refined as much as neoclassical theory. The material here is not the last word, then, but is ripe for further development. Because of the necessarily unpredictable effects of entrepreneurship, it will probably never find itself incorporated into as rigorously elegant a framework as neoclassical growth theory, but it does offer more insight into the foundations of economic progress.

Progress and policy

Entrepreneurship and economic progress could be studied for the purely academic satisfaction of gaining insight into the reason that the material well-being of mankind has increased, but another reason for this line of inquiry is to use that insight as a foundation for developing policies to foster economic progress. For hundreds of years, economists and governments have been looking for policies that could foster economic progress. The corn laws were passed in Britain beginning in 1804 with the intention of protecting and enhancing the productivity of Britain's farms, and David Ricardo argued against them saying that free trade was a better policy for promoting the well-being of the British and everyone else. The Progressive era around the beginning of the twentieth century brought with it antitrust laws, regulation of food and drugs, and central banking (in the form of the Federal Reserve System) to the United States, again with the idea that these policies would enhance people's economic well-being, and Franklin Roosevelt's New Deal was a set of policies intended to stabilize the capitalist system and produce prosperity. In the Cold War era from the 1950s through the 1980s there was a serious debate regarding whether central planning was a better way to run an economy than leaving matters to the uncertainties of the market system; after central planning was discredited Japanese industrial policy was touted as a better way to run an economy until the slowdown of the Japanese economy in the 1990s. A major goal of economic analysis always has been to implement policies that promote prosperity and enhance people's economic well-being. Thus, the answers to the issues discussed here lead directly to important issues of economic policy.

The analysis presented here shows not only that in many cases policies intended to create more economic prosperity are counterproductive, but that contemporary economic analysis tends to lead policy makers astray. Following the implications of the mainstream contemporary theory of economic growth can lead to policies that hinder growth and progress. That claim is a bold one, so at this point it is time to start supporting it by looking at the concepts of economic growth and progress.

2 Growth versus progress

Modern economic progress began with the start of the Industrial Revolution in eighteenth-century Britain. Prior to about 1750, economic progress was so slow that people would have to be very observant to see any progress during their lifetimes. Everywhere in the world, the standard of living and the quality of life was much the same in 1750 as it was in 1650, and it was much the same in 1650 as it was in 1550. Indeed, it was much the same in 1550 as it was in 550. The remarkable transformation in the world economy that began with the Industrial Revolution is often couched in terms of growth in per capita income, and when looked at only in those terms, income growth has been remarkable. Prior to the Industrial Revolution, there was virtually no per capita income growth,[1] but growth has accelerated since, so that by the beginning of the twenty-first century, growing economies could expect their per capita incomes to double every three to four decades. For most of human history, people struggled to get enough food to survive, but by the beginning of the twenty-first century, developed economies found obesity to be a greater problem than hunger. Obesity was barely possible prior to the twentieth century, except for the wealthiest individuals, and before the twentieth century obesity was a sign of prosperity. By the end of the twentieth century, poor people in the United States weighed, on average, more than the rich.[2] The income growth that has been generated since the Industrial Revolution has, indeed, been remarkable.

As remarkable as that income growth has been, it is only a small component of economic progress. More significant are the changes that have occurred in the types of goods and services that the economy offers, and changes in methods of production. Those changes have brought with them income growth, but the factors underlying the growth in income are the result of progress in the types of output and production methods in the economy. The growth in income cannot properly be understood without understanding how changes in types of output and production methods have occurred. This chapter contrasts the growth in income, which is how economists typically evaluate economic progress, with the more qualitative changes that constitute progress, and that have been responsible for income growth.

Indicators of progress

Modern economic progress began in the eighteenth century with the Industrial Revolution, but economic progress was greater in the nineteenth century than the eighteenth, and greater in the twentieth century than the nineteenth.[3] Because this progress is generated by entrepreneurship, and because the economic environment is increasingly favorable to entrepreneurship, there is every reason to think that economic progress will continue to accelerate in the twenty-first century.[4] Economic progress is often measured in terms of income growth, and in the United States, per capita GDP (Gross Domestic Product) was nearly seven times greater at the end of the twentieth century than it was at the beginning; yet to summarize economic progress by looking only at the growth in the value of economic output seriously misrepresents the nature of the economic progress that took place in that century.

At the beginning of the twentieth century, only about 1 percent of American households had cars; by the end of the century, 91 percent of households had them. Largely because of advances in medical technology, life expectancy in the United States rose from 47 years at the beginning of the century to 77 years by the century's end.[5] Telephones were rare at the beginning of the century, but commonplace by the end of the century. Information acquisition and entertainment were completely transformed in the twentieth century. At the beginning of the century there were no movie theaters, no radio broadcasts, and no television. By 1900 electricity was available to some, and was used primarily for lighting. By 1950, electricity powered radios, washing machines, and refrigerators for the masses in developed economies. By 2000, most people classified as poor in the United States had indoor plumbing, air conditioning, telephones, and automobiles. The internet revolutionized communication and allowed business ventures to span the globe. While only a few computers existed in the world in 1950, many people had more than one computer in their homes by 2000. Computers did not become common until the 1980s, and the World Wide Web did not exist until the 1990s. The first airplane had not yet flown at the beginning of the twentieth century, but by the end of the century travel throughout the world in a jet aircraft was routine. Despite the tremendous GDP growth over the twentieth century when one reflects on economic progress over the century it is apparent that the primary component of economic progress is not the amount of income growth, as impressive as it was, but rather the substantial change in the qualitative nature of the economy's output.

Progress is apparent not only in the types of goods and services available for consumption, but also in other dimensions of the quality of life. At the beginning of the twentieth century the average work week in the United States was about 50 hours, and by the end of the century it had fallen to about 35 hours. Again, this quantitative change in hours worked, while impressive, does not reflect the changing nature of work, which became less dangerous and less physically demanding. People worked more with their minds and less with their bodies by the end of the century, and this is reflected in the fact that at the beginning of the century only 22 percent of adults in the United States had completed high school, while by the end of the century 88 percent had a high school degree. Accidental deaths, including those on the job, fell from 88 per 100,000 people to 34 per 100,000 over the course of the century. Again, while people work fewer hours for more income, the more significant element of progress in the work people do is not the quantitative reduction in work hours or increase in output, but rather the qualitative changes in the nature of work.

At the beginning of the century the reward for work was money, and most jobs were mainly manual labor. While money was still a primary motivator at the end of the century, people considered the pleasantness of a job, including intellectual stimulation, challenges, and workplace amenities as significant rewards for employment. Many people enjoy the work they do: something that would have been much rarer in 1900, when work was often physically demanding, dangerous, and tedious. One can look at growth in terms of increased output per hour of work, but the progress in terms of qualitative changes at the workplace is at least as significant as the quantitative growth.

This type of economic progress would only have been visible to people after the Industrial Revolution. The advent of factory production and the use of steam power in manufacturing transformed the nature of work, and allowed substantial improvements in productivity. By 1850 the range of manufactured goods available to people was unprecedented, and by 1900 the use of steam power to drive the railroads and waterborne shipping had revolutionized transportation. People's income levels increased throughout the past 250 years in nations that had market economies, but even more striking than the growth in income has been the change in the nature of the types of goods and services people consume. These changes in lifestyles of the typical citizen, the types of goods and services consumed, and in the way that goods and services are produced, are the manifestations of economic progress.

The cumulative nature of progress

The growth of the automobile industry in the twentieth century illustrates the importance of changes in both production processes and the types of goods produced. Economic progress meant enhancing people's transportation options by making automobile travel available to a large segment of the population, changing the type of output. Assembly line production allowed a substantial increase in the output of automobiles per worker. But focusing on the growth in output per worker obscures the more important fact that the types of goods produced, and the way they were being produced, had been substantially transformed within that span of a century.

Progress in one area often leads to progress in others.[6] The widespread availability of the automobile has changed the way people shop and the way that goods are sold. Supermarkets, shopping malls, and large discount stores would not be feasible if people could not drive their own cars to transport substantial quantities of goods. The corner grocery, while just a convenient walk away, was more expensive and had less variety. The supermarket can draw from a larger number of customers because more people are within driving distance than are within walking distance. Customers can buy more each time they shop, because they can carry more in their automobiles than they could transport without them. For many reasons, supermarkets can offer a greater variety of goods at lower cost. The same is true of large discount stores like Wal-Mart. These innovations in retailing would not have been possible without innovations in personal transportation, and illustrate how innovations in one area of the economy lead to innovations in other areas.

New modes of shopping include not only larger more centralized stores but also catalog shopping and, more recently, internet shopping. These innovations have also led to increased product variety by, to use Adam Smith's phrase, expanding the extent of the market. The advent of long distance telephone calling – and the steep decline in its price – made it feasible for potential customers to call sellers thousands of miles away to order products immediately, and the sharp decline in transportation costs made it feasible to ship individual purchases thousands of miles to buyers. This allows greater variety in the types of goods and services offered for sale, and gives entrepreneurs an incentive to introduce products that might have an insufficiently small market if they were just sold in one town, but have a large enough market if they can be sold nationwide, or even worldwide. Progress in one area leads to progress in others.

There are limits to the utility of consuming increasing quantities of currently produced goods, which limits potential growth. Although income grew by about seven times in the twentieth century, Americans in 2000 would have found limited utility in having seven times as much food as Americans in 1900. But there are no limits to progress, because there are no limits to the types of new goods and services that people might benefit from consuming. Growth without progress is self-limiting, whereas progress brings with it growth.

The economic analysis of progress

Despite this remarkable progress in so many dimensions, economic analysis of these changes tends to focus on the growth in the level of output rather than the changes in the nature of the output.[7] This results in a limited understanding of both the cause and the effect of economic progress. The effects have already been considered by noting that the changes in the types of goods and services consumed and in the nature of work are more remarkable – and have had a bigger impact on people's lives – than the growth in the amount of consumption. The causal factors behind economic progress are more significant than just the growth in income because the changes in both the nature of output and the processes of production are what have caused this remarkable economic growth. Put plainly, the quantity of output would not have grown as it has without changes in the nature of both the processes of production and the type of output being produced.

Economic growth is only one component of economic progress, but the changes that will allow progress to continue are far from obvious. It takes insight to perceive changes that might alter the nature of production processes, or that might lead to the introduction of new goods and services. Without people who have these insights, and who have the incentive to act on them, economic progress would not take place. Perceiving and acting on such a profit opportunity is entrepreneurship, which is the engine of economic progress. Economic analysis has tended to focus on growth – the production of increasing amounts of output – so it is important to see the distinction between growth and progress, and to see that in the long run, progress brings with it growth, but growth without progress will be self-limiting.

Growth versus progress

As defined by the economics profession, economic growth means increasing income, or GDP. This vision of growth is reinforced by the way we measure income, as a homogeneous dollar amount – an idea that is explored further in Chapter 9. Measured in dollar terms, the seven-fold growth in income in the twentieth century is impressive,[8] but as already noted, vastly understates the progress that has occurred. Cox and Alm make the point that by many measures, poor Americans in 1994 had a standard of living similar to the average American in 1971.[9] Goods that were unavailable to anyone at one time become available to the wealthy, then to people of average means, and within a few decades to everyone. In 1971 only the very wealthy could have had microwave ovens or cellular telephones, and nobody had personal computers, but all were widely available in the United States – even to poor people – just 30 years later. The change is not primarily quantitative (more income) but rather qualitative (the consumption of different goods that were previously unavailable). And as Cox and Alm point out, even looking at major categories of goods understates the degree of progress that has been made. For example, while automobile ownership is rising, variety in the types of automobiles available is also rising, giving consumers more choices and a better opportunity to get a vehicle that is more specifically suited to their needs. In 1970 there were 140 different varieties of automobiles available to American consumers, and that number had risen to 260 by 1997.[10] The same is true of other goods. By the late 1990s, there were almost twice as many new book titles available as in the early 1970s, there were 340 different types of breakfast cereals in the late 1990s, compared with 160 in the early 1970s, and there were 285 different types of running shoes, compared to only 5 types available in 1971. Of course, some goods, such as personal computers, and internet web sites, were not available at all a few decades earlier.

Most common measures of economic progress, such as GDP growth, measure growth in the level of income, but do not measure economic progress. From a policy standpoint, a focus on these measures of income points toward measures that can increase the level of output of currently produced goods, rather than improving the variety and quality of output, and introducing new goods. Economic policy can be distorted by the way that we measure the productivity of the economy; so making the distinction between growth and progress is more than just an academic distinction. The policy implications will be examined more critically later in the book, and in Chapter 9 in particular.

Progress and the division of labor

Adam Smith begins his monumental treatise, *The Wealth of Nations*, by saying, "The greatest improvement in the productive powers of labour, and the greater part of the skill, dexterity, and judgment with which it is any where directed, or applied, seem to have been the effects of the division of labour."[11] Smith goes on to discuss the division of labor at length, explaining that when people can subdivide tasks into smaller tasks and specialize, they can be more productive. Smith offers a wonderful example of a pin factory and suggests that somebody not familiar with the trade could probably not make even one pin a day, and surely not twenty. Smith continues,

> But in the way in which this business is now carried on, not only the whole work is a peculiar trade, but it is divided into a number of branches, of which the greater part are likewise peculiar trades. One man draws out the wire, another straights it, a third cuts it, a fourth points it, a fifth grinds it at the top for receiving the head; to make the head requires two or three distinct operations; to put in on, is a peculiar business, to whiten the pins is another; it is even a trade by itself to put them into the paper; and the important business of making a pin is, in this manner, divided into about eighteen distinct operations... [12]

Smith goes on to say he has observed a pin factory in which ten people were employed, and where some workers therefore performed more than one of the tasks enumerated in the extract, produce 48,000 pins a day. That comes out to about 4,800 pins per worker per day. He then suggests that if a person unfamiliar with pin-making could make only 10 pins a day, each worker would be 480 times as productive because of the effects of the division of labor, and even if an unskilled worker could make 20 pins a day, the division of labor would still be responsible for an increase in productivity by 240 times.[13]

When one reflects on it, Smith's numbers seem a reasonable estimate of the increase in productivity afforded by the division of labor. When one considers how much in terms of material goods people in market economies have at the beginning of the twenty-first century, Smith's numbers take on more of a concrete appearance. How much would you, the reader of this book, be able to consume if you had to produce everything you consumed? What would you be eating if you had to grow your own food? What would you be wearing if you had to make your own clothes? What kind of car would you be driving if you had to make it yourself, starting by digging up iron ore and smelting it into steel? Even if you had a car, how much would you be driving if you had to refine your own gasoline to power it? People in market economies have so much because the division of labor has made everyone more productive.

Besides just an increase in the volume of production, Smith sees other advantages to the division of labor. Invention of new machines and processes are also due to the division of labor.

> Men are much more likely to discover easier and readier methods of attaining any object, when the whole attention of their minds is directed towards that single object, than when it is dissipated among a great variety of things. ... A great part of the machines made use of in those manufactures in which labour is most subdivided, were originally the inventions of common workmen, who, being each of them employed in some very simple operation, naturally turned their thoughts toward finding out easier and readier methods of performing it.[14]

The innovation that leads to economic progress is thus the result of the division of labor.

Consider a few more examples. Workers can excavate with shovels, but once each worker has a shovel, there will be little change in labor productivity from increasing the number of shovels. But if the shovels are replaced (or supplemented) by a backhoe, labor productivity will increase. This change in the nature of capital requires someone to have the insight that backhoes can be profitably produced, and even if backhoes are readily available on the market, requires the insight that a particular job could be more profitably done with a backhoe. Output can be increased some by increasing the quantity of capital and labor, but most of the increase in output comes from changing the nature of capital, not just increasing its quantity. Henry Ford's introduction of the assembly line into automobile manufacturing is another example of a change in the nature of capital, as is the substitution of solid state components for vacuum tubes in electronic devices.

Ford's introduction of the assembly line to produce automobiles could be viewed as an increase in the amount of capital per worker, but productivity with the assembly line increased not simply because there was more capital, but because there was a different kind of capital. Similarly, solid state components allow for a different type of capital to be produced. Computers once ran on vacuum tubes, but modern microprocessors have the equivalent of millions of transistors on them. It is difficult to imagine a computer with millions of vacuum tubes, and solid state components made portable computers possible, opening up new markets and new uses for computers. The models of economists often look at investment growth in terms of monetary amounts of investment, and rarely look at investment growth as a qualitative change in investment goods. Investment in most economic models is completely homogeneous, and even when economic analysis recognizes that different types of investment goods are used in different industries, there is no analysis of how investment goods change within an industry. Analyzing investment in this way completely overlooks progress when analyzing growth.

One can see similar changes in the nature of output. Automobiles are very different now from what they were only a few decades ago, and computers have changed even more than automobiles. In addition to the just-mentioned change in design from tubes to solid state components, the user interface is much improved (older readers will recall writing programs on punch cards), interconnectivity is much improved, and the speed and capacity of computers has grown tremendously even as the size of computers has been reduced. The quantity of both items has also increased – there are more automobiles and more computers – but changes in the characteristics of output contribute at least as much to economic progress as changes in the quantity of output.

Qualitative changes are even more evident over longer periods of time. Compare the roads, the aircraft, and the telephone system of 1950 to those half a century later. Even the characteristics of food, and in particular, food packaging, have changed substantially. Perhaps the most dramatic improvements in output have come in health care, where conditions that were life threatening a century, or even half a century, ago are now remedied by routine treatments. The largest increases in health care output have come not from building more hospitals and training more doctors, but from qualitative improvements in the nature of health care. At the beginning of the twentieth century, there were no antibiotics, joint replacements, open heart surgery, or cancer treatments. By trying to analyze economic growth within a framework where growth is represented by an increase in the quantity of output, the essential characteristics of growth are lost. In the production function framework, growth looks like an increase in the quantity of output, but the essence of growth is a change in the qualitative nature of inputs and outputs more than just a change in their quantities.

Knowledge and progress

These changes came about because of an increased division of labor that, first, made labor more productive as individuals specialized in particular jobs, and second, as those who engaged in specialized work discovered new ways to enhance their productivity. Nobel Prize-winning economist Friedrich Hayek discussed individuals being able to utilize economic knowledge that was not generally available, but that was visible to people in a specific time and place.[15] The division of labor increases the specific knowledge of time and place available to each individual and offers more opportunities for innovations that lead to progress. An individual doing a particular job on an assembly line, for example, has some specific knowledge of time and place that may enable him to come up with methods to increase his productivity, and over time an increasing division of labor may mean that designing the equipment that designs assembly lines even becomes a specialized line of work. Adam Smith's pin factory example shows how the division of labor makes labor more productive, and the economy progresses by making an ever-finer division of labor.

Economic analysis has neglected the role of knowledge in the generation of economic progress. The growth of knowledge is typically presented within the framework of research and development, where R&D is produced much like other goods and services.[16] But discovering new ways of producing goods and developing new goods for market is not a routine business activity, as Chapter 3 argues in more detail, even though all businesses must continually implement innovations to remain competitive. Furthermore, the production of research and development – while it does often lead to spectacular innovations – overlooks the innovations that are implemented by people with some specific knowledge of the jobs they are doing, as noted by Adam Smith and Friedrich Hayek. To really understand the process of economic progress, the analysis must look beyond firms simply investing more to produce more output and examine the process by which innovations lead to fundamental changes in goods and services produced and the processes that produce them.

Economic progress before and after the middle ages

While there was little economic progress in the millennium prior to the Industrial Revolution, in many parts of the world economic development had advanced sufficiently to allow people to live well beyond a primitive existence. Prior to 550, the Roman Empire produced economic progress, partly manifested in the development of a system of public works, including aqueducts and roads that connected much of that part of the world, and by developing a system of government that could oversee a substantial amount of territory. Both of these factors allowed for an increased division of labor, which Adam Smith described as the cause of economic progress. China, too, developed a transportation network and a government that produced the highest standard of living in the world at that time. But in China, as in Rome, despite remarkable progress thousands of years ago, economic progress ceased, and life in China in 1750 was little different from life in China in 550.

Economic progress stagnated for fifteen centuries prior to the Industrial Revolution that began in the mid-1700s because the level of economic development had reached the limits of what could be supported by the existing institutions. In Rome, and in China, strong governments created an orderly society, and unified sufficient territory to allow for a relatively free movement of goods over a large area. Specialization was possible, allowing for the increases in productivity that come from an increased division of labor. This allowed their economies to produce a level of prosperity not previously attainable, yet further progress did not occur because innovation was hampered by restrictive institutions and cultural obstacles. People's economic roles were assigned by custom and tradition, hampering labor mobility, and economic institutions did not allow individuals to capture the gains from any innovations they introduced. Not until the eighteenth century did modern markets for factors of production emerge, where labor could be sold for wages without other restrictions on the labor contract, where capital markets allowed relatively unrestricted borrowing at market interest rates, and where land was bought and sold in an open market. These institutional changes allowed the emergence of a market economy, and allowed economic progress to move beyond what had been accomplished by the Romans and Chinese so many centuries before.[17]

With regard to cultural obstacles, in Europe the church objected to sellers charging more than the "just price" for goods, limiting profits, and objected to the charging of interest on loans, again impeding potentially profitable exchanges and inhibiting the development of capital markets. Labor markets were undeveloped prior to the Industrial Revolution as well. For centuries, slaves had worked for slave owners, serfs had worked for landowners, and apprentices had worked for masters. All of these labor relationships allowed for a significant division of labor and specialization; in that respect so were advances over more primitive societies where people mostly produced for their own consumption, but people still engaged in specialized activities because that was what their parents did, or because that was the labor that was done by their class or caste. Labor relationships like apprenticeship and serfdom allow for a division of labor, but are significantly different from the buying of a person's labor on the labor market. Prior to the Industrial Revolution, labor was not viewed as a commodity, and those who employed the labor of others had responsibilities toward those they employed beyond just paying them.

These types of labor relationships inhibit the productive use of labor for several reasons. When those commanding the labor of others have the responsibility of taking care of that labor beyond just compensating it, those additional responsibilities place additional burdens on those who employ the labor of others, inhibiting labor exchange. When guild masters are responsible for the welfare of their apprentices, for example, a master might be reluctant to take on apprentices even when it appears the relationship would be beneficial for both, because of the risk that the master could be saddled with the burden of supporting the apprentice if things do not work out. Even in a slave relationship, the slave owner is likely to see the relationship as creating a responsibility for the master to look out for the welfare of the slave, if for no other reason than that the slave is an asset whose value must be maintained. The creation of a labor market where labor can be exchanged for wages, with no other obligations on either side, greatly facilitated the productive use of labor.[18]

Another problem with these types of labor relationships is that workers have a minimal incentive to be productive. They may fulfill their obligations by completing the jobs assigned them, but it costs workers little to shirk, and they have little incentive to look for ways to do their work more productively. A labor market, which provides compensation proportional to the productivity of the worker, does provide incentives to workers to be more productive, and to look for more effective ways of doing their jobs.

Prior to the Industrial Revolution, capital markets were similarly hampered. Moral and theological restrictions on lending at interest obviously hampered lending markets, but even without such restrictions, capital markets were not well-developed enough prior to the Industrial Revolution to match up potential borrowers with potential lenders. Excess wealth ended up as conspicuous consumption for the wealthy rather than being employed as productive capital in the economy. The market for land was little different. Land went with families, as part of their estates, and owners were reluctant to sell except under duress. When labor could be bought and sold as a commodity, when interest became accepted as a fair payment in exchange for the use of resources, when capital markets matched up borrowers with lenders, and when market prices became recognized as fair prices, many cultural obstacles hindering profitable activity were removed, allowing entrepreneurial activity to take place.

The institutional obstacles were just as serious. Profitable activity requires a well-developed market system where goods and services can be bought and sold; it requires the protection of private property so that people can capture the benefits of their profitable activity, and it requires a legal system that can settle disputes impartially in a manner that participants view as fair. Nowhere in the world did these institutional and cultural conditions exist before eighteenth-century England, and this combination of institutional and cultural conditions that allowed people to engage in economic activity, and to profit from activities that promoted economic progress, set the stage for the Industrial Revolution. People were free to engage in economic activity unfettered by the dictates of the church, or the state, or by the constraint of tradition.[19]

In a monarchy, where nominally everything belongs to the crown, there are limited incentives to introduce improvements into productive processes. There may even be disincentives. Serfs working for their masters did not get to keep the fruits of their labors, beyond what they needed to survive and continue producing, so their incentives were to shirk in their work as much as possible. If they innovated and found a way to be more productive, the rewards from the additional productivity would go to their masters. More broadly, any innovation would be subject to appropriation by the crown, so people had no incentives to innovate, and no incentives to take risks. The hierarchical economic system enabled people to be more productive and more civilized than primitive people, but by the end of the Roman Empire that economic system had reached the limits of its productivity.

Yet another factor that inhibited progress was a clear system of class in which the lower classes labored and engaged in productive activity. Upper classes lived off the productivity of those below them, and avoided productive activity because it was beneath their status. Prior to the Industrial Revolution, even the most productive individuals could produce relatively little, and those in power could have a far better standard of living by receiving transfers from workers. While the economic activities of the lower classes necessarily were oriented toward producing for their own survival, the economic activities of the upper classes were oriented toward trying to gain political and military power, which would enable them to take a little from a large number of people, making them much better off materially. The incentives of the time were such that politics and violence offered a higher payoff than productive activity.

Many other factors could be cited as contributors to the centuries of economic progress following the Industrial Revolution. Scientific advances opened the door for new products and production processes, but scientific knowledge alone does not produce economic progress. China was more scientifically advanced in 700 than Britain was in 1700, yet the Industrial Revolution began in Britain, not China.[20] Smaller innovations also played a major role. The invention of clocks enabled people to schedule activities at a specific time, and the invention of eyeglasses enabled people to remain productive at detail work, and to read, much later in life.[21] Enhanced agricultural productivity freed up more resources for manufacturing.[22] These inventions were widely available well before the Industrial Revolution, but the Industrial Revolution began in eighteenth-century Britain because it was there that the institutional and cultural barriers to the creation of a true market economy were first removed. The market economy made it profitable to develop the inventions of engineers and scientists into innovations embodied in marketable goods and services.

Economic progress did not begin with the Industrial Revolution, but for a thousand years before the Industrial Revolution there was minimal economic progress. Prior to the middle ages, the economic history of the world involved increasing the division of labor through an increasingly command-oriented social organization. In primitive societies, small bands of hunters or farmers could cooperate together, much as families cooperate, without a formal organizing structure; but as larger groups worked together, the social structure developed more hierarchically, with some people leading and commanding others. This type of organization allowed a greater division of labor, which resulted in greater productivity. The great achievements of the Roman Empire appear to represent the limits of this type of hierarchical economic organization. As such an economy grows more specialized, those at the top of the organization find it increasingly difficult to monitor those at the bottom, resulting in shirking and low productivity. Furthermore, those who engage in production have no incentive to innovate, because the rewards from innovation accrue to those above them in the hierarchy.

After the fall of the Roman Empire, economic progress stopped until the Industrial Revolution, when a new form of economic organization – the market system – allowed a resumption of economic progress.

The growth of commerce

A foundation for the Industrial Revolution was laid by a commercial revolution that had been several centuries in the making. Commerce was well-developed in Roman times, but most people did not make their living in commercial activities. Producers produced for their own consumption, and to support those above them in the hierarchy. When people left European feudal manors to form cities around AD 1050–1150, commerce became the foundation of more people's livelihoods as more people created independent businesses that produced manufactured goods for consumption by others. Commerce was the source of the food, clothing, and other consumption items of these individuals working as manufacturers. Commerce took another boost as financial markets developed in Florence around AD 1200–1300 and spread through the Netherlands to other parts of Europe by 1600. Such markets were used to finance world exploration and trade, and trade with Asia and the New World further developed commerce.

The growth of commercial society laid the foundation for the Industrial Revolution. As Adam Smith noted, the division of labor is limited by the extent of the market, and the expansion of commercial activity led to an expansion of markets, allowing for a greater division of labor. This expansion of commerce provided an environment wherein economies could begin the spectacular economic progress that began with the Industrial Revolution; yet actual progress occurred in Britain while the rest of the world stagnated as Britain blossomed. As Joel Mokyr explains, before the Industrial Revolution, economies were subject to "negative feedback," where ". . . each episode of growth ran into some obstruction or resistance that put an end to it."[23]

Mokyr notes that the best-known negative feedback mechanism is the Malthusian mechanism in which economic growth leads to population growth, keeping everyone's income at a subsistence level. Yet in hindsight it is apparent that this Malthusian trap is not binding, because so much of the world has escaped it. More significantly, Mokyr notes,

> Prosperity and success led to the emergence of predators and parasites in various forms and guises who eventually slaughtered the geese that laid the golden eggs. Tax collectors, foreign invaders, and rent-seeking coalitions such as guilds and monopolies in the end extinguished much of the growth of northern Italy, southern Germany, and the Low Countries.[24]

Echoing Mancur Olson, Mokyr says,

> Sooner or later in any society the progress of technology will grind to a halt because the forces that used to support innovation become vested interests. In a purely dialectical fashion, technological progress creates the forces that eventually destroy it.[25]

Joseph Schumpeter made a similar argument in *Capitalism, Socialism, and Democracy*. He argued that the people who prospered under capitalism did not support its values, which would eventually lead to its demise.[26] But in eighteenth-century Britain, institutions had evolved to insulate the incomes of innovators from the predatory reach of government, of foreigners, and of competing domestic producers by protecting property rights and enforcing a rule of law, escaping negative feedback mechanisms and laying the foundation for economic progress. Is Mokyr correct that sooner or later innovation will grind to a halt because innovators become vested interests? Is Schumpeter right that capitalism is threatened with collapse because people in capitalist societies do not support its values? The institutional foundations that maintain economic progress are discussed in more detail in Chapters 8–10. It is apparent by looking at differences in levels of prosperity and at differences in economic growth rates in various places of the world that prosperity is not inevitable. The institutional foundations of prosperity may be more fragile than is commonly realized, in which case it is all the more important to understand its causes so that public policy will allow economic progress to continue.

Theories of economic progress

What causes economic progress? At the risk of some oversimplification, the answers economists have given to this question can be divided into two broad camps, one following the ideas of Adam Smith, and the other following the ideas of David Ricardo, the most prominent economist of the early 1800s.[27]

Adam Smith, whose overriding goal was to understand the wealth creation process, began his treatise with a discussion of the division of labor as the cause of economic progress. As markets grew, entrepreneurship would lead to innovation, which would lead to an increasing division of labor and increased productivity. Smith's view of progress was optimistic, and envisioned the division of labor as an engine that would generate ever-increasing progress as the division of labor became increasingly more fine. In Smith's words, the division of labor is limited by the extent of the market. One could not have a pin factory producing 48,000 pins a day, to use Smith's example, to supply the needs of a small town, because the town would not consume that many pins daily. But if the factory could sell its output throughout a nation, or export its output to other nations, the greater extent of the market would allow more specialization and greater productivity. Greater productivity would lead to higher incomes, and income growth itself enlarges the extent of the market because higher incomes produce a larger market for goods and services. Thus, income grows, enlarging the extent of the market, which encourages the further division of labor, which increases productivity and income, which increases the division of labor again. Economic progress can continue to occur through this self-reinforcing process.

David Ricardo, in contrast with Smith, had a narrower model of the economy where he envisioned economic output as being a function of the inputs of land, labor, and capital. Investment could produce more capital, but because of diminishing marginal factor productivity and the existence of fixed factors such as land, population growth would always dominate economic growth, keeping most of the population at a subsistence level of income. Even if an increase in productivity led to an increase in per capita income, that increase would only be temporary, as higher incomes would allow more population growth which would push incomes back down toward the subsistence level. The constraints of limited resources coupled with the realities of population growth would stand in the way of increases in the general standard of living. The ideas of Ricardo and his friend and contemporary Thomas Robert Malthus, created the view of economics as the dismal science, which contrasts sharply with Smith's view of entrepreneurship and innovation that would lead to ever-increasing wealth.[28]

With hindsight, Smith's vision of economic growth was more accurate than Ricardo's, but the economics profession has followed Ricardo more closely than Smith in developing a theory of economic growth. Part of the reason is that the comparative static nature of economic modeling has made the production function approach of Ricardo amenable to economic modeling, whereas the innovation that leads to an increased division of labor is more difficult to model precisely. As economics became more scientific over the twentieth century, economists were more ready to attack problems that fit into a general equilibrium model of the economy than those that are more difficult to parameterize.[29] In the Ricardian production function approach, investment is the key to economic growth, whereas in the Smithian view, innovation leading to increases in the division of labor is the key, and growth comes as a part of progress. The Smithian answer seems right, but Smith did not fully explain the process by which that innovation occurs. This is taken up in Chapter 3, where the role of entrepreneurship is considered in more detail.

Smithian versus Ricardian growth

Perhaps the simplest way to differentiate Smithian from Ricardian growth is within the framework of the growth model of Robert Solow, which is the foundation for economic growth models in the early twenty-first century.[30] If output is denoted by Q, and capital and labor are represented as K and L, output is a function of the inputs of capital and labor, or in mathematical notation, $Q = f(K, L)$. This simple mathematical formulation allows considerable development by making simple assumptions about the production function.[31] The model can be used to derive the "golden rule" growth path, which implies that there is an optimal amount of investment, and can be used as a foundation for showing "convergence," which is the idea that economies with lower per capita incomes should grow faster than those with higher per capita incomes, so that over time incomes will converge. In fact, convergence has not occurred, casting some doubt on the basic framework of the Solow model, and creating its own strand of literature on convergence.[32]

Within the Solow model it has been relatively easy to formulate mathematical relationships among Q, K, and L, but modeling changes in the way that K and L are combined, perhaps by changing the form of the production function, or changing the nature of the output Q, have been more problematic. Often, L has been treated as exogenous, and if one is considering per capita income, it is easy to divide by L, meaning that per capita income depends on the amount of capital per worker.[33] The implication is that by investing, K can be increased, which will increase Q. This is the modern extension of the Ricardian view of economic growth.

The Ricardian model of growth has been taken seriously by both economists and policy makers. As development economist Anne Krueger notes, it was at the foundation of world economic development policy for three decades after the Second World War. The application of the Ricardian model points out the advantages of central planning over market allocation, because planners are in a better position both to increase a nation's saving and investment rate, and to direct investment toward those sectors that can be most productive.[34] Yet despite the advice of economic growth theorists, undeveloped economies remain undeveloped even though they have undertaken substantial investment initiatives. Furthermore, the data make clear that only a small part of economic growth can be explained by increases in investment. The answer must lie somewhere else.

Within the Solow framework the most frequently examined alternatives for the causes of growth are K or the functional form f of the production function. The effects of capital are easy to analyze, and so have been analyzed extensively, whereas the effects of changing the functional form are harder to analyze. Typically, changes in the functional form of the production function have been attributed to technological change, which has produced a substantial literature in itself. But technological advances by themselves will not produce progress, as examples from ancient China suggest, and as more recent examples from twentieth century centrally planned economies like the Soviet Union show. The Soviet Union tried to employ advanced technology, and invested heavily as the Solow model indicates it should to produce growth, yet its economy fell further and further behind world standards.

Other avenues might be taken within the basic Ricardian framework. Under different constraints, a Ricardian model need not imply convergence, suggesting that this framework might be able to be rehabilitated to conform more closely to reality.[35] Taking a different tack, Nobel laureate Robert Lucas suggests that the key may be L, not K, and that in particular human capital can play the major role in development.[36] Lucas discusses the idea of the external effects of human capital, and suggests that a higher population density may result in a finer division of labor and that the human capital of one person may make others more productive. Thus, Lucas takes an approach that moves the Ricardian framework a step toward the Smithian view of economic growth.

The Smithian view of growth focuses less on the quantities of factors of production and more on the processes that are used to combine them into aggregate output. Allyn Young viewed economic growth as occurring because of increasing returns,[37] and explicitly recognized the Smithian foundations of his analysis, but Nicholas Kaldor argued that increasing returns does not sit well in the neoclassical framework.[38] In frequently cited articles, Paul Romer has shown that growth can be modeled with a factor having increasing returns, and that in such a model growth rates need not converge over the long run, which fits the facts better than the simple Solow framework. Romer focuses attention on human capital, and argues that additional investment in research could promote more economic growth.[39] Like earlier developments from the Solow model, however, this line of reasoning focuses on the inputs into the production process rather than the process itself. In Romer's work, the idea of increasing returns that can be traced back to Adam Smith is depicted in a neoclassical and neo-Ricardian framework, but Smith's insight that people become more productive through an increased division of labor is omitted from this type of analysis.

The production process

The most basic facts of economic growth weigh against focusing on the inputs into the production process, and point toward an examination of the process itself. Within the neoclassical framework, changes in the form of the production function have had a bigger impact on economic growth than changes in the inputs into the production function. The quantity and quality of both human and physical capital are important, beyond a doubt, but they are a product of an economy and not factors given exogenously to it. Both existed in abundance in ancient China, and even today the pyramids of Egypt (physical capital) and the knowledge of Leonardo da Vinci (human capital) inspire awe; yet economic growth, as it is understood today, is a recent phenomenon. In 1989 Blanchard and Fischer noted,

> real GNP is about 37 times larger than it was in 1874, 7 times larger than in 1919, and 3 times larger than in 1950. Extrapolating backwards leads to the well-known conclusion that economic growth at these rates cannot have been taking place for more than a few centuries.[40]

Land, labor, and capital long predate the transformation to economic growth. It is the process by which they are combined that has created sustained economic growth.

Qualitative versus quantitative dimensions of progress

While recognizing that economic growth is only a part of economic progress, one might still believe that the growth in income or output can be analyzed by itself, without taking into account the other dimensions of progress. However, to do so is likely to turn up conclusions that are incomplete and misleading, and is likely to point toward policy implications that are not as effective as they could be, and that perhaps are even counterproductive. The reason is that the remarkable income growth that has taken place over the last several centuries would not have been possible without the qualitative changes in the nature of the output being produced. Growth in the level of income is driven by qualitative changes in the nature of the output produced.

If there is a naturally limited market for more of the same goods and services the market currently produces, then the potential for income growth will be limited unless new goods and services are brought to market. Economic growth in the twentieth century produced more output for consumers, but more significantly, it replaced horse-drawn wagons with automobiles, replaced typewriters and adding machines with computers, introduced television, telephones, air conditioning, and other innovations to the market. Without these qualitative changes, there would be much less room for quantitative changes in income, so one cannot really understand the quantitative changes without understanding the qualitative changes that cause them.

Different economic processes are at work to produce increases in the level of output and qualitative changes in the nature of output. The qualitative innovations are a product of entrepreneurship, which is left out of models that do not recognize the qualitative dimensions of economic progress. If quantitative changes in output are driven by these qualitative changes, then to understand the quantitative changes one must understand the causes of qualitative changes. Economic growth, narrowly defined as increases in income and output, cannot be understood except within the broader framework of economic progress. It is not just that focusing narrowly on growth leaves out some aspects of progress; rather, it is that focusing narrowly on quantitative growth in output and income leaves out the very factors that cause that growth.

For policy purposes, models that narrowly focus on income and output growth without taking into account the broader environment of economic progress are unable to capture or analyze the fundamental factors that cause growth. In such models, the crucial factors are assumed away, so they cannot be analyzed or understood. Economic policies designed to produce prosperity must, therefore, be formulated within the broader framework of economic progress, and not simply focus on growth in income and output.

Growth versus progress

Economists' theories of economic progress have, for the most part, taken a Ricardian production function approach and focused on income growth, where growth is depicted as a result of increases into the inputs into the production process. Investment leads to an increase in capital, and education augments human capital, making the economy more productive and creating growth. Technological advancement also plays a key role, but here again, the production function approach to growth takes the center stage, as technological progress is produced by research and development activities, and research and development is itself an output produced by inputs of capital and labor. In this Ricardian view, increases in output are the result of increases in human and physical capital and technological advances. Despite the recognition that technological advances are a key element, economic progress is depicted as an increase in the quantity of output rather than a change in the nature of the output.

The main point of this chapter is that economic progress is much more than just an increase in the quantity of output. While increases in output are significant, they are only a small part of the story, and even then, any significant increases in the quantity of output will almost necessarily be accompanied by changes in the nature of the output. If one reflects on the statistic that over the twentieth century income increased by about seven times, it is hard to imagine consuming seven times as much of the same output that people consumed a century earlier. Rather than eat seven times as much food, people eat different types of food, prepared differently. People travel in personal automobiles and jet aircraft rather than on horse-drawn carriages and sailing ships. People communicate via e-mail rather than by letter, and get information through television or the internet rather than from a newspaper. The changing nature of output is one of the factors that have propelled the quantity of output to increase so substantially.

Seeing the process of economic progress this way turns attention away from the inputs into the production process toward the causes of innovation. The Ricardian production function approach to growth naturally focuses attention on ways that investment in human and physical capital could be increased, and on ways in which technological advances can be made. The Smithian view of the process focuses attention on the factors that lead people to introduce innovations into the economy. Progress occurs because innovators introduce new goods and services, improve on existing goods and services, and introduce ways to more effectively produce existing goods and services. The factors that lead to innovation are likely to be different from the factors that lead to growth in inputs and technology.

Progress and growth are not the same things. Growth is but a small part of progress, and whereas progress naturally leads to growth, growth without progress is self-limiting. Progress occurs because of innovations introduced into the economy, and innovations are the result of entrepreneurship. Prior to the development of the capitalist economic system in the 1700s, entrepreneurship was stifled because there were incomplete markets for factors of production, and because innovators could expect no reward for their entrepreneurial activities. The idea that the emergence of a market economy laid the foundation for the Industrial Revolution and an unprecedented three centuries of economic progress is not new, but much of the economic analysis of this progress overlooks its fundamental cause. The qualitative changes that underlie economic progress are the product of entrepreneurship, which ties together the concepts of entrepreneurship and economic progress.

3 Entrepreneurship versus management

Entrepreneurship is the act of observing an unexploited profit opportunity, and then exploiting it. Israel Kirzner defines entrepreneurship more narrowly, as simply the act of noticing a profit opportunity that has previously gone unnoticed.[1] The actions the entrepreneur takes to exploit the profit opportunity are then, following Kirzner, acts of production rather than entrepreneurship. While this book views entrepreneurship more broadly than Kirzner, there is some merit in considering Kirzner's more narrow definition, because it focuses on the fact that entrepreneurship is the implementation of an innovative idea rather than the production based on the idea.[2] Kirzner's narrow definition of entrepreneurship clearly distinguishes entrepreneurship from the routine activities of production, and also distinguishes the approach to entrepreneurship and economic progress used here from the Ricardian production function approach to economic growth discussed in Chapter 2. Entrepreneurship means finding new ways to employ inputs and finding new markets and new types of output, and is not captured well in the Ricardian approach to economic growth which focuses on the quantities of inputs and advances in technology, as Chapter 2 explained.

While there are good arguments for using Kirzner's definition of entrepreneurship, the argument for broadening the definition is that unless an entrepreneurial insight is acted on, the simple noticing of an unexploited profit opportunity will have no effect. Furthermore, until an idea is acted upon, it is unclear whether it is, in fact, a profit opportunity. There is a natural tendency to focus on entrepreneurial successes, but there are undoubtedly a higher number of cases in which individuals believed they had an idea that could be implemented to bring them profits, but when they actually tried to implement the idea it resulted in losses. The idea itself may have been good, but the enterprise was mismanaged, or the idea may have had some subtle flaws that later innovators were able to correct and actually implement profitably. However, if the entrepreneurial act is spotting an unexploited profit opportunity, there is no real way to know whether the idea really is a profit opportunity until it passes the market test and actually generates profits.

This chapter contrasts the concept of entrepreneurship with management, which is the efficient use of resources within a given production technology. Adopting the simple mathematical notation of Chapter 2, where output, Q, is a function, f, of the inputs of capital, K, and labor, L, so that $Q = f(K, L)$, management means choosing the optimal quantities of K and L to produce the optimal amount of output Q, and doing it in such a way that no resources are wasted. That is, given the production function f, the profit-maximizing quantities of K and L are chosen, and K and L are combined without waste such that the maximum amount of Q is produced from the K and L employed. Good management means doing what one is doing as efficiently as possible. Entrepreneurship means implementing something new.

The distinction is important because the institutional structure that leads to effective management is different from the institutions that lead to entrepreneurial activity, and if entrepreneurship is the key to economic progress, the differences must be recognized. The economic theory of growth has developed in a framework that focuses attention on the managerial aspects of firms as opposed to their entrepreneurial aspects, so differentiating management from entrepreneurship points toward a better understanding of the foundations of economic progress.

Entrepreneurship as arbitrage

The surest way for an entrepreneur to make profits is through arbitrage. If an entrepreneur notices that a seller is willing to sell a good for less than a buyer is willing to pay for it, the entrepreneur can buy it from the seller, and sell it to the buyer, reaping a profit and making both the buyer and seller better off as a result. Such arbitrage profits are easy to notice, tend to be small, and tend to be rapidly competed away. Nevertheless, especially in financial markets, arbitrageurs are able to make steady, and occasionally spectacular, profits. Most entrepreneurial activities involve production and time, however, and these two elements mean that when an entrepreneur acts on an entrepreneurial insight, the entrepreneur's profit is not a sure thing.

Consider, for example, a person who notices that a particular type and quality of apples are selling for $0.25 each in city A, and are selling for $0.50 in city B. Further assume that apples can be transported from city A to city B for $0.10 each. An entrepreneur can buy apples for $0.25 in city A and sell them for $0.50 in city B, making a profit of $0.15 per apple, after transportation costs. However, the entrepreneur must consider that some apples may be damaged or spoiled in shipping, which could lower or completely eliminate the profit. Furthermore, prices may change so that by the time the entrepreneur actually gets the apples to city B, they may be selling for $0.35 or less. Unless the transaction is instantaneous and the transaction costs are zero (or certain), what appears to be a profit opportunity may not be one in fact.

Production might be analyzed as just a more complicated type of arbitrage. An entrepreneur notes that enough capital to produce 100 units of some output can be rented for $50, and enough labor to produce 100 units of that output can be hired for $100, while the output can be sold for $2 per unit, which would result in a profit of $50. If the entrepreneur acts on this observation, a number of factors could cause that apparent profit to disappear. The prices of the inputs or output may change, or it may turn out that it takes more capital and/or labor to complete the job than at first it appeared. If the production process is well-established, keeping costs in line may be a matter of good management, but if the entrepreneur is acting on an opportunity to produce something that never has been produced before, there may be considerable uncertainty with regard to the production methods and costs. In the real world, one will rarely observe a profit opportunity that is a sure thing.

Entrepreneurship can be viewed as an extension of arbitrage, in that the entrepreneurial insight always involves noticing that some particular things can be bought in particular locations for some particular prices, perhaps then be combined in a production process to generate something that can be sold in a particular location, perhaps at some later time, for an amount greater than the cost of the inputs. Yet with production and time intervening between the purchase and sale, entrepreneurship also involves taking a risk that the profit will vanish. Still, the depiction of entrepreneurship as arbitrage helps identify the essential entrepreneurial insight: a particular combination of goods and services could be purchased, and perhaps combined in a production process, and could then be sold for more than the purchase price. The entrepreneurial insight could be as simple as noticing price discrepancies in the market – pure arbitrage opportunities – or could be as complex as envisioning a new production process, or a new type of good or service that could be offered on the market. In all cases, it is the observation that goods and/or services can be bought at some price, perhaps combined in a particular way, and then sold for more than the purchase price.

Management, economic efficiency, and the profitability of firms

The methods of modern economics tend to overlook the significance of entrepreneurship in creating economic progress. Economic theory focuses on the properties of economic equilibrium, and in the theory of competitive markets, actions of firms are completely constrained by the parameters of the market. Firms are assumed to maximize profits, and in a competitive equilibrium, profits are competed down to zero, so firms must choose the optimal mix of inputs and combine them as efficiently as possible in order to minimize costs to remain in business. In a typical formal presentation of the theory of competition, the firm buys inputs of capital and labor which are combined in a production function to produce output, so as depicted above, $Q = f(K, L)$. The firm must pay interest at rate r to hire capital and wages at rate w to hire labor, so the firm's costs are $rK + wL$, and its revenues are the price of its output, p, times the quantity sold, or pQ. The firm's profit , Π, is its revenues minus costs, or $\Pi = pf(K, L) - rK - wL$. Within this framework, the only things the firm can choose are its levels of K and L, so profit maximizing means choosing the levels of inputs that maximize profit. Profit is maximized by hiring inputs up to the point where their marginal products are equal to their prices.

People who run the competitive firms in this framework are managers who have producing the optimal amount of output at minimum cost as their goal. This entails choosing the right combination of inputs, and also entails seeing that inputs are used as productively as possible. Workers need to be kept from shirking, and more generally, inputs must be used effectively to maximize profit.[3] Good management means efficiently combining inputs to produce output. With good management the firm will maximize its profits; with poor management it will not, and will be competed out of business by other more efficient firms.

In an economy characterized by economic progress, this type of management will be insufficient for a firm in a competitive market to survive. Over time, entrepreneurs uncover new and more effective ways of combining inputs and outputs, so the manager who simply prevents shirking and waste will be left behind by firms that adopt new production processes. More significantly, entrepreneurs will discover new types of output that will better satisfy consumer desires, so the manager who keeps producing the same type of output will be left behind by firms that offer more innovative products. Examples can be seen throughout the economy, in instances as varied as changes in fast food restaurant menus and food preparation methods, new styling and features in automobiles, and of course, in the substantial advances in computer and communication devices. This entrepreneurial theory of the firm is substantially different from the neoclassical model that serves as the foundation for mainstream economics.[4] One key difference can be found in the assumptions underlying these two approaches to analyzing economic competition. Consider two areas of entrepreneurship – finding more profitable methods of production, and discovering better product characteristics for consumers – within the standard competitive model.

The discovery of more profitable methods of production might arguably be able to be represented in the standard competitive model, by noting that there may be alternative methods of production, g, such that $g(K, L) > f(K, L)$. Framed in this way, the shortcomings of the standard approach are apparent. While the firm's management can choose levels of K and L from a continuous scale to solve the maximization problem, there is no menu of production functions f, g, h, and so on that offer alternatives from which the firm can choose. After the fact one might represent a new production technique as a different production function, but the theory offers no hints as to whether an alternative production function exists, and if it does, how a profit-maximizing firm might go about discovering it. Entrepreneurship, represented this way, is exogenous to the model.

The discovery of new and improved products and product characteristics is even further outside the model, because it is assumed away. In the standard model, firms in a competitive industry are assumed to produce a homogeneous product, and any deviation from this assumption is a movement away from competition toward monopoly. In contrast, an entrepreneurial view of product homogeneity sees product differentiation as a competitive strategy designed to try to gain market share and produce a competitive advantage. The managerial view of competitive markets sees product differentiation as anticompetitive, whereas the entrepreneurial view sees product differentiation as an integral part of the competitive process.

People who run firms serve both managerial and entrepreneurial functions. As managers they try to minimize costs by choosing the optimal levels of inputs, and try to avoid the inefficient use of resources. As entrepreneurs, they look for new and improved methods of production, and they look for ways to improve the characteristics of their output. For a firm to survive in the long run, good management is helpful, but successful entrepreneurship is essential. When one factors in the impact of economic progress on firms over time, it is apparent that a firm, no matter how efficiently managed, cannot survive by minimizing costs and eliminating waste. It must continually improve its methods of production, and it must continually update its product, or its business will be eroded by other firms that do. This is obvious when one looks at the difference between products in the computer and telecommunications industries now versus ten years ago. Similar progress, though slower, is also apparent in automobiles, apparel, entertainment, and just about any industry. Even in an industry as basic as food, restaurants continually update their menus and preparation methods, and grocery stores continue to offer new products and packaging.

Conceivably, an innovative firm could continue to stay ahead of its competition despite some inefficiency, but an efficient firm will continue to lose ground in the marketplace if it does not innovate, or follow innovators closely by adopting the innovations of competitors. Henry Ford, who had the brilliant innovation of using the assembly line to produce automobiles, and who was notorious for monitoring employees to prevent shirking and waste, once said his customers could have any color car they wanted, as long as it was black. But faced with eroding sales to General Motors, which offered a variety of colors, Ford changed his mind. This is one example of a more general observation that firms cannot hope to remain profitable by finding a successful formula and sticking to it. They will be left behind by competitors who discover improved production methods and improved product characteristics.

To emphasize, for firms to succeed in a competitive market, efficient management is helpful, but entrepreneurship is essential. With this in mind, one must question an economic model of competition that assumes that competition is characterized by firms producing homogeneous products, and that depicts a competitive industry as one in which there are no profits. The first step to take to rectify this is to recognize the distinction between management and entrepreneurship; the second step is to orient the theory of competition to recognize the importance of entrepreneurship relative to management.

Circumstances of time and place

Friedrich Hayek emphasized the particular circumstances of time and place that provide knowledge to some people that is unavailable to others.[5] While Hayek was discussing the role of the market system in coordinating the activities of individuals with this type of specific knowledge, his observations are directly relevant to entrepreneurship. Individuals without such knowledge cannot simply rely on their alertness to spot profit opportunities, because information about a profit opportunity may not be sufficient without a context of knowledge which allows individuals to see what actions might result in profits.[6] For example, it would be difficult for an auto mechanic to spot a profit opportunity in the pharmaceutical industry, and it would be difficult for a dentist to spot a profit opportunity in the automobile industry, even if they might wish for a product with certain currently unavailable characteristics. Some examples can help illustrate the role of knowledge in the distinction between entrepreneurship and management.

Pierre Desrochers, in a very insightful article, offers many examples.[7] One relates a story about a demonstration Steve Wozniak, a co-founder of Apple Computer, saw of a color monitor connected to a computer in a meeting of a silicon valley computer club. Wozniak was so impressed that he decided the Apple II – their first successful commercial product – had to have a color monitor. Wozniak says that had he not seen the demonstration, Apple computers probably would have had monochrome monitors, and the product probably would not have been as successful. The color monitor differentiated his product from other personal computers at the time, which was the type of competitive action that (1) results in economic progress, and (2) would be called a deviation from competition by neoclassical economics, because of the product differentiation. Had Wozniak not lived in silicon valley where he had access to knowledge concentrated in that geographic area, he would not have seen that demonstration. He did not attend the meeting with the intention of determining what type of monitor to use on his computer, yet because he was there and happened to be exposed to that information, he was able to make use of it even though he was not seeking it out and had no prior idea of its significance. Desrochers offers many other examples showing how specific knowledge of time and place leads to entrepreneurial activity.

Another example of entrepreneurship appeared in *Flying* magazine, in an article that discussed changes in production methods for Piper aircraft. Typically, aircraft manufacturers have different assembly lines for different aircraft models. The article notes,

> In the new plan, all the different models go down the line together – a turboprop Meridian following a Warrior, for example ... The first thought is that the Meridian would take a lot more time at each station, so it would slow the moving of the line. That doesn't happen because if the technicians finish on the Warrior and the Meridian isn't ready, they go to that station to help complete the task ... I've been looking at aircraft plants for years, and this is the best-looking system I have ever seen. New Piper estimates that it will result in a significant decrease in the man hours required to build an airplane.[8]

The end product – the airplane – is the same, but a more efficient production model produces it, yielding an example of the shift from $f(K, L)$ to $g(K, L)$. A profit opportunity like this is not just something that an observant individual could notice. It requires specific knowledge of time and place – in this case, knowledge about aircraft manufacturing – for one to recognize that a different production process might be more efficient.

Adam Smith notes the same thing when he says,

> Men are much more likely to discover easier and readier methods of attaining any object, when the whole attention of their minds is directed towards that single object, than when it is dissipated among a great variety of things... It is naturally to be expected, therefore, that some one or another of those who are employed in each particular branch of labour should soon find out easier and readier methods of performing their own particular work, whenever the nature of it admits of such improvement.[9]

Thus, Smith recognizes how the specific knowledge of time and place leads to entrepreneurial discovery, and why entrepreneurial discovery is necessary for a business to survive. Because competitors will be taking advantage of this type of knowledge to act entrepreneurially, the firm that continues to employ the same methods of production will be left further and further behind others in the industry with the passage of time.

Henry Ford's adoption of the assembly line to manufacture automobiles is an example from the beginning of the twentieth century of innovations in both the type of output, with the Model T differentiated from other automobiles, and in the process of manufacturing. Clayton Christensen gives several examples from the computer industry in the late twentieth century of the same type of innovation.[10] He notes several examples where successful firms retained their successful formulas too long, only to be left behind by the progress of the market. For example, IBM focused on their mainframe computer business as their market was being eroded in the 1970s by companies like Digital Equipment Corporation (DEC) that produced lower-cost minicomputers. DEC in turn stuck with their successful minicomputer line in the 1980s as the market was shifting to personal computers. In both cases, the firms ran into financial troubles as progress in the market made their once-successful formulas increasingly less successful. Even experts in an industry, who are in an excellent position to see information about the direction of the market, may find themselves unable to place it in the context of knowledge that shows them the entrepreneurial actions that must be taken for a successful firm to continue to be successful. Existing firms then find their businesses disrupted by changes in the market, resulting in what Joseph Schumpeter described as creative destruction.[11] When one looks at the march of economic progress, Schumpeterian entrepreneurship that disrupts the existing order is an integral part of the process.

The process of entrepreneurial discovery

Entrepreneurial discovery is depicted by Israel Kirzner as the costless act of noticing a profit opportunity, in contrast to William Baumol who depicts technological advancement as the result of the intentional investment decisions of profit-maximizing firms.[12] As Baumol describes it, entrepreneurial insights of the type Kirzner discusses are becoming increasingly rare as firms create bureaucratized research and development programs that produce innovations in the same way that firms produce other products. These two views lie at the extremes as models of entrepreneurial discovery. For Kirzner, the entrepreneur just notices a previously undiscovered profit opportunity, whereas Baumol argues that entrepreneurial actions have a minimal effect on economic progress compared to the routinized research and development activities of firms. In fact, the process of entrepreneurial discovery is a combination of both of these extremes. There is more to entrepreneurship than just noticing that a profit opportunity exists. Entrepreneurs undertake many activities to search for entrepreneurial opportunities, and to make it more likely that they, rather than someone else, will be the discoverer. Undertaking research activities may produce entrepreneurial opportunities, as Baumol emphasizes, but does not guarantee that they will be recognized.

An example that brings together the views of Baumol and Kirzner is the innovation of the graphical user interface on computers. The concept was invented at the Xerox Corporation, where research and development activities were undertaken. Xerox came up with the idea of windows on the computer screen and the mouse as an input device to navigate the windows operating system, but failed to commercialize their invention. Steve Jobs at Apple Computer saw Xerox's invention as a profit opportunity and created the Apple Macintosh computer with the new concepts at its foundation, followed by Bill Gates who adapted the graphical user interface as Microsoft Windows. Joseph Schumpeter made the distinction between invention and innovation, saying that innovation only takes place when an invention is incorporated into a product that is brought to market. Using Schumpeter's terminology, the invention was made at Xerox, but the innovators were Steve Jobs at Apple and Bill Gates at Microsoft.[13]

Baumol's view, where investment in research and development produces technological change, which then results in economic growth, leaves out the crucial step where invention becomes innovation. In the graphical user interface example, Xerox invested in the research and development, but nobody at Xerox was able to capitalize on the commercial potential of their invention, and without a market economy conducive to entrepreneurship, the story might have ended there. Jobs and Gates, though not the inventors of the concept, were the innovators, who recognized an unexploited profit opportunity and acted entrepreneurially to capture it in the manner described by Kirzner. But those entrepreneurs did not simply happen to notice what nobody before them had seen; they had systematically built up their bases of knowledge, and were using their knowledge of the computer industry as a base to actively seek profit opportunities from innovations in the computer market. They had invested resources in generating what Hayek called that specific knowledge of time and place, so that when the profit opportunity presented itself, they had both the alertness and the deliberately acquired stock of knowledge to recognize it.[14] Entrepreneurship is not produced, but the environment within which entrepreneurial discoveries are more likely can be produced, and entrepreneurs do invest in producing the knowledge base that will allow them to make future entrepreneurial discoveries.

When analyzing the entrepreneurial process, the actions of entrepreneurs can be broken down into three components along the lines of the previous example. First, entrepreneurs can undertake activities like research and development that may generate profit opportunities. Second, entrepreneurs can build their stock of knowledge so that when a profit opportunity does appear, they will be in a position to recognize it. Third, there is that elusive characteristic of alertness that enables an entrepreneur to spot what others have not recognized.

There is a second aspect to the entrepreneurial process that goes beyond the actions of the entrepreneur and extends to the entrepreneur's economic environment. Knowledge can be tacitly shared and obtained by those who are in close geographic proximity, increasing the overall level of entrepreneurial activity.[15] Also, entrepreneurial actions on the part of some generate entrepreneurial opportunities for others, creating an environment in which entrepreneurial activity is more likely.[16] Some economic environments are more conducive to entrepreneurship than others.

The environment for entrepreneurial discovery

The environmental factors that foster entrepreneurship might be broken down into three components. First, there are those aspects of the economic environment that produce profit opportunities; second, there are those aspects of the environment that make it easier to recognize those profit opportunities that exist; and third, there are those aspects of the environment that create the incentive for entrepreneurs to act on those profit opportunities they spot. A complete understanding of the entrepreneurial process requires a recognition of both the way in which the economic environment generates entrepreneurial opportunities and invites entrepreneurs to take advantage of them, and the way that entrepreneurs themselves act to increase the chances that they will make an entrepreneurial discovery.

Some aspects of the environment that produces entrepreneurial opportunities are income growth, technological developments, and the actions of other entrepreneurs. Income growth creates entrepreneurial opportunities because it opens up additional markets. Higher income creates the demand for not only more goods and services, but also for different types of goods and services. Relative price changes create entrepreneurial opportunities for the same reason. Technological developments also generate economic opportunities, for obvious reasons. Entrepreneurial action also generates further entrepreneurial opportunities because new markets create the opportunity for complementary goods, new manufacturing processes, and more. These issues will be considered further in Chapter 6. Entrepreneurs can create an environment for discovering entrepreneurial opportunities within their own firms by pursuing research and development activities, and when they do so, they create an environment in which knowledge spillovers can enhance the environment for entrepreneurship well beyond their own firms.

The existence of entrepreneurial opportunities is no guarantee that they will be recognized and acted upon. While entrepreneurs can act themselves to become more alert to entrepreneurial opportunities, an environment within which more entrepreneurial activity is taking place makes it more likely that entrepreneurial opportunities will be recognized. In a stagnant economic environment (or a steady state as described by neoclassical economics), there are few entrepreneurial opportunities, and so little reason to remain alert to those that may arise. Furthermore, because there will always be some risk that what appears as a profit opportunity will not, in fact, generate profits, entrepreneurial actions will be inhibited. An environment in which the examples of others show that there are entrepreneurial opportunities to be exploited, and show by example how to exploit them, make it more likely that entrepreneurial opportunities will be recognized and acted upon.

Entrepreneurship also requires an institutional environment in which institutional barriers do not prevent the benefits of such action from being appropriated. Stable legal institutions, the protection of property rights, and low barriers in the form of taxation and regulation, create an environment within which entrepreneurship can take place. Such institutions minimize the risk of entrepreneurial action – which is already an inherently risky activity – and preserve the profits from successful entrepreneurship.

Competition and entrepreneurship

Israel Kirzner's book with the same title as this section, offers a theory of the competitive process as an alternative to the neoclassical theory of competition which depicts competition as an equilibrium outcome. The neoclassical model of competition depicts an economy already at equilibrium, with no profit opportunities for firms. The only role for firms is efficient management. If a competitive market is not at an equilibrium, how would it get there? Kirzner answers that entrepreneurs notice unexploited profit opportunities that firms can act on, leading markets to equilibrium. Entrepreneurs serve this equilibrating function in response to any factors that might disturb a market equilibrium. Yet, more along the lines of Schumpeter, entrepreneurs must also be innovators, and must find new and improved types of output, and new and improved ways of producing their output, to survive.

The competitive process is the force that propels economic progress, and because the competitive process generates progress, firms must be entrepreneurial to survive. Firms cannot simply minimize costs and hope to remain profitable in a market where their competitors are offering innovations in output, and are discovering innovative methods of production. Firms must continually innovate – or imitate the innovations of other firms – to remain profitable. Entrepreneurship might be thought of as arbitrage, where the alert entrepreneur notices that a good can be bought for less in one location than it can be sold for in another, but this greatly oversimplifies the entrepreneurial role. In most cases, entrepreneurship is much more complex than arbitrage. It is more than just being alert to price discrepancies in the market. It is spotting alternative methods of production, and spotting ways in which output characteristics can be altered to better satisfy the demands of purchasers. Those entrepreneurial activities will typically require what Hayek called the specific knowledge of time and place. Simply being alert is not sufficient. One must have the appropriate context of knowledge within which to place new information in order to recognize that a profit opportunity exists.

Because an entrepreneurial opportunity has not been previously acted upon, there is always some uncertainty involved in an entrepreneurial undertaking, to use Frank Knight's term,[17] so without some reward for entrepreneurship, there would be no reason to accept the uncertainty. There is a tendency to look at successful examples of entrepreneurship and overlook the failures, but entrepreneurial actions almost always entail the likelihood of failure. Entrepreneurial action does not guarantee profits, but in a competitive market, a lack of entrepreneurship assures that profits will be eroded over time until they disappear and then turn into losses.

The competitive process can be described briefly as follows. At any point in time, the economy tends toward an equilibrium, and if it is not exactly at that equilibrium, entrepreneurial actions, as described by Kirzner, pull the economy toward equilibrium. That equilibrium is always changing, partly because of changes in preferences, resource prices, and other factors exogenous to the producers in the market. When these factors – exogenous to the firms – in the market change, Kirznerian entrepreneurship is the equilibrating force, as Kirzner describes.[18] A market's equilibrium will also change because of the entrepreneurial actions of the firms in the market. The process of competition implies innovations in production that lower production costs, and innovations in output characteristics, so competitive firms must always be alert to these innovations and must match them or improve on them to remain in business. Entrepreneurial innovations are always upsetting the previous equilibrium and creating a new one, and each new equilibrium offers consumers lower costs and/or more desirable products. What appears in neoclassical theory as an unchanging equilibrium is in fact a moving target, and in this sense is not an equilibrium at all. The neoclassical competitive outcome, where firms produce a homogeneous product according to a given production function, is completely unrelated to the competitive process where firms differentiate their products to enhance their appeal to consumers, and where they change their production processes to lower their costs.

Competitive firms cannot survive without being entrepreneurial. If they simply act as the neoclassical theory describes, producing according to a given production function, choosing the optimal levels of inputs, and minimizing input waste (such as shirking employees), they will fall further and further behind as the market adopts new production processes and offers new output characteristics. Entrepreneurship is an integral part of the competitive process, and an essential ingredient in any competitive firm, even though it is not represented in the neoclassical theory of the firm. The competitive process is driven by entrepreneurship that produces continually better products – as judged by the consumers of those products – and that produces those products at costs that continue to fall over time because of innovation in production techniques. In this way, entrepreneurship produces economic progress.

Three differences

To highlight the significance of this entrepreneurial approach to competition and economic progress, this section considers three aspects that differentiate it from the equilibrium approach to competition and growth that dominated twentieth-century economic analysis.[19] Product differentiation is viewed differently in the two approaches, the implications of profit are different, and most significantly, the entrepreneurial approach offers a substantially different view of optimality. There are other differences, but by focusing on these three significant differences, one can see that this approach offers not just a critique of existing theory, but an alternative way of viewing competition and economic progress.

Product differentiation

The issue of product differentiation really goes back to the distinction between growth and progress. If one proxies progress by growth, as in the standard view, and sees improvement as represented by higher income levels, then product differentiation is a means by which consumers can have more variety. Because differentiated products give sellers some monopoly power and allow them to price above minimum average cost, differentiated products result in an inefficiently large number of producers each producing a suboptimal level of output, resulting in inefficiency, according to the standard view. There is a trade-off between benefits of greater variety and the costs of some monopoly power that goes with differentiated products, and whether product differentiation is desirable according to the neoclassical approach depends upon how one evaluates this trade-off.

In contrast, when one sees progress as more than just income growth, product differentiation is a competitive strategy that generates progress. One of the most significant ways in which progress manifests itself is through improvements in the types of output offered in the market, in the form of either new products or improved characteristics in existing products. Improvements in output occur when entrepreneurs see that it would be more profitable to change a product's characteristics, or offer a different type of product on the market. Product differentiation is the route through which innovation expresses itself, and through which progress occurs. The process of product differentiation is the process of improving the characteristics of economic output. Without firms that are continuing to differentiate their products, there would be no improvement in the types of output the market offers.

Michael Cox and Richard Alm show the substantial increase in product differentiation over just a few decades at the end of the twentieth century.[20] As noted in

Chapter 2, they document the greater variety in automobile models, foods and beverages, shoes, and many other products. Cox and Alm emphasize the advantages of this variety in terms of an expansion in consumer choices, but as beneficial as the increased number of choices is, the real long-run advantage of this product differentiation is that it introduces improvements in products available to people, yielding economic progress. If firms introduce differentiated products into a market that are different, but not better, those firms do not gain any competitive advantage over rival producers, because each firm's product is equally different from the other's. If firms differentiate their products to make them better and more desirable, then the innovating firm has a competitive advantage. Competitive forces push firms to introduce products that are not just different, but better.

Product differentiation is not just an outcome that gives consumers more choices, it is a process that creates improved options for purchasers and generates economic progress. If one takes a static equilibrium view of the economy, product differentiation at any point in time appears to be the variety of choices that is offered to purchasers.[21] When one puts product differentiation within the context of economic progress, new variants of products improve upon previous offerings, leading to economic progress. Product differentiation is an essential component of a dynamic economy that increases people's well-being by offering them increasingly better products.

Profit

Another difference between the managerial and entrepreneurial views of the firm's activities is in the role of profit. In the managerial model, there is no profit in competitive markets because all profit is competed to zero. Because the competitive equilibrium is the benchmark for efficiency, profit is a sign of inefficiency and an impediment to welfare maximization.[22] The general equilibrium approach to economics depicts the concept of equilibrium as more than just a state toward which the economy is tending, and represents an economy as always in equilibrium, which means always without profit.[23] But profit is the lure which entices entrepreneurs to innovate. As Schumpeter notes in his *Theory of Economic Development*, without profit there will be no entrepreneurship, and without entrepreneurship, there will be no profit.

Do profits enhance economic welfare, or degrade it? From the managerial perspective, profits lower welfare because they raise prices, lowering the quantity demanded, keeping the economy from achieving Pareto optimality. Monopolies are the extreme case.[24] In competitive markets, profits are a sign of disequilibrium which, again, lowers welfare. From an entrepreneurial perspective, profits are the reward for welfare-enhancing innovation. They reward the entrepreneur for improving resource allocation, and create an incentive for further innovations to generate economic progress, so profits enhance economic welfare, and are necessary for economic progress.

Optimality

In the neoclassical framework, optimality means allocating resources such that nobody could be made better off without making someone else worse off. This is the economist's definition of Pareto optimality, which is almost always the concept of optimality that economists use. Pareto optimality is a static concept that judges the way that resources are allocated at any one point in time, but a static criterion for optimality is inappropriate for evaluating the characteristics of an economy that is continually improving its performance over time. Some characteristics of an economy prevent it from attaining Pareto optimality, but enhance economic welfare, so a Pareto optimal allocation of resources is not the welfare-maximizing allocation. Two characteristics that fit this description are product differentiation and profit, as just described. Competitive markets allocate resources Pareto optimally when they offer consumers homogeneous products, and when firms are making no profits, but welfare would be reduced in an economy that did not have these non-Pareto optimal characteristics. For economic progress to occur, which improves people's welfare, both profit and product differentiation are necessary. Profit guides entrepreneurs to better satisfy people's wants, and product differentiation is the vehicle that improves the characteristics of the economy's output. An economy that satisfies the static criterion of Pareto optimality is therefore not maximizing people's welfare.

The neoclassical framework depicts welfare maximization as the Pareto optimal allocation of resources, and twentieth-century growth theory, built on the foundation of Solow's growth model, extends this framework to a dynamic setting so that there is a Pareto optimal growth path. That framework is mathematically elegant and logically correct, but it is flawed because it represents economic progress as growth in a homogeneous measure of output.[25] Because changes in the characteristics of output are more important components of economic progress than income growth, the concept of optimality must be modified, and a Pareto optimal allocation of resources eliminates some of the features of an economy that generates economic progress. If resources are allocated Pareto optimally, the conditions of Pareto optimality take away the incentive to act entrepreneurially.[26] The concept applies to a static steady-state economy, but not to one in which welfare improvements are generated by economic progress.[27]

If welfare maximization means making people as well-off as possible, economic progress is crucial to welfare maximization, and aiming for the goal of a static Pareto optimal allocation of resources hinders welfare maximization.[28] Welfare maximization is a process, not an outcome, and the process is driven by entrepreneurship, and manifests itself as economic progress.

Conclusion

This chapter presents a description of the competitive process that is based on entrepreneurship, and that produces economic progress. The framework described here differs substantially from the neoclassical competitive framework for two main reasons. First, the neoclassical framework assumes away any role for entrepreneurship, so the people who run firms in that theory are managers, not entrepreneurs. Second, in its dynamic form, the neoclassical framework focuses on growth in the quantity of output, rather than on progress, which consists primarily of changes in the types of output produced. The difference is progress versus growth, and entrepreneurship versus management. One of the key questions in economics, described well by the title of Adam Smith's *The Wealth of Nations*, is how nations become prosperous. The ideas presented in this book suggest that twentieth-century equilibrium economics missed two key aspects that underlie prosperity. Chapter 2 argued that by focusing on income growth rather than progress in the types of goods and production methods, economics has analyzed the wrong indicator of prosperity. This chapter has argued that by focusing on efficiency in production rather than innovation, economic analysis has missed the key factor that generates economic progress.

Progress can be made in economics just as it can in the market economy, and this analysis suggests that progress in the theory of economic growth can best be made by recognizing that the scope of economic progress is much broader than income growth, and that entrepreneurship is the activity that generates economic progress. This chapter describes how theories of entrepreneurship can be completely incorporated into a model of the competitive process to show that entrepreneurship is the engine of economic progress, to show that entrepreneurship is necessary for firms to survive in competitive markets, and to show that product differentiation is one of the competitive strategies that produces economic progress. The result is not a steady-state competitive equilibrium, nor would such a result be optimal. The result is a competitive process where firms continually improve their production processes and the characteristics of their output in order to remain competitive, and this process results in continual economic progress.

4 Equilibrium versus the invisible hand

An economy populated by entrepreneurial firms will be different from one populated by managerial firms, to continue with the theme of Chapter 3. Of course, in the real world, firms act both managerially and entrepreneurially, but economic theory has tended to focus on the managerial functions of the firm, and has neglected the entrepreneurial activities of firms that are essential for the firms' survival. The distinction is important from the standpoint of public policy because government policy toward business has been designed around a managerial theory of the firm developed by twentieth-century neoclassical economics. Often, the result has been policies that stifle entrepreneurial activity. Economic analysis has an impact on economic policy, so it is important to orient economic analysis so that it leads to policies that are conducive to economic progress.

Two concepts that play a central role in economic analysis are those of equilibrium and the invisible hand. Equilibrium is that state toward which an economy is pulled by economic forces, and the invisible hand refers to those forces that pull the individuals in an economy. Seen this way, the two concepts are consistent with each other, and are even jointly necessary to have a complete understanding of the way an economy works. How could an economy tend toward equilibrium without forces that pull it there? Looked at in another way, if the invisible hand, as described by Adam Smith, is leading the economy in a systematic direction, the path along which the invisible hand leads the economy ends at an economic equilibrium. The desirable outcome that Smith argued is produced when individuals are led by an invisible hand is, in the framework of twentieth-century economics, a competitive equilibrium. Each concept points toward the other.

While the two concepts can be seen as complementary, there is an inherent tension between them, because equilibrium suggests the result of an economic process, while the invisible hand suggests the process itself. One does not necessarily exclude the other, but the developments of mainstream economics in the twentieth century have focused almost entirely on deriving a more precise and rigorous description of the conditions of equilibrium, leaving the study of the invisible hand process in comparative neglect. Models that study these equilibrium conditions typically assume complete information on the part of all market participants and a condition of zero economic profit, which eliminates two important factors that drive the invisible hand process. Thus, the assumptions of equilibrium models not only neglect to examine the market process, but rule out important aspects of it by assumption. This neglect of the market process has obvious implications for the study of the market forces that constitute what Adam Smith referred to as the invisible hand, but if the two concepts are as interconnected as suggested, it also means that the economist's comprehension of concept of equilibrium has suffered as well.

Does this tension between these two concepts really exist? In part, it depends upon how one defines the concepts of equilibrium and the invisible hand. Both concepts can be defined differently, and viewed in different ways. This chapter makes no attempt to find the best definition for either concept, or attach any kind of definitive meaning to the terms. Rather, after examining different ways in which the concepts can be understood, the chapter argues that the way they actually are understood by most economists at the beginning of the twenty-first century places them in an almost adversarial position. Economic theory at the beginning of the twenty-first century has accepted the tenets of equilibrium over the invisible hand, and this development of economic theory has significant implications for economic policy. Definitional matters will be discussed in the following pages in order to clarify what is meant by the two concepts, but the definitions, by themselves, are of secondary importance. The key argument of the chapter is that the theoretical emphasis on equilibrium over the invisible hand has important policy implications.

Twentieth-century equilibrium economics

The development of twentieth-century equilibrium economics began late in the nineteenth century with the discovery of the concept of marginal utility in independent works by Carl Menger, William Stanley Jevons, and especially Leon Walras, and quickly became the centerpiece of economic theory with the publication of the first edition of Alfred Marshall's *Principles of Economics* in 1890.[1] Economic theorists, trying to make economics more scientific, adopted the mathematical techniques of physics, resulting in an emphasis on equilibrium, partly because it conformed with the available mathematical tools, and partly because the equilibrium framework provided an elegant description of the condition toward which the economy tends at any point in time. Economic theory made great strides early in the twentieth century, armed with new tools of analysis produced within this equilibrium framework.

The development of this equilibrium framework was well along in the 1930s when a more practical reason for emphasizing equilibrium arose. With the world economy in recession, economists were grasping for explanations for the prolonged economic downturn and the apparent failure of the invisible hand, when John Maynard Keynes, in his *General Theory of Employment, Interest, and Money*, explained how an economy could remain at an underemployment equilibrium, and offered suggestions for re-equilibrating the economy at full employment.[2] From a practical policy standpoint, the main issue in economics in the 1930s became how an economy apparently at a stable equilibrium near full employment could become destabilized and eventually arrive at an underemployment equilibrium, and what policy tools could be utilized to stabilize the economy again at a full-employment equilibrium. The urgency of the policy issue laid the foundation for theoretical developments that could incorporate into economic theory a better understanding of the stability properties of economic equilibrium.

By the 1960s, the most important policy issues in economics were analyzed entirely within a static equilibrium framework. Macroeconomics was dominated by the issue of how to maintain an equilibrium with both low inflation and low unemployment, while microeconomic policy was based on the foundation of neoclassical welfare economics that emphasized the static optimality conditions of competitive equilibrium, and attempted to design policies to move the economy toward that unique Pareto optimum.[3] Optimal public policy within this framework meant correcting market failures so that the economy could move toward the welfare-maximizing Pareto optimum. Despite the wide gulf that separated macroeconomics from microeconomics during this period, both had the common methodology of identifying an optimal static equilibrium, and both sought to identify policies that would be able to create and maintain that equilibrium. Even when the economy was not at the optimal equilibrium, its condition was described in equilibrium terms, as a Keynesian underemployment equilibrium in macroeconomics, or as a Pareto-inefficient allocation in microeconomics, because of monopoly, externality, or other market failures.

Economic theory has advanced significantly since the 1960s, but retains its equilibrium emphasis. Modern growth theory, begun by Robert Solow,[4] uses the same equilibrium framework to describe a growing economy, and the new growth theory, discussed later, retains this equilibrium framework. Even the Austrian school of economics, which more than other schools of thought emphasizes the market process that leads to equilibrium rather than the state of equilibrium itself, still relies on the notion of equilibrium to describe where the process leads. In the most complete and systematic treatments written on Austrian economics, Ludwig von Mises and Murray Rothbard both describe an "evenly rotating economy" exhibiting the properties of equilibrium.[5] Thus, despite the existence of many different schools of economic thought and methods of analysis, by the end of the twentieth century the concept of equilibrium had become the foundation upon which most of economic theory was supported. This focus on equilibrium has, in turn, clouded the economist's understanding of the invisible hand process described by Adam Smith.[6]

The concept of equilibrium

In the competitive model of neoclassical economics, equilibrium exists when all prices are set such that they just clear the market, so for all markets the quantity supplied equals the quantity demanded.[7] This neoclassical competitive model makes a number of unrealistic assumptions in its depiction of equilibrium, including that there are a large number of small firms in all industries, that each producer in an industry produces a homogeneous product, that all resources are freely mobile, and perhaps most important for present purposes, perfect knowledge on the part of all market participants.[8] These assumptions assure that the economy will always remain in equilibrium, for if it were out of equilibrium, that would produce a profit opportunity, and perfect knowledge would mean that it would be instantly observed, and seized and acted upon immediately.[9] Thus, if the extreme assumptions of the neoclassical model of pure competition are met, equilibrium is the only possible state of affairs.

Part of the elusiveness of the concept of equilibrium is that even those who are firmly convinced of the merits of equilibrium modeling recognize that the economy itself is not always in equilibrium, even if their models are. Rather, the economy tends toward equilibrium, and the proponents of equilibrium modeling argue that the forces pulling it there keep it close enough that the state of the economy can be understood by understanding the properties of the equilibrium toward which it tends. This is far from self-evident, because it may be that by ignoring the forces that push an economy toward equilibrium and focusing on the properties of equilibrium instead, one leaves out key components of the equilibrating process. Nevertheless, the properties of equilibrium still remain important, and casual observation suggests that the economy does remain close to equilibrium following the neoclassical definition, because most markets come close to clearing most of the time. Conditions of excess supply or excess demand are so rare (except when caused by government intervention) that they can be considered anomalies. This equilibrium outcome tends to be produced despite the fact that it is obvious that the neoclassical assumptions regarding competitive equilibrium are not met.[10]

The assumption of perfect information is especially relevant to understanding the market process. Under what conditions would a model economy in which economic actors had less than perfect information actually be in equilibrium? That depends upon how one defines equilibrium. Friedrich Hayek, Frank Hahn, and Peter Lewin define economic equilibrium as a condition in which the plans of all individuals in the economy are mutually compatible.[11] Joseph Stiglitz defines equilibrium differently, as a condition "... where no economic agents have an incentive to change their behavior."[12] Under many conditions, including the neoclassical model of pure competition, there will be no practical difference between these two concepts of equilibrium, in the sense that a situation that satisfies one definition will also satisfy the other. However, there are conditions under which the economy could be in equilibrium following one definition but not the other, and a discussion of these conditions lends some insight into the invisible hand process.

Israel Kirzner, who emphasizes the equilibrating role of entrepreneurship, takes a view like Stiglitz on equilibrium, although he begins with the Hayekian idea. Kirzner says, "Equilibrium simply means a state in which each decision correctly anticipates all other decisions."[13] Left there, Kirzner and Hayek are completely consistent. In the next sentence, Kirzner continues, "In such a situation, decision making involves nothing more than the calculation of the optimum course available to the chooser, within the constraints imposed by the correctly anticipated decisions of others. No room exists for the entrepreneurial element." This must mean that there are no unexploited profit opportunities, because otherwise there would be room for entrepreneurship, so Kirzner's vision of equilibrium is consistent with the Stiglitz definition. Regardless of whether individual plans are mutually consistent, the existence of an unexploited entrepreneurial opportunity would rule out calling such a situation an equilibrium, according to Kirzner.

Because unexploited profit opportunities always provide an incentive for people to change their behavior in order to capture the profit, the existence of unnoticed profit opportunities would be inconsistent with equilibrium as Kirzner or Stiglitz defines it even if everybody's plans were mutually consistent. An economy could be in Hayekian equilibrium, in the sense that all individual plans are coordinated and everyone correctly anticipates the actions of others, and yet not be in equilibrium as Stiglitz and Kirzner envision the concept, if there are unnoticed profit opportunities that provide an incentive for people to change their behavior. In an economy with perfect information, the two definitions of equilibrium would be the same. However, both Kirzner and Stiglitz have emphasized information or knowledge problems as important aspects of the economy,[14] so it seems implausible that either would want to assume, in general, that all economic agents were perfectly informed. David Harper eloquently explains why there will always be some unexploited profit opportunities in an economy,[15] and based on similar reasoning, Kirzner has explicitly stated that an economy never can actually arrive at equilibrium.[16]

Hayek too has emphasized the role of the market in effectively utilizing information that is not generally known,[17] so these two different concepts of equilibrium do not seem to stem from the different assumptions that economists (these economists, anyway) want to make about whether all information is generally available to all economic actors. Rather, all would acknowledge that an economy may be in a situation where the plans of all economic actors are consistent with each other; yet there remain undiscovered profit opportunities. Hayek, Hahn, and Lewin would call this an equilibrium, but Stiglitz and Kirzner would not. Thus, unexploited profit opportunities are consistent with an economy in equilibrium, if Hayek's definition of equilibrium is accepted, but not if equilibrium is defined following Kirzner.[18] The distinction is worth making because the chapter argues that unexploited profit opportunities, and the responses of entrepreneurs to those opportunities, are a key element in the invisible hand process. Using Kirzner's definition of equilibrium resolves much of the tension between equilibrium and the invisible hand, but Kirzner's view is probably different from the concept of equilibrium that most economists envision. This conclusion is hedged because if perfect information is assumed, the neoclassical, Hayekian, and Kirznerian views amount to the same thing, and because of this, many economists may not have thought about the implications of imperfect information on equilibrium in any detail. But it is probably a safe conjecture that if imperfect information about entrepreneurial opportunities were introduced into the neoclassical framework, most economists would then envision equilibrium as closer to Hayek's description than Kirzner's.

Another reason to use Hayek's definition of equilibrium rather than Kirzner's is because it more closely approximates the actual state of the economy. It is reasonable to view a healthy economy, in which markets clear without excess supply or demand, as approximately in equilibrium, in the Hayekian sense that people's plans are consistent with one another. Furthermore, Hayek's definition fits better with the neoclassical depiction of equilibrium. All of these definitions identify the same thing when an economy is characterized as having perfect information. However, there are always unexploited profit opportunities waiting to be discovered, and the discovery of some leads to the creation of others. Thus, the way that Kirzner and Stiglitz define equilibrium implies that the economy will never be close to equilibrium, and may even be drifting farther away if new profit opportunities are arising faster than they are being acted upon, even if everyone's plans are mutually consistent. Twentieth-century economics has focused on the concept of economic equilibrium as coordination among the plans of all economic actors so that all markets clear, and when imperfect information is introduced, the essence of equilibrium models of all types is better captured by Hayek's notion of equilibrium.

Entrepreneurship and equilibrium

Kirzner characterizes entrepreneurship as acting to equilibrate markets, and contrasts his equilibrating view of entrepreneurship with Schumpeter's depiction of entrepreneurship as disequilibrating,[19] but as the previous section suggests, whether one views entrepreneurship as equilibrating or disequilibrating depends in part on how one defines equilibrium. In Kirzner's view, an economy is in equilibrium only when there are no unexploited profit opportunities, which by definition requires an economy to be out of equilibrium for entrepreneurship to take place. Hayek defines equilibrium differently, as the condition where "...the different plans which...individuals...have made for action in time are mutually compatible."[20] Similarly, Hahn says equilibrium exists when "...the intended actions of rational economic agents are mutually consistent and can, therefore, be implemented."[21] Lewin says "equilibrium is understood to be the consistency of actions and the plans on which they are based."[22] One could envision a situation where everyone's plans are mutually consistent, and so are in equilibrium according to the definitions of Hayek, Hahn, and Lewin, yet there are unrecognized profit opportunities so the Kirznerian criterion for equilibrium is not satisfied. Kirzner's and Schumpeter's views on the way entrepreneurship affects markets differ more than just terminologically. Kirzner's description of entrepreneurship evokes the image of entrepreneurial actions leading toward an evenly rotating economy, to use the terminology of Mises and Rothbard,[23] where nothing changes period after period, whereas Schumpeter's description of entrepreneurship depicts actions that would disrupt the equilibrium of an evenly rotating economy. Kirzner's entrepreneur pulls an economy toward the existing equilibrium, while Schumpeter's entrepreneur pushes the economy away from the existing equilibrium.

From a terminological standpoint, the difference between Kirzner's and Schumpeter's view of entrepreneurship and equilibrium can be resolved by noting that the new equilibrium created by Schumpeter's entrepreneurship is actually a preexisting equilibrium the way Kirzner defines the term. Kirzner alludes to this as he differentiates two different types of Hayekian knowledge problems.[24] The previously unnoticed profit opportunity implies, following Kirzner's use of the term, that the economy was not in equilibrium prior to the action of the Schumpeterian entrepreneur. While one could look at it either way, depending upon how one defines a state of equilibrium, within the context of economic progress discussed earlier, the Schumpeterian view of the effect of entrepreneurship on markets better describes the long-run impact of entrepreneurship. In the short run, if the economy is not in equilibrium, entrepreneurship moves the economy toward equilibrium, as Kirzner describes. But in the long run, the creative destruction of entrepreneurship is what generates economic progress.

Kirzner recognizes that the underlying economic data defining equilibrium are continually changing, so equilibrium is a moving target, but Kirzner notes that he focuses on entrepreneurial action with given underlying economic data and an unchanging underlying equilibrium. However, one of the factors that causes the underlying equilibrium to change is the actions of entrepreneurs,[25] so Kirzner focuses on one part of the entrepreneurial story but not the part that interested Schumpeter. This is not to say that one view of entrepreneurship is more correct than the other, but to suggest that Kirzner focuses on the short-run equilibrating actions of entrepreneurs, whereas Schumpeter's sees the longer-run impact of the actions of entrepreneurs as disrupting the existing equilibrium and producing the changes that create economic progress.

Whether the invisible hand, thus envisioned, is at odds with the concept of equilibrium depends in part on how one views the concept of equilibrium. Following Kirzner's idea that equilibrium exists only when there are no unexploited profit opportunities, entrepreneurship will be equilibrating because it moves the economy toward that condition where no profit opportunities remain.[26] Following the Hayekian definition of equilibrium, if entrepreneurial acts are unanticipated, entrepreneurship will upset the coordination of plans of those in the economy, and at least initially, will be disequilibrating. Whether one views entrepreneurship as equilibrating or disequilibrating thus depends at least in part on which definition of equilibrium one uses.

There is some ambiguity in the way Kirzner describes disequilibrium. After discussing equilibrium, Kirzner goes on to note,

> In contrast, a disequilibrium market means a state of affairs in which decisions do not correctly anticipate all the other decisions being made. Clearly, scope exists here for exercise of the entrepreneurial alertness to opportunities for more advantageous decisions than those currently embraced.

Kirzner describes the situation where people's plans are not coordinated, as in Hayek's concept of equilibrium, but following his own concept of equilibrium, he should also include the case in which everyone correctly anticipates everyone else's decisions and yet there are still unnoticed and unexploited entrepreneurial opportunities. The first sentence of Kirzner's definition of disequilibrium corresponds to Hayek's definition, but the second qualifying sentence corresponds to Stiglitz's. Which definition of equilibrium one accepts becomes relevant when considering the conditions under which entrepreneurial activity can be disequilibrating.

While this might appear to be a technicality or a definitional matter, differentiating these two definitions of equilibrium helps illustrate the relationship between the invisible hand concept and the concept of economic equilibrium. Using Hayek's definition, equilibrium is that destination toward which the invisible hand is always pulling an economy, given what economic actors know at the time. But with Kirzner's definition, entrepreneurial opportunities might remain unnoticed, so everyone's plans are compatible and the economy, in Hayekian equilibrium, is not being pulled toward Kirznerian equilibrium. An entrepreneurial discovery could then produce incompatibilities as the entrepreneur acts on it, which would be disequilibrating under Hayek's definition of equilibrium but equilibrating under Kirzner's. If one makes the neoclassical assumption of perfect information on the part of all market participants, whenever any unexploited profit opportunities appear, everyone knows about them, and the market rapidly equilibrates using both Hayek's and Kirzner's definitions. Of course, perfect information also means everyone knows the plans of everyone else, enabling them to perfectly take them into account with regard to their own actions, making equilibrium a tautological concept.[27]

Using Kirzner's definition of equilibrium, entrepreneurial opportunities cannot exist in equilibrium, but using Hayek's definition, unnoticed profit opportunities can exist in an equilibrium condition when everyone's plans are mutually consistent. When information is costly to obtain, or when there is ignorance so that people do not even realize they are uninformed, equilibrium can coexist with unexploited profit opportunities. Under the often-used assumption that all economic agents have full information, while the distinction between these two concepts of equilibrium disappears, key elements of the invisible hand process are assumed away. Thus, identifying the relationship between the concepts of equilibrium and the invisible hand requires a clearer notion of the concept of equilibrium than would be needed in the neoclassical full information setting. But subtle distinctions are unnecessary to identify the fundamental tensions between the concepts of equilibrium and the invisible hand. Equilibrium modeling, as it is done at the beginning of the twenty-first century, rules out the entrepreneurial actions that are the essential part of the invisible hand.

Entrepreneurship and the invisible hand

As the previous section suggests, there are subtle differences in the way in which economists understand the concept of equilibrium. This is even more true of the concept of the invisible hand. Whereas the concept of equilibrium has been extensively and rigorously analyzed in the twentieth century, the invisible hand has not. At its most basic level, the invisible hand refers to those forces that guide the economic behavior of those in an economy. In equilibrium, many of those forces have been assumed away, leaving the invisible hand outside the domain of much of economic analysis. In an equilibrium setting, the invisible hand might be thought of as those forces that keep people from straying from equilibrium, but as is argued later, this meaning is much too restrictive, and is not in the spirit of what Adam Smith had in mind when he popularized the phrase centuries ago.

The invisible hand concept arises from the incentives that are provided in a market economy for efficiency-enhancing actions, but those actions can be divided into two different categories. In one category are the maximizing actions that are a part of neoclassical economics – the management that was discussed in Chapter 3, along with maximizing behavior on the part of consumers. The other category consists of entrepreneurial actions. In the neoclassical framework, individuals maximize utility by allocating their endowments (which in a production economy includes their labor and human capital) over a given opportunity set. Firms maximize profits by choosing the optimal quantity and mix of inputs that will be combined in a production function to generate output. Profit maximization for firms must be a shorthand description, because firms do not act as independent entities. Rather, people act. In a neoclassical setting, profit maximization means that the firm's decision-makers choose the optimal quantities of inputs and then produce the maximum possible amount of output given the inputs employed.

In this neoclassical setting, people who run firms must be good managers, but there is no room for entrepreneurial activity. Good management, as the concept was described in Chapter 3, is not a trivial task, but the optimal course of action for the firm is always dictated by market conditions and by the firm's production function. Market prices reveal supply and demand conditions for the firm's inputs and output, and the production function reveals the most efficient way of combining inputs to produce output. Incentives facing both firms and individuals pull them toward equilibrium, and in equilibrium firms, behaving optimally, are just able to make normal profits. There is no room for bad management within the neoclassical framework, because firms that do not maximize profits suffer losses and are driven out of business by those that do. The role of the invisible hand in equilibrium is to keep economic actors from straying away from equilibrium. Even in a dynamic equilibrium model, the invisible hand merely keeps economic actors from straying away from the equilibrium path as the economy grows. Much like a sheep dog watching over a herd of sheep, in equilibrium models the invisible hand keeps people from straying away from the general equilibrium, but does not lead anyone anywhere.[28]

If Adam Smith really meant that people were being led by an invisible hand, which is what he actually said, rather than being held in place by it, there is an inherent tension between the concept of equilibrium and Adam Smith's concept of the invisible hand. Smith's *Wealth of Nations* makes it clear that he had in mind the invisible hand leading people toward new activities, and not just pushing them back toward an equilibrium allocation of resources. Smith began his monumental treatise with a discussion of how an increasing division of labor increases the productivity of the economy and enhances the wealth of nations. If Adam Smith is the father of economics, and his *Wealth of Nations* is the first real treatise on economics, then the first lesson of economics is that the wealth of nations is created and enhanced by the division of labor. Smith uses the example of a pin factory to show how much more productive people can be when they specialize in narrow tasks, and he argues that as markets grow, increased specialization becomes possible, leading to ever-increasing productivity. But this increasing specialization amounts to more than just making sure inputs are being used efficiently, or that the right combination and quantity of inputs are being employed. An increase in the division of labor requires the entrepreneurial insight to envision how a job done by one person can be subdivided into different tasks, changing the nature of the production function as the division of labor is increased. This may require new capital goods and new production processes. It does not mean doing the same things better, it means doing different things that create more value than the previous way of doing things. It requires entrepreneurship.

As people who run firms look for ways to enhance their profits, Smith emphasizes not the management aspects of profit maximization but the entrepreneurial aspects. Rather than looking for the most efficient way of combining a given set of inputs using a given production function to produce a given output, as a good manager would do, those who run firms engage in the entrepreneurial actions of looking for better inputs, different methods of production, and new and improved outputs. They look for ways to increase the division of labor, and this requires entrepreneurial insight beyond that required for management. Of course, profit maximization is enhanced by good management, but without entrepreneurship, even firms that are superbly managed in a growing economy will stagnate and die as they are surpassed by more entrepreneurial firms.

In the neoclassical model, the essence of what those who run firms do is management, but in Smith's vision, the essence of what those who run firms do is entrepreneurship. In the neoclassical model, the essence of what the economy does is sustain (or fail to sustain) an equilibrium. In the Smithian model, the essence of what the economy does is grow. The invisible hand leads people, pursuing their own interests, to do what is best for the entire economy, but in Smith's vision, the invisible hand does not pull people toward equilibrium, but rather leads them toward activities that enhance the wealth of nations. To do this requires entrepreneurship.

Within the neoclassical framework, one might picture the invisible hand as holding economic agents close to equilibrium, but this is not in the spirit of Adam Smith's depiction of the economy as an engine of wealth generation. Smith talked about a growing economy characterized by an ever-increasing division of labor, and an economy in which the invisible hand led to new ways of doing things. Entrepreneurship and economic progress are key components of Smith's vision of the economy, and the invisible hand concept is, in this sense, completely at odds with the neoclassical equilibrium framework. The concept of the invisible hand could mean different things to different economists, and with the preoccupation with equilibrium in twentieth-century economics, economists may think of the invisible hand as the equilibrating force in the economy. But the invisible hand is much more than this, and mainly consists of those forces that push individuals to seize entrepreneurial opportunities, and that as a result foster economic progress. In this sense the invisible hand may play a disequilibrating role, as argued by Schumpeter, as entrepreneurial discoveries upset the previous plans of those in the economy, even as they open up new opportunities for further entrepreneurship and further progress. But the key idea is that Adam Smith was describing an invisible hand that led people to engage in entrepreneurship and to promote economic progress, not an invisible hand that holds people close to equilibrium.

Equilibrium versus progress

The emphasis on equilibrium in twentieth-century economics has tilted the interests of the economics profession toward the study of the outcomes of economic processes rather than the processes themselves, and this has led to the neglect of the study of the causes of economic progress. Surely the title of Adam Smith's book, *The Wealth of Nations*, indicates his emphasis on the causes of progress, and one of the most-discussed economics books in the late 1800s, just before the economics profession was transformed by the marginal revolution, was Henry George's *Progress and Poverty*.[29] But the development of equilibrium economics changed the focus of the economics profession away from the causes of progress, and toward the causes of stability.

Economic growth occurs because the invisible hand is pulling individuals in an economy to engage in entrepreneurial insights that change the nature of inputs and outputs. The result is called growth by economists, but as Chapter 2 notes, it is better referred to as economic progress. The economy may grow, in the sense that national income accounts measure increasing income, but the changes that occur because of the changing nature of production and the increased division of labor result in economic progress, not just growth. Individuals, led by an invisible hand to engage in entrepreneurial acts, produce this progress. When looking at the theory of economic growth, the inherent tension between equilibrium and the invisible hand becomes clear.

Policy implications

The distinction between viewing the economy as in an equilibrium state rather than focusing on the invisible hand process is in one sense artificial, because the economy both equilibrates and stabilizes as it leads the plans of economic agents to be mutually consistent, and it promotes economic progress by providing the incentives and institutional structure for entrepreneurship and innovation. The two concepts are in this sense complementary. Yet the development of economic models in the twentieth century has focused on the equilibrium properties of the economy, almost to the exclusion of the entrepreneurial aspects of economic activity. This is more than just a theoretical point. Because economic theory has focused on the concept of equilibrium, economic policy has focused on factors that help generate Pareto optimal resource allocation rather than on factors that encourage entrepreneurship and economic progress.

This is most evident in the area of macroeconomics. Keynesian macroeconomic policy focused on trying to manipulate aggregate demand in order to arrive at full employment with low inflation.[30] The emphasis was on arriving at a full-employment equilibrium as an end state, rather than examining the forces that lead the economy to progress. Recent developments in macroeconomics have focused more on growth issues, but the equilibrium framework is explicitly retained, so the issue remains as to how to increase inputs in order to get more output. The literature, typified by works by Paul Romer and Robert Lucas, recognizes the importance of human capital, including education and on-the-job training, and that technological advances are a key element.[31] But within the production function framework, technological advances are the product of investment in research and development rather than of entrepreneurial insights. Romer explicitly allows for the possibility of new goods being developed,[32] yet all within a production function framework that leaves out the role for entrepreneurial activity.

To the extent that this literature offers policy recommendations, it is to increase human and physical capital, and to produce technological advances through encouragement of research and development. While it is generally true that more inputs and better technology can produce more output, economic progress in the real world is mostly due to innovations and the application of entrepreneurial insights, not additions to physical and human capital.[33] New growth models improve upon the old, but remain similar in their major shortcomings. They depict growth, but not the essential elements of economic progress.

If these policy recommendations are taken literally as a blueprint for generating economic growth, they are likely to generate poor policies that will inhibit economic progress. The former Soviet Union emphasized investment in human and physical capital, and the adoption of advanced technology, yet its poor economic performance led to the dissolution of the nation. A similar story can be told about centrally planned economies around the world. Clearly, providing the inputs of human and physical capital along with the promotion of technological advance was not enough in those cases. What was missing was the institutions that fostered entrepreneurship, which is the key to economic progress. Yet even the most contemporary economic growth models suggest that the types of policies followed by centrally planned economies should lead to growth. As Anne Krueger notes, these same types of recommendations were offered to less developed economies as a blueprint for economic growth, yet economies whose leaders chose to centrally direct resources to those areas that economic models suggested would be most productive ultimately languished.[34] The bad advice those economies received came directly from theoretical models of economic growth that were firmly grounded in twentieth-century equilibrium economics.

In contrast, there is a more recent body of research on economic growth that leaves the equilibrium framework behind and looks instead at the institutional framework that promotes growth.[35] This literature finds that an institutional environment conducive to entrepreneurial activity leads to more economic growth, and conversely, that even when the inputs for economic growth are present in an economy, without the market institutions that promote entrepreneurial activity, an economy will not grow.

The distinction between equilibrium and the invisible hand is made as clearly in microeconomics as it is in macroeconomics. Much actual microeconomic policy is based on the framework of theoretical welfare economics that emphasizes the efficiency of a competitive equilibrium, and views deviations from competitive equilibrium as market failures. Thus, market concentration is viewed as undesirable, rather than as a sign that some firms have found better ways to satisfy the demands of many of the market's customers, and product differentiation is seen as a source of inefficiency rather than as evidence of economic progress.[36] In the competitive equilibrium framework that is the basis for policy recommendations, all economic profits have been competed away, and without the possibility of profits, there is no incentive for entrepreneurship. If a thought experiment is undertaken where the economy is placed in disequilibrium, equilibrating forces bring it back to the unique equilibrium depicted in the model. Depicting the economy as having a unique equilibrium rules out the possibility of allowing the invisible hand to lead people to engage in any innovative entrepreneurial activity. Arbitrage is possible within the general equilibrium framework, but not innovation.

In the late 1960s the Department of Justice brought suit against IBM for monopolizing the computer industry, and indeed IBM did have an overwhelming share of the market when the suit was initiated. The suit dragged on until it was dropped in the early 1980s, because IBM's market share had also dropped. By the early 1990s, IBM had suffered such a loss of market share that some computer industry analysts were predicting that the company would go out of business. If the vantage point of equilibrium is replaced by the vantage point of the invisible hand, it appears that IBM's market share in the 1960s arose because of its innovation that allowed it to satisfy its customers, but through the 1970s the company's offerings stagnated when compared to new computer manufacturers, again as the result of entrepreneurship that led to better products. In the late 1990s the scenario was repeated again, as the Justice Department pursued Microsoft for monopolizing the same industry. These examples show that the policy implications one draws differ substantially depending upon whether one views the economy from the vantage point of equilibrium or from the vantage point of the invisible hand.

In the neoclassical equilibrium framework, competition requires homogeneous products, and product differentiation leads to inefficient resource allocation and excess capacity in firms.[37] Yet as Chapter 3 discussed, producers are always looking for ways to better satisfy their customers in order to increase their profits, and improving the characteristics of their products is a common method of competing for customers. From the vantage point of equilibrium, product differentiation should be discouraged as inefficient, and where it exists markets are not (perfectly) competitive, whereas from the vantage point of the invisible hand, product differentiation is one of the characteristics of market competition and the introduction of new products is one of the hallmarks of economic progress.

Neoclassical welfare economics identifies a unique, stable, Pareto optimal general equilibrium that provides the benchmark for economic efficiency. Public policy then tries to guide the economy toward this outcome. From the vantage point of the invisible hand, efficiency is not an outcome, but rather a process that encourages entrepreneurship and economic progress. It does not try to push the economy toward a unique point, because new knowledge is always being generated by market participants, and one can never anticipate where that knowledge will lead the economy.[38] Optimal policy is that which encourages the development of knowledge and the application of entrepreneurial insight to generate economic progress. A framework that offers a unique optimum, like the equilibrium framework, leaves out the possibility of economic progress.

This section on policy implications is intended to show that the differences between the equilibrium versus the invisible hand approaches to economics are more than just semantic, and that the different viewpoints on economic activity generate very different policy implications. With regard to monopoly, product differentiation, and even the underlying factors behind economic progress, these two vantage points on economic activity have quite different implications. The distinction is of more than just academic interest. It begins with the academic choice of how economists model the economy, but generally accepted economic models form the foundation for economic policy, which in turn determines how well the economy ultimately performs. An examination of some policy issues shows that there is good reason to take the competing visions of equilibrium versus the invisible hand seriously.

Conclusion

The concepts of equilibrium and the invisible hand are consistent with each other, and indeed it is not possible to fully understand one concept without understanding the other. However, the concepts depict different aspects of economic activity, and the perspective one gets on the economy is affected by the concepts one uses for analysis. The focus of twentieth century economics has been on the conditions for economic equilibrium, and twentieth century public policy reflects this focus. Some equilibria make better use of economic resources than others, and economic analysis has focused on removing sources of market failure such as externalities, public goods, and monopoly, and on arriving at a stable full-employment equilibrium. The nature of equilibrium analysis naturally directs the analyst's attention toward arriving at a desirable end state.

The invisible hand concept, in contrast, focuses on the ongoing and continuously evolving activities of the market. This focus on the market process naturally leads one to consider development and economic progress as key elements for economic policy. Ideally, the invisible hand will continue to lead an economy to ever-increasing economic well-being. The focus is on continual improvement rather than arriving at the best possible end state. Adam Smith optimistically titled his book *The Wealth of Nations*, and in it argues that with appropriate policy, ever-increasing economic well-being is possible. The division of labor is limited by the extent of the market, Smith noted. Growing wealth and expanding markets have the effect of extending markets beyond their current bounds, leading to an increased division of labor and continued economic progress. Contrast this with the twentieth-century Keynesian notion of underemployment equilibrium. The goal there is not growth or progress, but arriving at a full-employment end-state equilibrium.

While the concepts of equilibrium and the invisible hand are not inconsistent with one another, one gets a different view of the world, and different policy implications, by focusing on one or the other. The twentieth-century preoccupation with equilibrium in economic models has led economic policies toward correcting inefficiencies rather than toward creating an environment for economic progress. In the end, one can see that this preoccupation with the concept of equilibrium has stood in the way of the operation of the invisible hand.

5 Entrepreneurship and knowledge

Entrepreneurship is a creative activity. As such, it may not be possible to describe what entrepreneurs do. As William Baumol notes, "One can, indeed, describe what entrepreneurs *used to do*, but simply by virtue of having been reported in detail such an act is transformed into one that is no longer entrepreneurial."[1] Baumol's remark offers a number of insights. Accepted at face value, it suggests that after entrepreneurial acts have been undertaken, others can, through analysis of those acts, convert them to managerial acts. Brilliant and original entrepreneurial insights then evolve to become a routine part of business operations. Probing deeper, this suggests that a component of economic progress is taking entrepreneurial insights and making them into a part of the routine activity of businesses.[2] But where do these entrepreneurial insights come from in the first place? According to Kirzner, entrepreneurs uncover profit opportunities that previously went unnoticed,[3] but this does not explain how those profit opportunities came to be observed, and why they were spotted by one person when they were overlooked by others. In fact, people can – and do – take actions to make themselves more entrepreneurial.

Entrepreneurial opportunities tend to appear within the context of a specific time and place, so entrepreneurial opportunities are more likely to reveal themselves to people who are at the right "time and place" to make the discovery.[4] Everyone is not equally likely to notice an entrepreneurial opportunity: many people may be at the same location at the same time, but one person may notice it while it remains unseen by others. This chapter considers some factors that determine how individuals come to recognize these previously unnoticed profit opportunities, and what factors give individuals that specific knowledge of time and place that allows them to make entrepreneurial discoveries.

As Kirzner describes it, entrepreneurs happen to notice what nobody has noticed before. Whether an entrepreneurial opportunity actually is noticed depends on many factors, but those factors can be divided into two general categories: factors specific to the individual, and factors related to the individual's economic environment. Many individuals might observe the same information revealing an entrepreneurial opportunity, yet only a few may have the wisdom to actually act on it. One focus of this chapter is on how individuals transform the economic data they observe into a systematic body of knowledge that allows them to spot entrepreneurial opportunities. A second focus of the chapter is on the role the economic environment plays in signaling that certain data actually represent a profit opportunity. A growing economy is more conducive to revealing profit opportunities to potential entrepreneurs, for reasons that will be discussed in detail later, and within an economy, those areas that are growing more rapidly will offer more profit opportunities. Entrepreneurial activity in an economy creates data about profit opportunities that potential entrepreneurs add to their knowledge base, which then makes it easier for them to recognize other unexploited profit opportunities. This chapter discusses how entrepreneurs acquire information about entrepreneurial opportunities, and how entrepreneurial activity itself generates information that fosters additional entrepreneurial activity.

Information, knowledge, and wisdom

Peter Boettke notes that economists are inconsistent in their use of the terms information and knowledge.[5] For present purposes, and consistent with Boettke's use of the terminology, *information refers to data that an individual can collect.* Individuals can search for information, and may be aware of information they are lacking that, if attained, could help them achieve their goals. For example, people might read newspaper ads looking for information about prices for goods they intend to buy. They may be unaware of other information that would help them if they had it. *Knowledge refers to the incorporation of information into a framework where it can be used for decision making.* Information about the price someone charges will be of little use unless the person with the information can place it in context. For example, what do other sellers charge for the same or similar goods? Is this price likely to fluctuate, so that next week's price might be considerably higher or lower? Do some sellers offer non-price advantages that might make it desirable to look at other information besides prices before deciding whether to buy? These are the types of factors that enable an individual to place information in a context that makes that information a component of the individual's knowledge. *Wisdom refers to the use of knowledge to make good decisions.* Because many factors must be weighed to arrive at a decision, and because some of those factors may be difficult to articulate or weight in a mathematical sense, many people may have the same knowledge, but even with identical knowledge, some will make better decisions than others.

Boettke notes that "information is a flow concept, while knowledge is a stock notion."[6] By extension, Boettke observes, "Knowledge is ever changing and is multifaceted, while information is something fixed."[7] The flow of information adds to the stock of an individual's knowledge, but new information may also change the context within which old information is interpreted. Knowledge is more than just the sum of all information possessed by an individual. If one pictures a pitcher of water, and an individual adding a flow of water to the stock of water already in the pitcher, this analogy inadequately describes the relationship of flow information to the stock of knowledge. Instead, picture someone adding flour, water, yeast, and the right amount of heat, to produce bread. In the kitchen, the flow of ingredients yields a stock of food that is qualitatively different from the flow of ingredients that produced it. Just as bread is not some flour, some water, and so forth, a person's knowledge is not just all the information the person possesses. And just as some chefs are more successful than others at producing meals even with the same stock of ingredients, many individuals might have similar stocks of knowledge, yet some have the wisdom to make better economic decisions with their knowledge.

Kirzner makes a similar distinction between knowledge and entrepreneurship.

> But as closely as the element of knowledge is tied to the possibility of winning pure profits, the elusive notion of entrepreneurship is, as we have seen, not encapsulated in the mere possession of greater knowledge of market opportunities. The aspect of knowledge which is crucially relevant to entrepreneurship is not so much the substantive knowledge of market data as *alertness, the "knowledge" of where to find market data.*[8]

Kirzner means by data what this section refers to as information. But knowledge as Kirzner describes it in this passage is knowledge about where to find information. One must put that information in context to have knowledge, and must be able to use that knowledge productively to have wisdom.

In most instances, acting on an entrepreneurial insight is a risky undertaking. The well-known fact is that most new businesses fail within their first five years, illustrating that in many cases, what appears to some as an unexploited profit opportunity turns out not to be profitable after all. When Kirzner talks about someone noticing a previously unexploited profit opportunity, what the potential entrepreneur notices is information. The entrepreneur must be in a position to turn that information into knowledge, and to apply wisdom to that knowledge. The setting within which the information reveals itself plays an important role in whether the information about a profit opportunity ultimately is transformed into knowledge, and then wisdom, leading to action to exploit the opportunity on the part of the entrepreneur.

Consider the example from Chapter 3 of an individual who notices that apples can be bought for $0.25 in city A and sold for $0.50 in city B. These prices are information. The individual can place this information into a framework that can lead to an entrepreneurial insight: a profit opportunity may exist by buying apples in A and selling them in B. More must be known than just the prices, however. The potential entrepreneur would have to factor in transportation costs, and for a true profit opportunity to exist, not only would the entrepreneur need this information on prices, but also a reasonable expectation that the price differential would continue to exist long enough for the entrepreneur to complete a transaction. If an apple can be shipped from city A to city B for $0.10, there is still the possibility for a profit, if after buying apples for $0.25 in city A and shipping them to B, the price in B has not fallen below $0.36. The entrepreneur may have information about the propensity for apple prices to fluctuate in the short run, or may be able to avoid the risk of fluctuations in the spot market by contracting ahead of time with a buyer in city B. Prices by themselves provide information, but as this simple example shows, information by itself does a potential entrepreneur little good. The entrepreneur must be in a position to place that information in a framework that yields knowledge before a profit opportunity can be spotted.

In this sense, Hayek's 1945 article, "The Use of Knowledge in Society," was discussing the use of knowledge in society, as his title says, not the use of information. Wisdom goes a step further, and is the ability to use knowledge to make good decisions. The high failure rate of new businesses suggests that many people incorrectly believe they have discovered profit opportunities. For example, the apparent profit opportunity in the example might be undone if too many apples are spoiled or damaged in transit, or if the entrepreneur failed to account for the possibility that transportation costs might fluctuate even while taking account of price fluctuations for the apples themselves, or any number of other complications. Wisdom lowers the probability that one is wrong when making a decision based on knowledge.

With hindsight, one can separate good decisions from bad decisions on the basis that good decisions yield profits while bad decisions produce losses. One can never know whether a decision was "optimal," in the sense that it was better than other available alternatives, because one can never know what would have been the outcome of a foregone alternative.[9] Information is relatively easy to evaluate, in the sense that one can check on its validity, despite the fact that people can obtain information that is wrong, incomplete, or faulty in some other way. Knowledge is more difficult to evaluate, because one must be aware of the context within which information is used, and it is easy to envision how someone's knowledge could be faulty because the person is lacking some information he/she does not even realize would be useful. Wisdom is more difficult to evaluate than knowledge, because even in hindsight one cannot compare the outcomes of decisions people make with what would have been the outcomes if they had chosen differently.

If one views entrepreneurship as seeing and acting upon a previously unnoticed profit opportunity, it is apparent that two people could observe the same information, and one would see it as an unexploited profit opportunity while the other might not, either because the second person did not have the knowledge to place that information in context, or did not have the wisdom to see that the information does, in fact, reveal the opportunity to make a profit. Of course, the opposite may be true, and the person who sees that no profit opportunity exists may be the one who has the wisdom to realize that the opportunity will not cover its costs, while the person who believes the profit opportunity exists has faulty information, or incomplete knowledge, or insufficient wisdom. Not every apparent profit opportunity will actually produce profits, which makes entrepreneurship an uncertain undertaking.

Ray Kroc, who built the McDonalds restaurant chain, sold restaurant equipment before he took over McDonalds. He had an order for 10 milkshake mixers from a restaurant in San Bernadino, California, and went to the restaurant started by brothers Richard and Maurice McDonald to see personally how a restaurant could be selling so many milkshakes. What he saw was an innovation in restaurant operation. Before McDonalds, most restaurants got customers' food orders and then prepared the food, but McDonalds had the entrepreneurial insight that they could prepare the food before it was ordered so customers could get their food right away. This system required that management be good at predicting the number of customers and food orders so the right amount of food would be on-hand, and hindsight shows that they had a good system.

Ray Kroc did not develop this system himself, but he recognized it as a profit opportunity. He had the information from seeing the operation of McDonalds, he had the knowledge from years of experience in the restaurant industry, observing many different types of operations, and he had the wisdom (moreso than the original innovators) to see this as a profit opportunity. Kroc partnered with the the McDonald brothers and opened his first McDonalds in 1955 in Des Plaines, Illinois. He bought out the McDonald brothers in 1961, purchasing the restaurant from the innovators and establishing it as a worldwide chain.

Perhaps Kroc was just lucky. It is difficult for an outside observer to separate out luck from wisdom, because there is no formula for identifying how individuals can use knowledge to make good decisions. It is easier to see how knowledge can prevent people from making bad decisions, by identifying potential problems before they arise, but how did Ray Kroc have the insight to see what a profit opportunity McDonalds presented when the innovators who started the restaurant were (using their sale as evidence) less optimistic. Part of the answer likely lies in the different knowledge bases of Kroc and the McDonald brothers. The McDonalds may have had the knowledge to start and operate a restaurant, and the brilliant insight to prepare the food before the customers ordered it, but Kroc, as a vendor selling to many restaurants, had a broader knowledge of the industry. Regardless of whether this speculation on the differences in knowledge between the McDonalds and Kroc is true, this is an example of how two people could have the same information about a profit opportunity, and yet because the two individuals had different knowledge bases, one saw it as a more profitable opportunity than another.

Perhaps Kroc was lucky, but there is an old slogan, "Luck is when preparation meets opportunity," and it seems to apply here.[10] Kroc was prepared because of his background in the restaurant industry, and had the opportunity when the McDonald brothers were willing to sell him their restaurant. But many people believe they have spotted profit opportunities that result instead in losses. Perhaps their knowledge was faulty, but consider companies like IBM on the brink of bankruptcy in 1991, or Xerox and Polaroid on the brink of bankruptcy in 2001. Surely the management in those companies had ample knowledge of the computer, photocopying, and photography industries, respectively, but that knowledge did not translate into the wisdom that led to profitable decisions. In the real world (unlike the neoclassical model of the firm), profitability is a moving target, and activities that were profitable a decade ago – or even a year ago in rapidly evolving industries – may not be profitable today. As Clayton Christensen notes, decision-makers can be misled by their past successes into thinking that strategies that brought them profits in the past can continue to do so in the future.[11] As the IBM, Xerox, and Polaroid cases show, more than knowledge is required to spot profit opportunities. Entrepreneurship is built on a foundation of knowledge, but also requires the wisdom (or luck) to be able to sort the good strategies from the bad.

Can entrepreneurship be produced?

As Kirzner defines entrepreneurship, the entrepreneurial act itself is costless, and uses no resources. It is simply the act of noticing what nobody has noticed before. But people can invest resources into activities to make it more likely that they will make an entrepreneurial discovery. Research and development activities are not entrepreneurship, but R&D creates an environment within which entrepreneurial opportunities are more likely to present themselves. Research and development generates information, which can add to knowledge. Within a neoclassical framework, where things are produced by combining inputs in a production function, research and development is undertaken by combining land, labor, and capital, to produce technological change. The successes attributable to investment in research and development are indisputable, but R&D expenditures cannot be the whole story, because once the research is done, the results need to be applied to make production less costly, or even more mysteriously, to produce goods and services that have never been produced before.

Joseph Schumpeter distinguishes invention from innovation.[12] Invention is a possible product of R&D, but inventions do not necessarily lead to economic improvements. The innovation is taking the invention and applying it to produce new products, or to produce existing ones more efficiently. The taking of inventions and making them into innovations is the role of entrepreneurship. Fifteen hundred years ago, China was the most technologically advanced nation in the world, but did not turn its inventions into innovations, whereas during the Industrial Revolution, Europe did. Similarly, Xerox invented the computer interface used on the Apple Macintosh and in Microsoft Windows, including the use of windows to show different tasks, and the use of the mouse to navigate the operating system and its applications, but Xerox did not turn its invention into an innovation. Steve Jobs of Apple, and Bill Gates of Microsoft, saw what Xerox had done, incorporated that information into their stock of knowledge, and with that knowledge had the wisdom to see that the commercialization of that interface was an unexploited profit opportunity. The information was revealed to those at Xerox first, but those who saw the information first failed to see the entrepreneurial opportunity that it presented.[13] The story of the development of the graphical user interface for the computer parallels the story of the development of fast food restaurants told in the preceding section.

While entrepreneurship may involve that flash of recognition that a profit opportunity exists, entrepreneurship can be produced, in the sense that individuals and firms can create an environment that is conducive to entrepreneurial discovery. People can search for information about market conditions, about production processes, and about possible innovations and new goods. Research and development can be viewed as the creation of an environment that produces information that could reveal entrepreneurial opportunities. Some information about an entrepreneurial opportunity is available to everybody. Price discrepancies and arbitrage opportunities fall in this category, and those most alert will notice them. Some information is available only to a few, and the object of commercial research and development is to generate information that nobody else has. This gives the researcher a substantial advantage in transforming the proprietary information into a profit, but as the Xerox example shows, it is not an insurmountable advantage. Despite the fact that Xerox developed the information to produce the graphical user interface for the computer, the company did not have the wisdom to be able to implement it as a profit opportunity, so those profits from the information Xerox generated ended up going to Apple Computer and Microsoft.

Information about entrepreneurial opportunities can be produced, and firms actively undertake activities to produce that information. The knowledge to place the information in context can also be produced. Businesses go to great lengths to try to understand not only the engineering aspects of the products they produce, but also the nature of the market within which their products are sold. Firms always run the risk of misunderstanding their markets, even when they are market leaders, and sometimes past successes lead firms to overlook the future direction of the market.[14] But firms do try to understand their markets so that they can remain successful. Understanding the market means taking available information and placing it in context so that the firm's decision-makers can make successful decisions. To that end, firms undertake marketing research, engineering research, and other information-gathering activities, and consolidate that information to try to acquire the knowledge to make managerial decisions. This knowledge is necessary for entrepreneurship.

Information about entrepreneurial opportunities can be produced, and that information can be aggregated into knowledge about entrepreneurial opportunities. In that sense, entrepreneurship can be produced. But the wisdom to use one's knowledge effectively is more problematic. It can be produced by experience, but some people seem more adept at making wise decisions than others. Entrepreneurship is more than just good management – finding ways of minimizing costs and combining inputs efficiently. Entrepreneurship means finding a better way of doing something, and there is no benchmark for comparison. Can entrepreneurship be produced? Information that can help people act entrepreneurially can be produced, and the knowledge to place that information in context can be produced, but there is no clear-cut way to produce the wisdom that leads to entrepreneurial discoveries. Entrepreneurship is more than just noticing something, as the record of business failures suggests. It involves having the wisdom to separate actual profit opportunities from tempting options that will not generate profits.

Information, wisdom, and the process of entrepreneurship

Entrepreneurship creates new entrepreneurial opportunities, but how do entrepreneurs gain the knowledge to spot those opportunities once they are created? In a static setting, because there is little change, there will be relatively little in the way of entrepreneurial opportunities. Those opportunities that might be lying in wait must be relatively obscure to have remained unnoticed, and the static environment precludes the creation of new opportunities. Schumpeter, discussing a framework in which all profit is competed away in equilibrium, and in which profit is the return to entrepreneurship, observed, "Without development there is no profit, without profit no development."[15] Economic progress relies on an economy that is not in neoclassical general equilibrium to generate the profit opportunities necessary for development to occur.

A key question is, where do potential entrepreneurs get the knowledge to utilize information about entrepreneurial opportunities? As noted in Chapter 4, one view of equilibrium, shared by Stiglitz and Kirzner, is that equilibrium implies that there are no unexploited profit opportunities. By definition, entrepreneurship is ruled out in equilibrium, and a Solow-type growth model is inconsistent with entrepreneurship. Another view of equilibrium, shared by Hayek, Hahn, and Lewin, defines economic equilibrium as a condition in which the plans of all individuals in the economy are mutually compatible. If this latter definition of equilibrium is taken, entrepreneurial opportunities can exist in an economy and lie unnoticed for an indefinite period of time as individuals continue making mutually consistent plans, oblivious to the existence of profit opportunities. The potential for entrepreneurship exists, but how would opportunities be observed?

Consider a traditional economy in which heredity and institutions assign people their economic roles.[16] Institutional constraints prevent entrepreneurial activity. The same would be true in a centrally planned economy, where profits are institutionally ruled out. Now consider an economy in general equilibrium. Period after period, economic agents undertake the same activities, earning a normal rate of return for their efforts. There are no economic profits, and much like the traditional economy, nothing in the economic environment changes period after period. In such a setting, individuals must be suspicious of any potential opportunity that would appear to be profitable. An old joke goes, Economist 1: "Look, there's a $20 bill on the sidewalk!" Economist 2: "Couldn't be. If there was, somebody would have picked it up." The punch line exactly applies to profit opportunities in general equilibrium. If there really was a profit opportunity, why had nobody seized it before?[17] Most businesses fail within their first five years because what appeared to the business's founder as a profit opportunity turned out not to be. In general equilibrium, market participants have the knowledge that apparent profit opportunities are likely to be illusory, and the most profitable course of action would likely be to ignore them.

Consider again the hypothetical example where one discovers the information that apples are selling for $0.25 in one location while buyers are paying $0.50 for the same type of apples in another location. Now consider two different scenarios in which that information is revealed. First, imagine a setting of general equilibrium. The same economic activities happen period after period, leading the potential entrepreneur to think that if this really was a profit opportunity, someone would have already acted on it. If one were to factor in transportation costs, shipping damage, possible price fluctuations, and a host of other factors, the apparent profit would probably disappear. When the information about prices is incorporated into a body of knowledge, that body of knowledge weighs against acting on what initially appears to be a profit opportunity. Now, consider another setting where entrepreneurship is rampant: perhaps the microelectronics industry at the end of the twentieth century. The innovations of entrepreneurs are creating new entrepreneurial opportunities, and the observer's body of knowledge now incorporates that environment. Many people have spotted and acted on entrepreneurial opportunities, and profited from their actions. In this setting, the same information leads to a different sort of knowledge, and makes it more likely that the apparent profit opportunity really would lead to a profit.

An entrepreneurial environment changes the knowledge base of potential entrepreneurs, and makes it more likely that information about an entrepreneurial opportunity will actually be spotted and acted upon. If the same information about a potential profit opportunity surfaces in an economy stagnating in general equilibrium versus an entrepreneurial economy characterized by constant change, it will be more likely to be an actual profit opportunity in the dynamic entrepreneurial economy, so the information will be more likely to be acted on by an entrepreneur. The environment within which information presents itself affects the observer's knowledge base, and an entrepreneurial environment is more likely to develop the knowledge that leads people to act entrepreneurially. Entrepreneurship creates more entrepreneurial opportunities, but it also creates a base of knowledge that makes it more likely that entrepreneurial opportunities will be spotted and acted upon. Knowledge is more than just the sum of the flow of information that creates it. The market economy itself creates knowledge that would be unavailable in a different institutional setting.

Wisdom and entrepreneurship

A view that opportunities for entrepreneurial insights are produced exogenously and lie in wait for entrepreneurs to notice them would be fundamentally misleading. Furthermore, it would be misleading to think that at any point in time there is an abundance of entrepreneurial opportunities that are unnoticed, waiting to be discovered. Entrepreneurial opportunities constantly arise in a growing economy, and when they do they are, except in rare circumstances, rapidly acted upon. Entrepreneurial insights are produced in the process of economic advancement. More rapid advancement brings more entrepreneurial opportunities, and more entrepreneurial opportunities produce greater incentives for potential entrepreneurs to become more alert to them. The actions of entrepreneurs add to the knowledge base of potential entrepreneurs, so entrepreneurship generates more entrepreneurship. In contrast, a stagnant economy blunts the incentives for entrepreneurial activity, and can remain stagnant because it is more difficult to spot those entrepreneurial opportunities that actually exist.[18] Even if the information about a profit opportunity is revealed, a stagnant economy may not generate the knowledge sufficient to prompt an entrepreneur to act. The idea that entrepreneurial activities create more entrepreneurial opportunities endogenizes the creation of entrepreneurial opportunities, expanding Kirzner's model of entrepreneurship to explain the origin of entrepreneurial opportunities as well as the competitive process that results from their existence. This idea is explored further in Chapter 6.

Equilibrium economics offers little insight into entrepreneurship, precisely because of its equilibrium character. Twentieth-century equilibrium economics in all of its variants has viewed production in a Ricardian production function setting. In contrast, Eugen Bohm-Bawerk depicted a structure of production that would become more roundabout as more indirect methods of production were used.[19] Bohm-Bawerk's approach more closely follows Adam Smith, who emphasizes increases in the division of labor as the engine of economic progress.[20] Smith's division of labor finds a parallel in the Bohm-Bawerkian concept of extending the structure of production through increased indirect production. Within the neoclassical-Ricardian framework, the new production processes imply changing the functional form of the production function, which means changing the way that inputs are combined into outputs. In the neoclassical framework, this could happen in any way – it is more general than Bohm-Bawerk's approach – but because of its generality does not focus on the nature of changes (such as increasing the division of labor, or engaging in more indirect production).

The Smithian view of economic progress is based on the concept of increasing returns, and twentieth century contributors to the Smithian idea, like Allyn Young and Nicolaus Kaldor have explicitly acknowledged that they were building on Adam Smith's insights.[21] Yet increasing returns is a problematic concept in an economic framework because it implies that average cost continually declines. Kaldor notes the problems for general equilibrium models when firms are characterized by increasing returns, but another possibility is that the production functions of firms do not exhibit increasing returns. Rather, firms generate network externalities that lower the costs of production for other firms in close proximity.[22] Individual firms do not exhibit increasing returns, but the entire economy does. This is easy to visualize as a Smithian idea. The division of labor is limited by the extent of the market, so additional firms in an area enlarge the market and allow all firms to be more productive by becoming increasingly specialized. Increased specialization is but one way in which firms can become more innovative, so a more general way to envision this idea is that the knowledge created by firms benefits other firms in close proximity. When one firm innovates, other nearby firms find themselves in a better position to innovate also.

Paul Romer depicts the process as a knowledge spillover.[23] Knowledge, embodied in human capital, is the factor with increasing returns, meaning that investments in human capital make future investments in human capital more productive. Because human capital must be combined with other factors of production, there will be a tendency for productivity increases to be geographically concentrated, which result in some areas manifesting more economic growth than others. Along these lines, Krugman and Audretsch and Feldman develop models in which increasing returns occur in geographically concentrated areas.[24] Pierre Desrochers presents an excellent discussion about the way that tacit knowledge, as described by Hayek, is transmitted more effectively by people in close proximity to one another.[25] Some things can be observed more effectively than they can be described, so industries that are more entrepreneurial are more likely to reveal entrepreneurial opportunities to those in their own industry, and geographical areas that are more entrepreneurial are more likely to reveal entrepreneurial opportunities to those in their own area.

The wisdom to undertake effective entrepreneurship is not equally available to everyone, and entrepreneurial opportunities that may be easily obtainable for some will be out of reach for others. Much information is readily available to all, but as noted earlier, people also generate their own private information with the intention of using it entrepreneurially. Information is valuable only within a broader context of knowledge, and information that would have no meaning to some might suggest an entrepreneurial opportunity to others who are able to put that information in the context of their knowledge. Wisdom comes from the effective use of knowledge, and part of this is collecting sufficient knowledge to avoid making bad decisions. This section has suggested the important role of proximity in making wise decisions. Some information is difficult to communicate without firsthand knowledge. Those in a particular industry will have more wisdom about entrepreneurial opportunities in that industry, and following the arguments of a substantial literature discussed in this section, geographical proximity generates a significant amount of this type of knowledge. Desrochers gives a superb description of knowledge transmission through geographic proximity.

Earlier, the chapter showed that people can take actions that will increase the likelihood of their discovering entrepreneurial opportunities by, for example, undertaking research or studying industry trends and activities to build a knowledge base. But holding individual action constant, some economic environments generate information for all individuals in the environment that make it more likely that they will recognize entrepreneurial opportunities. An environment where there is a substantial amount of entrepreneurship creates a knowledge base that increases the probability that when people are exposed to information about entrepreneurial opportunities, they will recognize it as such and act on it. The market process itself generates information. Entrepreneurship creates more entrepreneurial opportunities, but entrepreneurship also generates information that adds to the knowledge base of potential entrepreneurs, making them more entrepreneurial. The same profit opportunity is more likely to be recognized in an entrepreneurial economic environment than in a stagnant one, or in an equilibrium setting. Entrepreneurship requires knowledge, but entrepreneurship also generates information that adds to knowledge, leading to more entrepreneurship.

The growth of time and place

Hayek has emphasized the importance of the specific knowledge of time and place that is available to individuals as a result of their specific economic activities, but that is not readily available to others, and that is not easily communicated to others.[26] That knowledge comes directly from their experiences in their own productive activities, so is not generally available, and cannot be reduced to a formula or be sufficiently articulated to communicate it to others who do not have the same background of knowledge. Hayek makes the distinction between scientific knowledge that can be expressed in rigorously precise terms and knowledge that is derived from experience and that often cannot be precisely communicated to others. This experience-based knowledge may not be able to be passed on to others because the person with the knowledge is able to recognize and understand what a desirable course of action is in certain situations, but cannot explain what specific factors lead to the understanding of what actions should be taken in those situations. While the market does not transmit this knowledge itself, it creates an institutional environment where individuals are able to make use of this specific knowledge of time and place held by others, though exchange.

Over time, one's specific "place," in Hayek's sense, has been enlarged by the development of transportation and communication technology. People can see more, and broaden their knowledge bases further, by being in close proximity to others who may actually be physically distant most of the time. In the same way that Adam Smith noted that the extent of the market can grow, allowing a greater division of labor, a person's place in the market system can be enlarged, giving that person greater knowledge about entrepreneurial opportunities.

The development of written communication is an ancient factor in this enlargement of place. While much of this specific knowledge cannot be communicated through writing, basic ideas can, so that a foundation of knowledge is available to everyone, potentially increasing their productivity. Because of written communication, no longer did people have to be somewhere to observe something firsthand, or have it explained to them by someone with such knowledge. Formal education does the same thing by allowing people to acquire information to enlarge their knowledge bases without firsthand experience. Education cannot pass on the specific knowledge of time and place that Hayek noted was essential to the functioning of the economy, but it can systematize information to provide a knowledge base to make people better able to utilize the specific knowledge of time and place to which they are exposed. This distinction between general knowledge, that Hayek refers to as scientific, and the specific knowledge of time and place, warrants further investigation.

Specific and general knowledge

A part of the growth of knowledge is the transformation of the specific knowledge of time and place into more general scientific knowledge. Hayek quotes Alfred Whitehead, who says,

> It is a profoundly erroneous truism...that we should cultivate the habit of thinking what we are doing. The precise opposite is the case. Civilization advances by extending the number of important operations which we can perform without thinking about them.[27]

Hayek goes on to say, "We make constant use of formulas, symbols and rules whose meaning we do not understand and through the use of which we avail ourselves of the assistance of knowledge which individually we do not possess."

A familiar example of the transformation of specific knowledge into general scientific knowledge is the development of the airplane. At the beginning of the twentieth century, many people were attempting to build working airplanes, and while many of the component pieces of knowledge were generally available, nobody was able to put them all together to build a flying airplane until the Wright brothers did so in 1903. A key knowledge component in their construction of a flying machine was their realization that in order to keep an aircraft aloft, it had to be controllable in three dimensions: pitch, roll, and yaw. The efforts of others had failed because even though they had wings that generated sufficient lift and an engine and propeller to generate sufficient power, they did not have the three dimensional aerodynamic control that would allow the airplane to remain aloft. The Wright brothers solved this problem through experimentation, and they were able to achieve stable and controllable flight.[28]

When originally developed, this was specific knowledge of time and place available only to the Wrights, and the way in which they achieved controllable flight was not readily communicated to others because it was a combination of factors that worked together to allow the airplane to fly.[29] The best science of the day could not explain it, and indeed, the Smithsonian Institution had invested a considerable amount of money and scientific expertise in designing a flying machine, only to be eclipsed by the Wright brothers' efforts. But it did not take long after the Wright brothers began producing airplanes for others to reformulate the Wrights' specific knowledge of time and place into general scientific principles that could be studied by others, and that could be duplicated by anyone investing the effort into understanding the science and engineering behind it.

The invention of the airplane is but one of a virtually infinite number of examples that show how the specific knowledge of time and place can be transformed into general knowledge. The Wright brothers had made earlier attempts at powered flight, and used their experience to refine their flying machine by trial and error until they were able to succeed. Others did not have the experience of the Wrights – their specific knowledge of time and place – so were unable to use the knowledge specific to the Wrights to design and refine a flying machine. After the Wrights succeeded, others could look at their design, replicate it, and try to systematically understand what made it work to reduce its success to scientific knowledge that could be recorded and communicated to others. Half a century after the Wright brothers had flown, aeronautical engineering was a well-established curriculum, and the Wrights' specific knowledge of time and place was not only transformed into general knowledge, but substantially improved upon so that anybody with the widely available training in aeronautical engineering could design airplanes far superior to the Wrights'.

The significance of specific knowledge

While eventually this specific knowledge of time and place was transformed into more general scientific knowledge that could be communicated to those without firsthand experience, at first it was not that way, and in general that is not the case even with developments in basic science. One might view the production of new knowledge as something that can be disseminated widely, for example in a book or over the internet, but there is often a large component of "learning by doing" that can only be picked up by firsthand experience. As Michael Darby and Lynne Zucker note,

> When a major scientific breakthrough occurs and creates a corresponding incumbent-enhancing or entry-generating technological breakthrough, it may be very difficult for anyone other than the discovering scientists or their close working associates to reduce the discovery to technological practice. ... Published results – including those in a patent – may not be reproducible unless the reproducing scientist goes to the discoverer's lab and learns by doing with him or her.[30]

Many times there is no substitute for firsthand experience, and that specific knowledge of time and place is crucial to innovation.

In a footnote, Darby and Zucker repeat a remark by a scientist who complains that competitors are stealing his best cloners. If cloning were a procedure that could be reduced to a formula and explained in a book, those cloners would be easily replaced, but if the process requires firsthand experience and observation, then there is no way to substitute for that specific knowledge of time and place. So while the widespread dissemination of knowledge through modern communication and transportation technologies is possible, and often turns specific knowledge of time and place into general knowledge, specific knowledge of time and place remains a feature of the economy, and it is difficult to envision that it would ever be eliminated. Future discoveries will always have a component of time and place specificity that will limit the set of individuals who will have the knowledge to take advantage of the entrepreneurial opportunities those discoveries imply.

The specific knowledge of time and place allows success that may be difficult to understand and replicate, but a study of those specific successes allows them to be understood in terms of more general principles that then can be taught to many people, transforming specific knowledge into general knowledge. This general knowledge then becomes a routine part of economic activity. Such specific knowledge does not have to be knowledge about science or technology. It could be business practices or marketing plans, product characteristics, or practices and procedures used routinely in one industry that can be adapted for others. As with MBA case studies, one examines the whole enterprise to try to identify those specific elements that make the enterprise successful, transforming specific knowledge into general knowledge.

The growth of knowledge occurs because what began as someone's specific knowledge of time and place becomes better understood so that it can be clearly articulated and shared among a larger group. Specific knowledge becomes general scientific knowledge. But as the economy progresses, people who take advantage of this growth of knowledge then find themselves in positions where new situations create specific knowledge of time and place. People utilize this information in innovative ways, generating economic progress and giving others an incentive to try to understand what allowed those innovators to succeed. Thus, specific knowledge continually is transformed into general scientific knowledge, changing the economic environment and producing new specific knowledge of time and place. The growth of knowledge in society goes hand-in-hand with economic progress.

Information generated by the market

People may gather information themselves to generate a base of knowledge that can enhance their opportunities for making entrepreneurial discoveries. Independent of any individual's actions, the market environment has a large impact on people's stocks of knowledge that can contribute to entrepreneurship. Entrepreneurial activity in an economy produces information that creates knowledge of time and place that helps to reveal entrepreneurial opportunities. Entrepreneurship produces information about entrepreneurial opportunities in several ways. An economy with little entrepreneurship, simply because of the lack of entrepreneurship, provides information that few entrepreneurial opportunities are available. In an economy in general equilibrium, all profit opportunities have been competed away, so what appears to be a profit opportunity may actually generate losses if acted upon. Few profit opportunities present themselves as sure things, and a potential entrepreneur will be less likely to take a risk on an apparent profit opportunity if it appears that most apparent profit opportunities are illusory. If entrepreneurship produces more entrepreneurial opportunities, then an extension of this argument is that an entrepreneurial economy will have more profit opportunities than a stagnant economy (or one in equilibrium). If this information is in the entrepreneur's stock of knowledge, then entrepreneurship itself produces knowledge that leads to more entrepreneurship. Entrepreneurial activity generates more entrepreneurship because opportunities are created, and because knowledge about those entrepreneurial opportunities is created.

The knowledge that is created is more than just information. It is a context within which information can be evaluated, and entrepreneurial activity adds to knowledge in several ways. First, it reveals that others have found profitable opportunities, encouraging potential entrepreneurs to be more alert. Second, it provides information on how previous entrepreneurs have seized profit opportunities, and this information generates knowledge for other potential entrepreneurs. For example, an entrepreneur could observe someone else's entrepreneurial activity and have the insight that if that person did something a little differently, the activity would be more profitable. The new entrepreneur could copy much of the predecessor's actions, changing only those things that the entrepreneur thought would warrant improvement. Or, an entrepreneur might observe certain changes in one industry and see that they could be adapted to generate profits in another. The point is that entrepreneurship does more than just generate additional entrepreneurial opportunities. It also generates the knowledge that leads people to be able to take better advantage of those entrepreneurial opportunities that exist.

Conclusion

Kirzner sees entrepreneurship as the recognition of a previously unnoticed profit opportunity, but he does not consider how entrepreneurs put themselves into positions where they are actually able to spot new profit opportunities. The information is often available to many people, but only a few have the knowledge to recognize the significance of the information. The wisdom to determine the appropriate course of action implied by the information is even more scarce. Entrepreneurial opportunities may not be easy to spot, even if they are lying in plain sight. As Hayek notes, everyone has some specialized knowledge of time and place that enables them to make use of market information in ways not available to others without that specialized knowledge. The same information about a profit opportunity could be revealed to many people, yet only a few with the appropriate knowledge will be able to place this information into a context so that the information suggests to them a profit opportunity.

The distinctions among information, knowledge, and wisdom help illuminate the nature of entrepreneurial discovery. Information includes much of the data of the market, but may also include other data not visible to everyone, such as production techniques, or even market data generated by surveys or statistical analysis. In order to yield any insight, information must be placed in the context of other information, and this aggregation of information that an individual possesses is knowledge. Entrepreneurial opportunities, as Kirzner describes them, are information, but Hayek was talking about how people use knowledge, which requires them to place information they receive in a broader context. Knowledge is insufficient to produce entrepreneurship. The individual must be able to evaluate that knowledge in subjective ways to determine whether an entrepreneurial opportunity actually exists. Wisdom is the product of knowledge, intelligence, and experience. This chapter cited several examples showing that when different people have the same information and knowledge, some may recognize the information as signaling an entrepreneurial opportunity while others may not.

Hayek noted that knowledge is often not easily transmitted from person to person. A person can have knowledge about a particular industry, process, or market, and yet not be able to articulate that knowledge to pass it along to others. It is at this point that knowledge becomes wisdom, and enables people to make better decisions than others who have all of the same information available to them. People can pick up wisdom from others by observing their actions and by collaborating with them, but this requires that interactions take place in close proximity. This is why areas that become entrepreneurial tend to generate more entrepreneurship. This is the knowledge of time and place that Hayek discussed, and "place" can be an industry, or a geographic area. More entrepreneurship occurs when both industry and geographic location coincide. This explains, for example, the concentration of entrepreneurship in semiconductors in Silicon Valley, in financing in New York, and in automobile development in Detroit. People are able to get ideas from others who have specialized knowledge in the same area in a way that would not be possible without the geographic proximity. Because of the geographic proximity, knowledge that is difficult to articulate can still be shared.

Entrepreneurship adds to the knowledge base, providing the knowledge that makes it easier to recognize profit opportunities when they arise. Kirzner depicts entrepreneurs as noticing profit opportunities that nobody has noticed before, which raises the question of why one person notices what others have missed. Hayek emphasizes the importance of individual knowledge of time and place, and this chapter shows that entrepreneurship in an economy produces knowledge for individuals that enhances their ability to recognize entrepreneurial opportunities. Entrepreneurial activity generates information that aids future entrepreneurial discovery.

6 The origins of entrepreneurial opportunities

Entrepreneurship occurs when an individual acts to take advantage of a profit opportunity that presents itself in the economy. The entrepreneur's activity benefits the economy by allocating resources in a way that increases their total value to the economy's consumers. Furthermore, the entrepreneur's profit signals potential suppliers and demanders about their market opportunities, and even signals other potential middlemen of the profit opportunity for facilitating exchanges. Eventually the ability to earn above-normal profits will be competed away, but only after those profits have served their role in signaling a way in which resources could be more efficiently allocated in the economy. Entrepreneurship is indispensable for economic progress, but entrepreneurial activity is possible only when profit opportunities are available to the entrepreneur. This chapter discusses the ways in which those profit opportunities can arise in an economy.

If one views the economy as tending toward equilibrium, and views entrepreneurs as the economic agents who act on profit opportunities that exist in disequilibrium in order to equilibrate the economy, then eventually all of those profit opportunities will be competed away, and the economy will remain in equilibrium. In this narrow conception, it appears that once the economy reaches equilibrium, all profit opportunities will have been used up, but in reality, they keep appearing. What produces the profit opportunities to begin with? This chapter identifies three major categories of factors that create profit opportunities: (1) factors that disequilibrate the market, (2) factors that enhance production possibilities, and (3) entrepreneurial activity that creates additional entrepreneurial possibilities. An analysis of each of these categories leads to the conclusion that by far the most significant cause of entrepreneurial opportunities is prior entrepreneurial activity. Entrepreneurship creates the opportunity for more entrepreneurship, which leads to economic progress. Entrepreneurship provides an important equilibrating function, but is also the crucial element in economic progress.

Paradoxically, while entrepreneurship had been becoming an increasingly important part of the economy in the twentieth century, it became increasingly less important as a part of economic theory, as Chapter 5 noted. Entrepreneurship occurs when an individual notices and acts on a profit opportunity, but in the equilibrium models that dominated economics at the end of the twentieth century, all profit opportunities had already been exploited, meaning that there was no role for entrepreneurship in this type of model.[1] To capture the role of entrepreneurship, economists must focus their attention on the process that leads individuals to seek profit opportunities, rather than on a state of equilibrium in which, by assumption, no profit opportunities exist. If equilibrium is a moving target that the economy always approaches but never reaches, it makes sense to devote some attention to the process that always is occurring, rather than focusing exclusively on the result that never occurs. Chapter 5 considered entrepreneurship from the standpoint of the entrepreneur, discussing how entrepreneurs come to obtain the knowledge that allows them to act entrepreneurially – to spot those previously unnoticed profit opportunities. This chapter looks at entrepreneurship from the standpoint of the broader market economy, to describe where those entrepreneurial opportunities come from in the first place.

The information needed to seize some entrepreneurial opportunities comes from sources available in principle to everyone, although recognizing that information that a person acquires constitutes an entrepreneurial opportunity may also require some specific knowledge of time and place. Ray Kroc turned McDonalds into a global fast food empire by buying an existing restaurant started by someone else, and recognizing its potential, expanding into new markets. Many people had the same information Ray Kroc had, but Kroc was the one with the entrepreneurial insight, built partly on his experience in the restaurant industry. At other times, the information is not generally available, as, for example, when it is generated by private research and development. But as already noted, technological advance is not entrepreneurship, and often those who develop the technology are not the people who make best use of it to provide marketable goods and services. Entrepreneurship is an economic activity. A profitable opportunity is spotted by an entrepreneur, and acted upon. The next several sections of the chapter provide a taxonomy of the origins of these market opportunities.[2]

Factors that disequilibrate the market

Kirzner's emphasis on the equilibrating function of entrepreneurship naturally focuses attention on factors that disequilibrate the market. The very notion of equilibrium suggests an economy that will continue on its present path undisturbed until it is shocked out of equilibrium. Then the equilibrating forces of the market take over to put the economy back on its equilibrium path. A number of factors could disequilibrate the market. For example, preferences could change, requiring resources to be reallocated to conform to the new pattern of preferences. From the perspective of economic modeling, one might question models based on autonomous preference changes, because such models explain little.[3] An explanation saying that some phenomenon occurred because preferences changed is not much different from saying one does not understand what caused the phenomenon to occur. The explanation is much more satisfying if it describes why people change their observed behavior based on some constant underlying utility function. Nevertheless, autonomous preference changes remain a possible disequilibrating force.

Other factors might be related to the environment within which production occurs. Farm production is affected by the weather, so that floods or draughts might lower farm output, and particularly good weather can raise it. Similarly, natural resources can be depleted, so that as oil wells run dry, continued production of oil is dependent upon the discovery of new reserves, which is an ongoing process. As landfills reach their capacity, new sites (or disposal methods) must be found. Thus, many factors can push an economy away from equilibrium, producing entrepreneurial opportunities. Despite the fact that the impending push away from the current steady state can often be foreseen, it is not always obvious what actions are appropriate to re-equilibrate the economy. One can foresee an oil well becoming exhausted or a landfill reaching capacity, but that does not make it obvious where the next landfill will be, or where new discoveries of oil, or substitutes for oil, can be made. Therefore, factors that disequilibrate the market call for entrepreneurship.

Entrepreneurial activities that respond to disequilibrating forces are vital to preserving the status quo, and thus are vital to the continued operation of the market. Yet taking a longer view, entrepreneurship results in much more than just maintenance of the status quo. When one thinks of entrepreneurs like Henry Ford, or Ray Kroc, or Bill Gates, one can see that entrepreneurship plays a crucial role in enhancing the status quo.

Kirzner contrasts his equilibrating view of entrepreneurship with Schumpeter's, which Kirzner characterizes as disequilibrating.[4] "Schumpeter's entrepreneur acts to *disturb* an existing equilibrium situation. ... The entrepreneur is pictured as *initiating* change and generating *new* opportunities."[5] Kirzner then quotes Schumpeter as concluding that entrepreneurship is at odds with equilibrating activity. Kirzner, in contrast, argues that the entrepreneur "... *brings into mutual adjustment* those discordant elements which resulted from prior market ignorance."[6] Kirzner raises the issue because he believes Schumpeter's discussion of entrepreneurship is "... likely to generate the utterly mistaken view that the state of equilibrium can establish itself without any social device to deploy and marshal the scattered pieces of information which are the only source of such a state."[7]

A key point is found in Kirzner's reference to the scattered pieces of information required to equilibrate the market. The necessary information is readily available in the form of market prices, but for entrepreneurship to equilibrate the market, there must be somebody with the knowledge required to take advantage of the information. If the market is disequilibrated through a shift in supply or demand, the change in the status quo should provide a relatively obvious signal of an entrepreneurial opportunity, and provides the most likely case that an entrepreneurial opportunity would be recognized. People who already trade in a market are likely to spot opportunities that are created by factors that disequilibrate the market as a by-product of their routine economic activity, so many people will have the required knowledge, and relatively little wisdom is required to spot such a profit opportunity.

Entrepreneurial opportunities are more difficult to spot when the disequilibrating factors occur in markets other than those an individual normally trades in. For example, if a product has been made of steel, but changes in the aluminum or plastics markets now make it more profitable to make the product out of a different material, an individual who does not see beyond the markets in which he trades would be unlikely to spot that profit opportunity. If the profit opportunity were not noticed, one could envision a situation in which all markets continue to clear, but in disequilibrium as Kirzner (but not Hayek) would use the term. Even though all markets in this scenario continue to clear, factors have disequilibrated the market, following Kirzner's terminology, creating an entrepreneurial opportunity.

Factors that enhance production possibilities

Some entrepreneurial opportunities arise as a result of factors that enhance production possibilities. Some factors that enhance production possibilities might also disequilibrate the market, if they are unanticipated, and the discussion of the previous section would apply. Other times, factors that enhance production possibilities are anticipated. An example is Moore's law, named after Gordon Moore, one of the co-founders of Intel. Moore's law states that the power of microprocessors will double every 18 months, and has held approximately true for three decades. Whether Moore's law will continue to hold is irrelevant for present purposes. In the computer industry, and in other industries, advances in production technologies are often anticipated, and are consistent with an equilibrium in which everyone's plans are mutually compatible.[8] In fact, one can imagine a situation in which anticipated enhancements in production possibilities were not realized, leading to a disequilibrium because people made their plans based on the anticipated technological advances that did not materialize. Enhancements to production possibilities may be disequilibrating, but when they are anticipated, they need not be.

Within the neoclassical production function approach to examining productivity, one might view output, Q, as a function of capital, K, and labor, L, so $Q = f(K, L)$. This approach immediately leads one to see that output can be increased if there is an increase in capital or labor, or if the production function changes form so that more output can be produced with a given amount of capital and labor. Changes in the production function are often the result of entrepreneurial activity itself, which will be discussed in more detail in the next section. In neoclassical models, this has led primarily to a focus on research and development as a method of enhancing production possibilities. Exactly how research and development yields greater output is a bit of a mystery, both in the model and in the real world. Sometimes substantial expenditures are undertaken with little or no payoff; at other times the simplest discovery can yield great returns.

The role of capital and labor in the production function are more clear. But this production function approach conceals the fact that if more capital and labor are available, they may be used in new and innovative ways, so a doubling of inputs may lead to more than a doubling of output. This can be "modeled" by depicting a production function with increasing returns to scale, but the model does not depict the essential fact that increasing returns to scale must imply using inputs differently depending upon the quantity of inputs available. The ability to use inputs differently, because more inputs are available, requires entrepreneurial insight. While it is relatively easy to envision increasing output by using more inputs to do the same thing, it requires some insight and imagination to see that with more inputs, there is a more efficient way of undertaking an activity.

A good example is Henry Ford's adoption of the assembly line to manufacture automobiles early in the twentieth century. As the demand for automobiles increased, more workers and more tools could have been purchased, and if any management and coordination problems could be avoided, a doubling of inputs could have produced a doubling of output. Entrepreneur Henry Ford envisioned that with more labor and capital, different inputs could be used in a different type of production process, increasing output more than in proportion to the increase in inputs. This entrepreneurial insight falls outside the model when taking a neoclassical production function approach.

The production function approach also conceals the fact that an increase in capital or labor could just be more people or more machines, or could be an increase in the quality of the inputs, quantity held constant. Thus, growth models using a production function like the one mentioned earlier have sometimes divided through by L to find that Q/L, output per capita, is then a function of capital and the technology available for production, leaving labor out of the picture altogether. Economists now understand the problem with this approach, and understand that L is more than just bodies, it also encompasses human capital. Thus, L can be increased through education, training, and even cultural norms (like showing up for work on time). When the quality of the labor force increases, or when the quality of the capital stock increases, that opens entrepreneurial opportunities to do things differently. To do so, however, requires someone with the insight to observe that with increases in inputs, a new process could be instituted that would result in more output from a given amount of inputs. This is a major source of increasing returns to scale.

Furthermore, sometimes advances in production technology enables lower-quality inputs to be used, enhancing production possibilities by lowering costs. For example, the development of high-level computer programming languages made programming easier, so that people with less human capital (in the form of programming skills) can program a computer. Cash registers that automatically calculate the change due back to customers mean that cashiers do not have to have the same arithmetic skills as they did when cashiers had to figure out the change themselves. Medical diagnostic software can make improved medical diagnoses and reduce errors, while at the same time lowering the human capital requirements of medical personnel. For example, NxOpinion is diagnostic software that asks questions of medical personnel, using the answers to generate more questions that narrow in on a diagnosis using Bayesian logic.

The economics literature associates progress with increases in human capital, and rightly so, but sometimes progress occurs by developing production processes that can produce more output with less human capital, or with less physical capital. The aluminum soft drink can was introduced into the market in 1957 – an innovation in itself – and continued to be improved with the invention of the pull-ring tab in 1962, so a can opener was not needed, and the stay-on tab in 1974. Readers who have been drinking soft drinks that long will recall that at one time crushing a soft drink can was a demonstration of strength, but cans have become increasingly thinner and lighter, using less aluminum but not producing any less utility to their users. Sometimes progress is generated by developing production processes that use smaller quantities of inputs, or lower quality inputs.

Production possibilities are enhanced when factors of production and production processes are improved, but increases in output by themselves generate entrepreneurial opportunities. The aggregate production function approach conceals the fact that if more output is available, consumers will not want the same mix of output. Even when many different outputs are depicted in economic models, it is common to use some sort of homothetic utility function (such as Cobb–Douglas or CES) for modeling simplicity, which assumes that when relative prices are unchanged, consumers will desire the same mix of outputs at any level of income. In an economy that produces many goods and services, it is implausible to think that a doubling of output would result in exactly twice as much of all existing goods and services. As less-developed economies increase their incomes, more automobiles are demanded relative to bicycles, and a smaller share of income is devoted to food relative to other goods. The changing mix of goods and services as income grows also produces entrepreneurial opportunities.

Adam Smith began his *Wealth of Nations* with the key insight that the division of labor is limited by the extent of the market. He explained that increasing specialization in production led to increased productivity, but that the potential for increases in output due to increased specialization was limited by the extent of the market. Thus, one of the key factors producing entrepreneurial opportunities is an expansion in the extent of the market. The market can be extended through population growth, by increases in per capita income, and by reductions in transportation and communication costs. Each of these factors increases the potential market for producers in any given location, and allows an increased division of labor.

When production possibilities increase, entrepreneurial opportunities are created in several ways. More inputs, including increases in the quality of physical and human capital, allow inputs to be combined in new ways. Income growth opens the possibility of marketing new goods, or expanding the market for goods that are income-elastic. Undertaking such activities requires the entrepreneurial insight to see that there are profits to be made from changing the way one does things. As the extent of the market increases, there are entrepreneurial opportunities to increase the division of labor, but again, such changes only take place as a result of an entrepreneurial insight that the changes have the potential to be profitable. Thus, increases in production possibilities provides an important source of entrepreneurial opportunity.

Most obviously, more production means people have higher incomes, so there is a profit opportunity to produce more output for them to purchase. More significantly, higher incomes will lead to changes in the mix of goods demanded. As income rises and people tend to demand more automobiles relative to bicycles, they may also demand automobiles with different characteristics, and may shift from auto or train travel to traveling by air. People may demand more steak relative to hamburger, and may demand more restaurant meals relative to home-cooked meals. Changes in the composition of demands for various types of output create profit opportunities. Perhaps more significant as a source of profit opportunities, a more productive economy has a greater role for the division of labor, as Adam Smith noted, so even if the output of all goods did increase proportionally, there would still be the opportunity to change production methods to produce more efficiently with a finer division of labor. As G.B. Richardson notes, in Smith's view "the division of labor is at once both a cause and an effect of economic progress."[9]

In this case, the exact nature of an entrepreneurial opportunity will not be as obvious as in the previous case (for factors that disequilibrate the market). If there is an opportunity to produce new goods to sell to a broader market, it is not always obvious what new goods it would be profitable to produce. Likewise, if there is an opportunity to profit from increased specialization in production, or by any other change in the production process, it is not always obvious how this could be done. Consider Henry Ford's insight that because of a growing market, automobiles could be mass produced on assembly lines to lower the cost and bring the opportunity of automobile ownership to the masses. Many people had the same market information as Ford, but he had the wisdom to seize that profit opportunity. While it looks obvious in hindsight, many automobile companies led by people with less wisdom than Ford failed in the early twentieth century.

For a similar example, consider the success of Palm Pilots – small handheld computers. Do readers recall the Apple Newton, which was Apple Computer's entry into that market only a few years before the Palm Pilot?[10] Apple introduced the Newton in 1993, and discontinued its sale in 1998. Meanwhile, the Palm Pilot was introduced in 1996. Apple spotted the information signaling a profit opportunity in that market before Palm,[11] Apple had the knowledge to see that there was a profit opportunity (the evidence is Palm's profit in that market), but Apple was unable to profit from it. In 2006, ten years later, the market for handheld computers was fading as their functions are being built into mobile phones, creating additional entrepreneurial opportunities.

To pick up on a theme from Chapter 5, profit opportunities created by enhanced production possibilities probably take more wisdom to turn into actual profits than those created by the other two categories. The process by which profit opportunities are generated is more evolutionary and continuous than in the other cases, the knowledge required to make a profit is typically substantial when its origin is in enhance production possibilities, and the wisdom necessary to make good decisions is substantial, as the Newton–Palm example illustrates. One interpretation of this example is that the failure of the Newton in this market provided information to Palm which helped them to succeed. These opportunities are considerably more complex than spotting a $20 bill lying on the sidewalk, or seeing that something can be bought for less in one location than it can be sold for in another, and the failure of the Newton to capitalize on the same profit opportunity later exploited by Palm illustrates the difficulty of seeing the exact nature of a profit opportunity.

It is easy to see how much more specialized retailers are in big cities relative to smaller towns. The variety of restaurants, shops, and other services is apparent. The variety of specialized business services is so much greater that many businesses would have trouble operating outside of a major city. Reductions in transportation and communications costs are making such services available to a wider market, however. One example is the proliferation of nationwide financial services firms (such as stock brokers) who rely on long distance telephone communication to stay close to their customers. Such services that are common in the twenty-first century would not have been financially viable in the 1950s only because communications costs were so much higher. Similarly, roadway improvements and the lower cost of air freight has extended the market for many firms. Some firms, like Federal Express, seized an entrepreneurial opportunity to extend the market, and this allowed other firms a larger market, which then allowed them to increase their division of labor and increase their productivity. This example leads directly into the next section.

Entrepreneurial activity as a source of entrepreneurial opportunity

As important as factors that disequilibrate the market and factors that enhance production possibilities are to the production of entrepreneurial opportunities, the most important source of entrepreneurial opportunities is the activity of other entrepreneurs. When an entrepreneur takes advantage of a previously unnoticed profit opportunity, this creates new profit opportunities, allowing other entrepreneurs to act, and the process continues cascading through the economy creating additional profit opportunities. The process of entrepreneurship itself is the most common source of new entrepreneurial opportunities.

As Kirzner depicts it, entrepreneurial opportunities lie unnoticed until entrepreneurs see and act on them. If this was all there was to it, entrepreneurial opportunities would be used up as entrepreneurs exploited them. Once the market reached equilibrium, no more opportunities would appear – unless, as noted in the previous section, factors disequilibrated the market, or production possibilities were enhanced. However, entrepreneurial actions themselves produce new entrepreneurial opportunities. Consider, for example, the cordless computer mouse. Some entrepreneur had the idea that computer users would prefer a mouse that was not tethered to the computer by a cord, and so created a battery-operated mouse that would communicate with the computer through radio waves or infrared light (there are at least these two types of cordless mice). That entrepreneurial insight would not have been possible had Steve Jobs and Bill Gates not had the entrepreneurial insight to adapt Xerox's graphical user interface to the PC. And in turn, the graphical user interface would not have been an entrepreneurial opportunity had not the PC been commercialized. And the opportunity to create the PC would not have been available had the microprocessor not been developed, and there would have been no opportunity to develop the microprocessor without the invention of the transistor. The point is that entrepreneurial actions do not use up entrepreneurial opportunities: on net they create more entrepreneurial opportunities. The main source of entrepreneurial opportunities is from the act of entrepreneurship itself.

Kirzner depicted entrepreneurship as the recognition of previously unnoticed profit opportunities, and emphasized, in contrast to Schumpeter, the equilibrating nature of entrepreneurship. Kirzner focused on how entrepreneurial activity exploited previously unrecognized profit opportunities to pull the economy toward equilibrium, rather than considering how these profit opportunities had been created, or why they had gone unrecognized. In fact, most profit opportunities had not been previously recognized because they were relatively new, and once created, they were rapidly exploited. By filling in the details about how profit opportunities are created, Kirzner's story becomes more complete. Kirzner described the process of entrepreneurship in response to those entrepreneurial opportunities that had not yet been noticed, and this chapter complements Kirzner's story by describing the origins of those entrepreneurial opportunities. Because most entrepreneurial opportunities are created by the actions of entrepreneurs, the same theory of entrepreneurship explains both the origins of entrepreneurial activity and the way in which entrepreneurs act on available opportunities.

If one concentrates only on the response of entrepreneurs to a stock of entrepreneurial opportunities, it appears as if there is a pool of opportunities from which entrepreneurs can draw, but as entrepreneurs act, the remaining number of entrepreneurial opportunities is reduced as the economy approaches equilibrium, and at equilibrium all of the entrepreneurial opportunities have already been exploited. Looked at in this way, the more entrepreneurial activity there is, the fewer entrepreneurial opportunities will be available. However, just the opposite is true. Each entrepreneurial action creates more entrepreneurial opportunities, increasing the pool of entrepreneurial opportunities as entrepreneurship takes place.

Mancur Olson's article, "Big Bills Left on the Sidewalk," argues that people just do not pass by easily exploited profit opportunities.[12] Olson is considering why some economies grow more rapidly than others, but he makes the important point that when the incentives are right, profit opportunities do not remain unexploited for long. If Olson is right, continuing entrepreneurial activity requires a continuing source of new entrepreneurial opportunities, and the key point of this section is that those new opportunities are created by entrepreneurs as they exploit existing opportunities.

In one way, this positive feedback mechanism where entrepreneurship creates additional entrepreneurial opportunities might be viewed as a kind of network externality that allows the culture of entrepreneurship to spread.[13] This is undoubtedly correct, but as this section notes, independent of any cultural effects (such as some entrepreneurs serving as role models for others) or community characteristics that might make people more likely to act entrepreneurially, entrepreneurial actions simply produce more entrepreneurial opportunities that will then be available to be exploited. Independent of any network effects, entrepreneurial actions create more entrepreneurial opportunities lying in wait to be discovered. Network effects work in the same direction, however, so the effects of entrepreneurship discussed in this section are reinforced by the network effects of entrepreneurship.

Consider some great American fortunes. Andrew Carnegie was able to build the foundations of U.S. Steel by capitalizing on the newly developed Bessemer process. John D. Rockefeller's Standard Oil Company developed because he was able to control the distribution network, which at the time relied on the recently constructed railroad infrastructure. Henry Ford's assembly lines were feasible only when there was enough of a mass market for automobiles, and the fortunes of Bill Gates rose along with the fledgling personal computer industry. None of these individuals invented the technology that made them wealthy, but they had the insight to take advantage of an entrepreneurial opportunity. Note, however, that in each case the opportunity was newly developed, and the entrepreneurial opportunity did not go unnoticed for long. Entrepreneurial opportunities are not just lying around waiting for someone to notice them. Rather, they appear and then entrepreneurs rapidly move to take advantage of them.

In each of the given examples, the entrepreneur had some specific knowledge of time and place as a context for new information revealed through the market about profit opportunities produced by recent entrepreneurial acts: the entrepreneurial act of seizing those opportunities that produces the engine for economic progress, and lays the foundation for more entrepreneurial discoveries.

One can analyze a single act of entrepreneurship, but to do so overlooks the cumulative nature of the ongoing process of entrepreneurship in the economy. In an economy that is relatively stagnant, or in a model in which the economy is in equilibrium, there are little or no entrepreneurial opportunities to be exploited. With little in the way of entrepreneurship, few new opportunities are being added to the pool, and it does not pay to be very entrepreneurial. Omniscient observers can tell real profit opportunities from apparent opportunities that look better than they really are, but in the real world entrepreneurs may take losses as a result of erroneously perceiving what appeared to be an opportunity. When few opportunities exist, the chances of being wrong increase, and entrepreneurial activity will be almost nonexistent. On the other hand, when there is much entrepreneurial activity, many new opportunities are being added to the pool, and entrepreneurial activity is more likely to pay off, creating an incentive to be more entrepreneurial.

When entrepreneurs take advantage of profit opportunities, they create new entrepreneurial opportunities that others can act upon. Entrepreneurship creates an environment that makes more entrepreneurship possible. Furthermore, in a more entrepreneurial environment, individuals know by observing the entrepreneurial successes of others that entrepreneurial opportunities are available. Thus, an entrepreneurial environment creates more alertness to the possibility of entrepreneurial opportunities.

Entrepreneurship is an integral part of the process of economic progress, but when considering the origins of entrepreneurial opportunities, economic growth and past entrepreneurship differ in important ways. Growth creates entrepreneurial opportunities by changing the type and mix of output demanded, and creating the opportunity to take advantage of scale economies. These opportunities are exogenous to the entrepreneurial process, and are eliminated as entrepreneurs act on them. Entrepreneurial opportunities created by entrepreneurship change the nature of the production process, and so generate additional entrepreneurial opportunities, making them an endogenous process that produces continuing growth.

Agglomeration economies

The effects of agglomeration economies and knowledge spillovers are important factors leading to economic progress. Agglomeration economies and knowledge spillovers are in part a function of geography.[14] One can see geographic concentrations of entrepreneurial activity in California's Silicon Valley, in North Carolina's research triangle, and in population centers such as New York, Tokyo, London, and Seoul. But one also notices the same phenomenon in industries. Entrepreneurial industries like electronics see spillovers across broad geographic areas, so that Austin, Boston, and Taiwan see innovative activity in the same industry. With increasingly better transportation and communication technologies, geographic locations can be widely separated and still take advantage of knowledge spillovers.

Hayek emphasized the importance of that specific knowledge of time and place, and agglomeration economies are a good application of Hayek's idea, and relates it to the idea that entrepreneurship creates more entrepreneurial opportunities. Potential entrepreneurs obtain some specific knowledge of time and place by observing other entrepreneurs acting in close proximity, and often this knowledge is "tacit" knowledge that cannot easily be communicated in ways other than direct observation. When entrepreneurial action creates entrepreneurial opportunities, those in close proximity will be in a position to react with entrepreneurial actions of their own. Agglomeration economies are a natural result of entrepreneurship generating additional entrepreneurial opportunities.

Entrepreneurship and equilibrium

Because twentieth-century economics was focused so much on understanding the properties of economic equilibrium, it is no surprise that the economist's understanding of entrepreneurship is closely related to equilibrium concepts, whether following Kirzner's idea of entrepreneurship as an equilibrating force in an economy or Schumpeter's idea of the disequilibrating activity of entrepreneurs engaged in creative destruction. Whether one views entrepreneurship as equilibrating or disequilibrating depends in part on how one defines equilibrium, as Chapter 4 discussed, but if the Hayekian definition of equilibrium as a condition where the plans of all individuals are mutually consistent is used, one can see from the taxonomy of the origins of entrepreneurial opportunities that entrepreneurship is sometimes equilibrating and sometimes disequilibrating.

The first source of entrepreneurial opportunities – factors that disequilibrate the market – describes the source of entrepreneurial opportunities in Kirzner's framework of analysis. A shift of a supply or demand curve creates a disequilibrium that calls for Kirznerian entrepreneurship to re-equilibrate the market. This source of entrepreneurial opportunities does not fit well within the Schumpeterian description of the origins of entrepreneurial opportunities, revealing why Kirzner was so ready to take issue with Schumpeter over whether entrepreneurship is equilibrating or disequilibrating.[15]

The second source of entrepreneurial opportunities – factors that enhance production possibilities – can be viewed as consistent with both Kirzner's and Schumpeter's visions of entrepreneurship, although with slightly different implications. Economic growth means that people have more income to spend, increasing demand in existing markets, and perhaps opening up new markets. In Kirzner's framework, this disequilibrates the market, producing entrepreneurial opportunities which, when acted upon, will pull the market toward equilibrium. Taking a Schumpeterian view, if demand increases in an existing market, that may create the opportunity to implement a new production process, such as moving from hand production to assembly line production, which will disrupt existing production technologies. Meanwhile, markets for new goods will be created, perhaps displacing production in some existing markets. In either case, the former equilibrium is disrupted.

While both the Kirznerian and Schumpeterian views seem to apply here, the Schumpeterian view seems more consistent with the notion of economic progress, because it depicts not just someone re-equilibrating the market, but someone seizing an opportunity to introduce an innovation into the economy that results in something different from the old status quo: new production processes, new goods, new methods of bringing goods to market.

The third source of entrepreneurial opportunities – the past entrepreneurial actions of others – is very Schumpeterian. One might, following Kirzner, say that the entrepreneurial actions of others have created a new equilibrium, allowing entrepreneurs to spot further profit opportunities to re-equilibrate the market, but this does not seem to do justice to the innovation that comes along with such entrepreneurship. Entrepreneurs in this case are not just equilibrating a market, they are producing new goods and services that bring qualitative improvements to people's lives.

Kirzner objected to Schumpeter's characterization of entrepreneurship as disequilibrating, and Chapter 4 suggested that the issue is at least in part definitional. But looking at the two contrasting views of Schumpeter and Kirzner, it is apparent that some causes of entrepreneurial opportunities lead to equilibrating types of entrepreneurial actions whereas others may be disequilibrating. The disequilibrating vision of Schumpeter paints a better picture of the entrepreneurial actions that lie at the foundation of the remarkable economic progress the market economy has generated for two and a half centuries.

If these innovations are introduced into an economy at a slow-enough pace that people have a chance to anticipate them and react to them, they will not necessarily lead to a disruptive disequilibrium situation – and the economy can respond quickly to new opportunities. The Kirznerian equilibrating forces of entrepreneurship can be sufficient to more than keep up with the Schumpeterian disequilibrating forces. So there is not much point in debating whether entrepreneurship is equilibrating or disequilibrating, because it can be both, but it is important to see that entrepreneurship is much more than just equilibrating markets, and that over the long run, innovation brings the benefit of economic progress.

Is knowledge entrepreneurship?

The answer to the question that heads this section obviously is no; yet economic models of growth and development often make the leap of assuming that if the knowledge of entrepreneurial opportunities is available to individuals, they will use that knowledge to be entrepreneurial. Without appropriate underlying institutions, this will not be the case. Chapter 8 considers in detail the conditions that lead people to act entrepreneurial, but it is important to see that the mere generation of knowledge is insufficient to produce entrepreneurship. Thus, economic models that focus on, for example, the production of research and development or the incorporation of technology into an economy leave out an important step.

One of the assumptions underlying the neoclassical model of perfect competition is that everyone in the economy has perfect knowledge about all economic opportunities.[16] This assumption rules out the possibility that any unrecognized profit opportunities could exist in the economy, but also points toward the perfect knowledge assumption as the key assumption to relax if one is trying to understand the origins of entrepreneurial opportunities. Superficially, it might appear that the production and dissemination of knowledge by itself will produce more of the entrepreneurship that will equilibrate the economy, and while an increase in knowledge will help foster entrepreneurship, the production of knowledge is not by itself an entrepreneurial undertaking. This might appear obvious when stated so plainly, but the new classical models of economic growth, such as those by Lucas and Romer, emphasize the importance of human capital and the production of technological advances in their growth models, without capturing at all the role of entrepreneurship.[17] Even Baumol, who has specifically studied the process of entrepreneurship, has minimized the role of entrepreneurship in the generation of economic progress.[18] Chapter 4 showed how the emphasis of twentieth-century economics on equilibrium tended to minimize the role of entrepreneurship in economic models – and the just-mentioned economists are examples. Chapter 5 looked at the way that entrepreneurs accumulate the knowledge to be able to perceive and act on entrepreneurial opportunities from the vantage point of the individual entrepreneur. This chapter looks at the issue from an economy-wide vantage point to explain how those entrepreneurial opportunities arise so that they can be exploited by individual entrepreneurs.

Spotting entrepreneurial opportunities often requires knowledge that is not easily transferable to others. It may be the ability to recognize certain patterns in market behavior (a simple example would be seasonal patterns), subtle differences in quality of goods, or ways to identify whether resources are being used efficiently. Such knowledge might be acquired by experience, and may be difficult to articulate to others. Thus, certain entrepreneurial opportunities will be more available to some people, while a different set of opportunities will be more available to others. Because the ability to recognize an opportunity will often come only from some specific knowledge of time and place, perfect knowledge, in the sense assumed in the neoclassical model of perfect competition, will never exist.

Kirzner depicts entrepreneurial insight as the recognition of a profit opportunity that was previously unnoticed, and as such, does not require, or even involve, any outlay of resources on the part of the entrepreneur.[19] In this way, entrepreneurial opportunities are differentiated from mere information, which people can and do seek out. Yet, it is possible for people to invest in activities that create a more fertile environment for observing entrepreneurial opportunities. Seeking information, investing in human capital, and systematically searching through promising ideas are not entrepreneurial acts in themselves, as Kirzner defines entrepreneurship, but they can create an environment where entrepreneurial insights are more likely to be generated. Similarly, research and development activity is not entrepreneurship. But such investment in the advancement of knowledge can create an environment in which entrepreneurial opportunities are more likely to be generated. Furthermore, knowledge is necessary for the entrepreneur to recognize an entrepreneurial opportunity when one appears. There is a direct connection between entrepreneurship and knowledge, as Chapter 5 showed.

Does research produce entrepreneurship?

When one looks at the entrepreneurship that occurs in high-tech areas such as medical care, pharmaceuticals, and electronics, it is apparent that entrepreneurial insights are more likely to come to individuals who have an intimate knowledge of the area. It is unlikely that a baker will stumble across a better method for etching circuits for electronic devices, or that an auto mechanic will discover a more effective medication for lowering cholesterol. Of course, the baker and the auto mechanic have their own specific knowledge of time and place, but the point of picking high-tech examples is to illustrate that while entrepreneurship is not directly produced by knowledge, knowledge is a key ingredient in the production of entrepreneurial insights. Without knowledge, how could one recognize whether the opportunity to take some action was likely to result in profit? Furthermore, marketing research can aid entrepreneurs in identifying the most promising ideas, and tailoring their offerings to more closely fit the actual entrepreneurial opportunity.[20] Henry Ford seized a very profitable opportunity when he began mass producing automobiles at a cost much less than the other available alternatives, but missed the chance to maintain his lead by not seeing the market for new models and more options for his cars.

Innovation and technological advance are not entrepreneurship. As noted in earlier chapters, most of the innovations introduced to the market on Macintosh computers, and that later migrated to Microsoft's Windows environment, were developed by Xerox, but the company that produced the innovation failed to capitalize on the entrepreneurial opportunity. At the time that Xerox developed this technology by investing substantial resources in research and development, no other entrepreneur had the opportunity to use it, because nobody else knew about it. However, apparently lacking the entrepreneurial insight, Xerox failed to capitalize on the entrepreneurial opportunity that only it had, and when the company revealed the idea, other entrepreneurs made use of it, capturing the profits Xerox was unable to produce. In this case, it is easy to separate the innovation and technological advance from the entrepreneurship. Research and development can produce inventions that can lead to entrepreneurship, but R&D does not, by itself, produce entrepreneurial innovations.

Two categories of entrepreneurial opportunities

This example of the graphical user interface for computers illustrates that entrepreneurial opportunities can be divided into two categories. Some opportunities might arise as a result of the innovative activity of the potential entrepreneur, making the innovator the only one who is in a position to observe the existence of the opportunity. The people at Xerox could have, had they been more entrepreneurial, recognized that they had a good idea for a computer interface, and implemented it in a profitable product, or sold the idea to another company. As the innovator, they had the first chance to seize the entrepreneurial opportunity from their innovation. Xerox did try to market some products based on their graphical user interface, but were unable to market a profitable product. This illustrates how difficult it is to spot the actual profit opportunity. It was not simply producing a computer with a graphical user interface, as Xerox did with the results of its research, but rather a computer with particular characteristics at a particular price. Xerox tried, but Apple and Microsoft succeeded by perceiving the other characteristics the product needed to make it profitable.

While some entrepreneurial opportunities are the result of knowledge available only to the entrepreneur, other opportunities arise from information that is widely available, although perhaps not widely recognized as signaling a profit opportunity. People may see that the market offers an entrepreneurial opportunity that could be as simple as buying something cheaply in one location and selling for more elsewhere, or as complex as buying inputs, combining them in a new manufacturing process, and selling a new product for a profit. The first type of opportunity is open only to the innovator, because nobody else is in a position to observe the innovation, whereas the second type of opportunity is open to anyone, because it relies only on seeing an unexploited market using generally available information.

Entrepreneurship as described by Kirzner is more in the spirit of the second type of activity. For it to take place, however, there must be a market in which the profit opportunity can be realized. The first type of entrepreneurship, resulting from innovation undertaken as a private activity, also depends on a market. Partly, this is because the innovation cannot be capitalized upon without a market (in the case of Xerox, while they did manufacture a computer with their windows interface, they did not correctly assess the market value of their innovation, but others did), and partly this is because there is little incentive to invest in innovative activity unless, eventually, there is a way for the activity to generate a return to finance it. Thus, there is a close connection between the advance of knowledge and the production of entrepreneurial activity. When entrepreneurship can be profitable, people have the incentive to invest in the advance of knowledge, which eventually can produce a payoff if it produces entrepreneurial opportunities. The production of knowledge is not entrepreneurship, but the two are closely linked, as Chapter 5 described. For knowledge to be used entrepreneurially, the institutional environment must be designed so that entrepreneurs can profit from acting on their knowledge, a topic discussed in more detail in Chapter 8.

Conclusion

Kirzner's theory of entrepreneurship focuses on the way in which entrepreneurial discovery reallocates resources, and on the role of entrepreneurship on equilibrating markets. Kirzner has little to say about where those entrepreneurial opportunities come from that allow entrepreneurial activity to take place. Because Kirzner does not discuss it, one could envision there being a fixed stock of entrepreneurial opportunities, and as entrepreneurs discover and take advantage of them, the opportunities for future entrepreneurship are diminished. In fact, the opposite is true. Entrepreneurial discoveries lead to more entrepreneurial opportunities, so the more entrepreneurship there is in an economy, the greater will be the opportunities for future entrepreneurship.

There are three basic sources of entrepreneurial opportunities: factors that disequilibrate markets, factors that enhance production possibilities, and the effects of entrepreneurial activities themselves. Disequilibrating factors can be easily understood within a neoclassical general equilibrium framework. Changes in tastes, technologies, or available resources push the economy out of equilibrium and create profit opportunities for those who reallocate resources. Market economies typically remain close to equilibrium precisely because entrepreneurship reallocates resources in a stabilizing way. This is one of the important lessons Kirzner emphasizes. Factors that enhance production possibilities imply a reallocation of resources because the mix of goods and services demanded will change as income grows, and because an increase in the extent of the market will make different production techniques more profitable. This is not so apparent in a general equilibrium context because general equilibrium models often employ homothetic utility and production functions. Even when models allow increasing returns to scale, the models do not make it apparent that entrepreneurial activity is necessary to increase output more than in direct proportion to an increase in inputs. Thus, the models overlook changes in the mix of outputs and overlook the fact that more efficient production techniques can be used as markets grow.

The most important factor creating entrepreneurial opportunities, however, is the act of entrepreneurship itself. When an entrepreneur seizes on a new entrepreneurial opportunity, new market possibilities are created. If an entrepreneur creates a new product, that creates the possibility of complementary products and increases the demand for inputs into the new product (but also may reduce the demand for other goods). If an entrepreneur discovers a better process for producing an existing product, this also creates opportunities for potential input suppliers. Thus, there is not a stock of entrepreneurial opportunities that can be used up as entrepreneurs take them; rather, when entrepreneurs act on one opportunity they create additional entrepreneurial opportunities, so the more entrepreneurship there is in an economy, the more entrepreneurial opportunities will be available for others. Entrepreneurship leads to more entrepreneurship.

Entrepreneurship cannot be produced in the same way that capital goods can, but it is possible for potential entrepreneurs to create an environment within which entrepreneurial discovery is more likely. Research and development is not the same thing as entrepreneurship, but by investing in research and development, businesses can create an environment conducive to entrepreneurial discovery. Entrepreneurship then generates more entrepreneurial opportunities. This suggests that an economy can produce entrepreneurial opportunities, but in a manner very different from firms engaging in research and development. An understanding of the origins of entrepreneurial opportunities is important in its own right, as a guideline for creating economic policies that will lead to prosperity. From an academic standpoint, an inquiry into the origins of entrepreneurial opportunities helps to develop a more general theory of entrepreneurship.

7 Markets, entrepreneurship, and progress

The first six chapters have laid out a theory of economic progress that differs in fundamental ways from the framework presented by mainstream economic analysis in the early twenty-first century. Many of the ideas presented here are not entirely new, and the general orientation of this analysis can trace its foundation back to more than two centuries, to the ideas of Adam Smith. But the economics profession has not uniformly followed Smith's lead, or built on his insights. Chapter 2 framed the issue by dividing the analysis of economic growth into two broad camps, one following the ideas of Smith, and the other following the ideas of David Ricardo. This volume takes the Smithian approach, building on Smith's insights along with the insights of other economists, most notably Joseph Schumpeter and Israel Kirzner. One goal of this chapter is to discuss the relationships among the ideas of Smith, Schumpeter, and Kirzner. Doing this points toward a more general entrepreneurial theory of economic progress, leading to a second goal of this chapter, which is to synthesize the ideas of the previous chapters and describe the process that generates progress. Because this approach to economic progress differs in fundamental respects from the mainstream approach, another goal of this chapter is to highlight those differences.

Adam Smith's invisible hand

Adam Smith's ideas have been discussed throughout this volume. Smith's views were contrasted with Ricardo's in Chapter 2, and Chapter 4 looked at Smith's idea of the invisible hand in a modern context. This section considers Smith's actual words in more detail. The full title of Smith's treatise, *An Inquiry Into the Nature and Causes of the Wealth of Nations*, reveals that the primary phenomenon Smith wanted to explain was the nature and causes of the wealth of nations. Perhaps the concept Smith is best known for is his idea of an invisible hand guiding the economy. The invisible hand concept was discussed in Chapter 4 from the vantage point of contemporary economics, and this section looks at Smith's actual words to relate that contemporary concept back to Smith's original idea.

Smith, introducing the concept of the invisible hand, says,

> As every individual, therefore, endeavors as much as he can both to employ his capital in the support of domestic industry, and so to direct that industry

that its produce may be of the greatest value; every individual necessarily labours to render the annual revenue of the society as great as he can. He generally, indeed, neither intends to promote the public interest, nor knows how much he is promoting it. ... he intends only his own gain, and he is in this, as in many other cases, led by an invisible hand to promote an end which was no part of his intention. Nor is it always the worse for the society that it was no part of it. By pursing his own interest he frequently promotes that of the society more effectually than when he really intends to promote it. I have never known much good done by those who affected to trade for the public good.[1]

There are several points to note about Smith's discussion of the invisible hand. First, he discusses the way an individual tries to allocate resources to produce output of the greatest possible value. As Chapter 4 noted, one might interpret this, in a twentieth-century context, to suggest that the function of the invisible hand is to equilibrate the market, but it is unlikely that even those who are thoroughly trained in twentieth-century economics have using their resources to try to equilibrate the market as a goal. Rather, they will be looking for opportunities to allocate their resources so that they can generate more profit than the resources are generating in their current use. In other words, they will be looking for entrepreneurial opportunities. The equilibrating forces of the market may be a by-product, but the invisible hand is not leading individuals to equilibrate markets, it is leading them to seek more profitable ways to employ the resources they control. Even through the lens of twentieth-century economics, the equilibrium interpretation of Smith's invisible hand does not seem to be plausible in the context in which Smith was employing it.

Second, it is interesting to note that Smith does not present the invisible hand as an analogy. Smith does not say that people are led "as if" by an invisible hand, but simply says they are led by an invisible hand. Smith is referring to real economic forces when he refers to the invisible hand, not developing an analogy. Considering the number of words Smith wrote in the volume, one might want to be cautious about placing too much emphasis on the use of specific words in a particular phrase, but as Smith wrote the phrase, the invisible hand is a real economic force, not a metaphor.

Third, Smith notes that people are more likely to further the interests of society when, within a market economy, they consider only their own interests than when they really intend to promote the more general interest. This third point is especially relevant when considering policies that generate economic progress. Progress is the result of people acting to maximize their own well-being, not people acting to further the public good. Ironically, international growth and development policies – especially since the mid-twentieth century – have been spearheaded by plans of some governments to try to do some good in other nations. Meanwhile, the nations that have achieved the most economic progress have done so independent of those efforts. While Smith was referring to individual behavior, his words also appear to apply to the collective actions of national governments.

In this passage, Smith is not very specific about what economic activities promote the wealth of nations, but that is the overall subject of his book, and he addresses the issue immediately. If Adam Smith is the father of economics, then *The Wealth of Nations* is the first book in economics, and the first lesson in that first book is that the division of labor is the engine of economic progress. The first sentence in *The Wealth of Nations* is, "The greatest improvement in the productive powers of labour, and the greater part of the skill, dexterity, and judgment with which it is any where directed, or applied, seem to have been the effects of the division of labour."[2] Smith then illustrates the division of labor with his example of the pin factory, marveling at how many more pins can be produced through this division of labor than if just one person had the job of making the whole pin. But the division of labor is limited by the extent of the market, Smith argues. As markets grow, an increased division of labor is possible, which increases productivity and allows markets to grow further. Smith described the economy as an engine of ever-increasing prosperity. An increasingly fine division of labor increases output and income, increasing the extent of the market, which allows for an even finer division of labor. There is no natural limit to the wealth of nations.

Prosperity is generated, then, not just by producing more and more of the same output using more and more of the same inputs, but by increasing the division of labor. To do so requires that individuals find new and better ways of doing things, and discover new goods and services that can be produced for profit. Smith's engine of economic progress, the division of labor, is antithetical to the production function idea that more output is produced by increasing inputs. Increasing the division of labor means doing things differently from the way they were done previously, not just adding more of the same inputs to the same production function. That requires some entrepreneurial insight. The invisible hand, then, must be that force that leads individuals acting in their own interests to discover and act on profit opportunities that had previously gone unnoticed. The invisible hand, in other words, leads people to be entrepreneurial. The ideas presented in this volume thus rest firmly on the foundation of Adam Smith's *The Wealth of Nations*.

Schumpeterian and Kirznerian entrepreneurs

Israel Kirzner's book *Competition and Entrepreneurship* contrasted his view of entrepreneurs who equilibrate markets with Schumpeter's entrepreneurs who generate economic progress through creative destruction, disequilibrating markets. This section considers in more detail the differences between Schumpeter's and Kirzner's depiction of entrepreneurial activity. Chapter 4 argued that at least part of the difference depends upon how equilibrium is defined, but even if this terminological difference is settled, there remains a fundamental difference between the functions that entrepreneurship accomplishes in Schumpeter's and Kirzner's analysis. Schumpeter's entrepreneurs change the nature of the underlying equilibrium in the economy, and Kirzner's entrepreneurs act to keep the economy close to that equilibrium. While Kirzner did find more commonality between his and Schumpeter's ideas in his later work, it does not appear that Kirzner made this distinction between these effects of the entrepreneurship that they both were discussing.

Kirzner distinguishes his view of entrepreneurship, which he envisions as equilibrating, with Schumpeter's, which he depicts as disequilibrating, saying "Schumpeter's entrepreneur acts to *disturb* an existing equilibrium situation. ... The entrepreneur is pictured as *initiating* change and generating *new* opportunities."[3] Kirzner then quotes Schumpeter as concluding that entrepreneurship is at odds with equilibrating activity. Kirzner, in contrast, argues that the entrepreneur "*...brings into mutual adjustment* those discordant elements which resulted from prior market ignorance."[4] Kirzner takes issue with Schumpeter because his discussion of entrepreneurship is "...likely to generate the utterly mistaken view that the state of equilibrium can establish itself without any social device to deploy and marshal the scattered pieces of information which are the only source of such a state."[5]

When Kirznerian entrepreneurship is considered within the framework of economic progress, there may be more common ground between Kirzner's and Schumpeter's views on entrepreneurship than Kirzner implies in the above passages. Kirzner's entrepreneurs explicitly begin their activity within a disequilibrium situation.

> It is necessary to postulate that out of the mistakes which led market participants to choose less-than-optimal courses of action yesterday, there can be expected to develop systematic *changes in expectations* concerning ends and means that can generate corresponding *alterations in plans*.[6]

In such a situation, entrepreneurial insights would bring individuals closer and closer to their optimal courses of action, eventually causing entrepreneurial opportunities to vanish. However, new opportunities could arise from Schumpeterian entrepreneurship, as Chapter 6 described, which would create a disequilibrium situation with new profit opportunities for Kirznerian entrepreneurs to act upon.

From the entrepreneur's standpoint, there is no real distinction to be drawn. In both cases, the entrepreneurs are seeking opportunities to reallocate resources to realize a previously unexploited profit opportunity. The distinction arises because of the differences in the nature of the profit opportunities that Schumpeter and Kirzner were envisioning. In Schumpeter's case, one can picture an economy in Hayekian equilibrium, where everyone's plans are mutually consistent. The entrepreneur spots a profit opportunity, and unless the entrepreneur's actions were anticipated by others in the economy, other people's plans will be disrupted by the entrepreneur's actions and some people will not be able to realize the plans they had previously made. The entrepreneurial act is disequilibrating. At this point there is an opportunity for Kirzner's entrepreneurs to step in and seize profit opportunities to reequilibrate the economy. The entrepreneur is acting on a previously unnoticed profit opportunity in both instances. But in Schumpeter's case, the entrepreneur disturbs an existing Hayekian equilibrium, whereas in Kirzner's case the entrepreneur moves toward Hayekian equilibrium.

The distinction between the two cases becomes somewhat more obscure in practice if one admits that an economy is never in Hayekian equilibrium, but the distinction remains clear in theory. In this context, Schumpeterian entrepreneurs have the effect of making individual plans less consistent with each other, whereas Kirznerian entrepreneurs have the effect of making them more consistent. There is a more important distinction to be made between the two cases, however. The key element Schumpeter was describing was the innovative activity of bringing a new product or production process to market, whereas the key element Kirzner was describing was spotting profit opportunities that would make people's plans more consistent and bring the economy closer to equilibrium. Because of the way Kirzner defined equilibrium, as discussed in Chapter 4, his vision of entrepreneurship encompasses the activities of Schumpeterian entrepreneurs, but Kirzner describes them differently, so the equilibrating nature of entrepreneurship is emphasized over the entrepreneur's innovative activities. Although neither vision of entrepreneurship excludes the activities described by the other, it seems descriptive to refer to the innovative activities of entrepreneurs that make it less likely for people to be able to realize their plans as Schumpeterian, and the equilibrating activities of entrepreneurs that make people's plans more consistent as Kirznerian.

In fact, there is no difference between the actions of Kirznerian and Schumpeterian entrepreneurs. Both are seizing unexploited profit opportunities, and in both cases the market environment will be different for all market participants in the future. One must note, however, that in any advancing economy, the equilibrium toward which the economy tends changes from day to day, and when the Kirznerian model is expanded to recognize this, the tendency toward equilibrium in a static sense is less important than the exploitation of new profit opportunities which implies greater gains from trade and economic progress. The difference that Kirzner emphasizes between his and Schumpeter's views largely arises because of the different objectives of the two writers. Schumpeter was discussing directly the role of entrepreneurship in economic growth, while Kirzner was interested in showing how entrepreneurship is an essential but underrecognized element in the allocation of economic resources.[7]

Integrating the ideas of Smith, Schumpeter, and Kirzner

Thinking about entrepreneurship in this way, Adam Smith's vision of an ever-increasing division of labor as the engine of economic progress can be described by integrating Schumpeter's entrepreneurs with Kirzner's. In Kirzner's model of entrepreneurship, Kirzner takes entrepreneurial opportunities as given, and describes the entrepreneur's reaction to the stock of existing entrepreneurial opportunities. While, in a sense, profit opportunities lie unseen until entrepreneurs observe them and capitalize on them, profit opportunities are not like a fixed stock of resources waiting to be claimed. Rather, they arise in the course of economic activity, and in many cases are seized shortly after they appear. As Chapter 6 explained, when looking at the causes of economic progress, the most significant entrepreneurial opportunities are created as a result of past entrepreneurship. Seeing entrepreneurship within the context of economic progress helps clarify the origin of entrepreneurial ideas, and the way in which entrepreneurs are able to spot them and act on them.

Kirzner's analysis of entrepreneurship does not describe the origins of entrepreneurial opportunities, which may give the impression that a stock of opportunities lies unnoticed, waiting for entrepreneurs to discover them, but this impression is fundamentally misleading. A view that entrepreneurial opportunities are somehow produced exogenously and lie in wait for entrepreneurs to notice them leaves out the most important product of entrepreneurship. Furthermore, it would be misleading to think that at any point in time there is an abundance of entrepreneurial opportunities that are unnoticed, waiting to be discovered. Entrepreneurial opportunities constantly arise in a growing economy, and when they do they are, except in rare circumstances, rapidly acted upon. Entrepreneurial insights are produced in the process of economic advancement. More rapid advancement brings more entrepreneurial opportunities, and more entrepreneurial opportunities produce greater incentives for potential entrepreneurs to become more alert to them. Entrepreneurship generates more entrepreneurship.

In contrast, a stagnant economy blunts the incentives for entrepreneurial activity, and can remain stagnant because few new opportunities are being generated by entrepreneurs.[8] Just as entrepreneurship generates more entrepreneurial opportunities, the lack of entrepreneurship puts a damper on future entrepreneurial actions. In a non-entrepreneurial environment, fewer entrepreneurial opportunities will be created, reducing the incentive to seek them, and increasing the probability that what may at first appear to be a profit opportunity will turn out to be unprofitable if it is pursued.

If one wanted to focus solely on the activities of entrepreneurs, then entrepreneurial opportunities might be viewed as exogenous creations that entrepreneurs act upon. However, when one examines the results of entrepreneurship, it is a straightforward conclusion that entrepreneurial activities create more entrepreneurial opportunities. This line of reasoning has the advantage of endogenizing the creation of entrepreneurial opportunities. Entrepreneurial opportunities are not used up as they are acted upon. Rather, the exploitation of one entrepreneurial opportunity leads to the creation of others, creating a more entrepreneurial environment in the process.

Schumpeter's discussion of entrepreneurship flows from his vision of economic progress as a spontaneous, revolutionary, and discontinuous process,[9] implying that the motive forces that produce growth are exogenous to his model of growth, if not to the economic process itself. From an initial equilibrium, entrepreneurial activity disturbs that equilibrium, leading Schumpeter to the idea that entrepreneurial activity is disequilibrating. Kirzner begins from a disequilibrium condition to show how entrepreneurial activity helps equilibrate an economy. Neither view is complete, because in Schumpeter's model some force must equilibrate an economy before entrepreneurial activity can disequilibrate it, and that force is Kirznerian entrepreneurship. Likewise, in Kirzner's model, if entrepreneurial activity continually works to equilibrate an economy, some force must push it away from equilibrium to allow the equilibrating process to operate, and that force is Schumpeterian entrepreneurship. Both forces have the same origin, however, which is entrepreneurs acting as Smith described, to allocate resources under their control in a more profitable manner.

Kirzner is justly concerned that Schumpeter ignores the equilibrating role of entrepreneurship, but at the same time Schumpeter does correctly note that entrepreneurial activity is essential for economic progress. Kirzner's theory of entrepreneurship gives no indication of the origin of entrepreneurial opportunities, and when Kirznerian entrepreneurship is depicted as an integral part of the process of economic progress, entrepreneurial opportunities can be seen as originating from past entrepreneurial activity, making Kirzner's theory of entrepreneurship more self-contained and complete.

Schumpeterian and Kirznerian entrepreneurship

While in one sense the entrepreneurial activities described by Schumpeter and Kirzner are the same – especially when viewed from the vantage point of the entrepreneur – in a larger sense they are different. In both cases entrepreneurs are searching for ways to employ the resources under their control in a more profitable manner, and entrepreneurship means noticing, acting upon, and seizing these opportunities.[10] But in Schumpeter's framework, one can picture an economy in Hayekian equilibrium, with everyone's economic plans being consistent with each other, when the entrepreneur's action disrupts those plans by introducing a new or improved product, or a new production technique, which means that as a result some people cannot realize their previous plans. An economy in equilibrium is disequilibrated by the creative destruction of entrepreneurship. In Kirzner's framework, one can picture an economy in disequilibrium,[11] creating a profit opportunity for the Kirznerian entrepreneur to seize and pull the economy toward equilibrium.

The overlap and consistency between Schumpeter's and Kirzner's description of entrepreneurship has already been noted, but for purposes of understanding the function of entrepreneurship in an economy, it is useful to exaggerate the differences between them to emphasize two different effects that entrepreneurship can have on an economy. Thus, Schumpeterian entrepreneurship can be viewed as entrepreneurial activity that pulls an economy away from a Hayekian equilibrium, that is, one that reduces the mutual consistency of individual plans in an economy and that reduces the coordination of individuals' economic activities. Before the Schumpeterian entrepreneurship, individuals had plans that were mutually consistent, and after the entrepreneurial activity, some people change their plans so that people's plans are no longer consistent. In contrast, Kirzner's entrepreneurs coordinate the plans of individuals. Kirznerian coordination could take place in two ways: by making individual plans more consistent with each other, or by facilitating Pareto-improving exchanges.

In the first instance of Kirznerian coordination, individuals might have inconsistent plans. Individuals may find themselves unemployed or underemployed, or may find resources they own unemployed or underemployed. An engineer might be working as a cab driver, or a retail storefront on a busy thoroughfare might be employed as a storage room. Entrepreneurial activity could match the engineer with employment that more fully utilized the engineer's skills, or could establish a retail outlet in that prime location (if in fact it was a better location for retail trade than for storage). Thus, the entrepreneurial activity matches suppliers and demanders so that individuals' activities are more coordinated. The example would be even more forceful if the engineer were unemployed, or if the retail storefront were vacant after its previous tenant left.

In the second instance of Kirznerian coordination, people's plans might be coordinated out of ignorance of a possible Pareto improvement, much like the arbitrage example used earlier, where apples sell for $0.50 in one location and $0.25 in another. The entrepreneur finds a Pareto improvement that leaves the buyers and the sellers in a market better off, enhancing the coordination of individual plans in the marketplace. These examples emphasize the equilibrating nature of entrepreneurship that Kirzner promoted.

In one sense this is an artificial distinction, because the economy is never in Hayekian equilibrium, where the plans of all individuals are coordinated and everyone's expectations can be realized. Entrepreneurial actions can often improve coordination among a subset of individuals in an economy while disrupting coordination among others, and if the economy is not at an equilibrium anyway, it may be difficult, even conceptually, to say that a certain action moves an economy closer to, or further away from, an equilibrium. Yet in another sense, by distinguishing the effects of these two different types of entrepreneurship, a clearer picture appears regarding the role of entrepreneurship in an economy.

If one pictures an evenly rotating economy in Hayekian equilibrium, a Schumpeterian entrepreneur can introduce a new product or a new production process, disturbing that equilibrium. Now, with disequilibrium and an economy in which individual plans are inconsistent with each other, Kirznerian entrepreneurs act on the profit opportunities created by the disequilibrium to pull the economy toward a new equilibrium. Schumpeterian entrepreneurship disrupts the plans of individuals and reduces coordination among individuals, disequilibrating the economy, and Kirznerian entrepreneurship acts in response to the disequilibrium to allocate resources more efficiently, to coordinate the plans among many economic actors, and to equilibrate the economy. Schumpeterian entrepreneurship disequilibrates the economy, and Kirznerian entrepreneurship re-equilibrates it.

Schumpeter, Kirzner, entrepreneurship, and progress

With this background, the relationship between entrepreneurship and progress can be described in a straightforward way by reference to Schumpeterian and Kirznerian entrepreneurship. Starting with the status quo, an entrepreneurial action disrupts the existing coordination of individual plans, disequilibrating the economy. The entrepreneurial action will improve the well-being of some economic actors by introducing a new or improved good or service, or by introducing a superior production process for an existing good or service. By so doing, people who planned to buy the old good or service now migrate to the new, and people who were engaged in the old production process find their business eroded by a superior process. Schumpeterian entrepreneurship thus disrupts an existing equilibrium.

A good or production process inferior to the status quo has a limited potential to disrupt existing economic arrangements. While some individuals might mistakenly buy the new good, or switch to the new production process, if it is not an improvement they will switch back once their mistake is realized, making changes that are not improvements self-limiting in their disruptive potential. Any initial disruption will find its effects dampened over time. Improvements, in contrast, will increase their disruptive effects as more people move from the old goods and methods to the new ones. The creative destruction of Schumpeterian entrepreneurship brings with it economic progress. It is not just that old goods and methods are replaced by new ones, it is that they are replaced by welfare-enhancing alternatives. Schumpeterian entrepreneurship is the engine of economic progress.

The disruptive effect of Schumpeterian entrepreneurship leads to some inefficiency in the use of resources, if inefficiency is viewed in a static sense. In the long run, welfare is improved, but in the short run, new conditions exist such that all resources are not employed as effectively as they could be if all resource owners – and all potential customers for those resources – had perfect knowledge. This disequilibrium creates profit opportunities, which opens the role for Kirznerian entrepreneurs to seize them and equilibrate the economy. This Kirznerian entrepreneurship also contributes to economic progress by allowing resources to be employed more efficiently.

The short story, then, of entrepreneurship and economic progress is that Schumpeterian entrepreneurs disrupt the existing allocation of resources, creating improvements in goods and production processes, which generates economic progress, and Kirznerian entrepreneurs react to the disruption in the allocation of resources by acting on profit opportunities to pull the economy toward an equilibrium and to pull the economy toward an efficient allocation of resources. Schumpeterian entrepreneurs disrupt market coordination, and Kirznerian entrepreneurs enhance market coordination, both leading to a welfare-enhancing allocation of resources.

Entrepreneurial foundations of macroeconomics

This merging of Schumpeterian and Kirznerian entrepreneurship into a more general model of economic progress can be applied more broadly to analyze macroeconomic instability. Macroeconomics became a separately identified subset of economics in the 1930s as a result of the Great Depression, and up through the 1960s macroeconomics was Keynesian economics. The unemployment of the

1930s was the macroeconomic problem that led to the creation of macroeconomics as a separate area of inquiry. Prior to the 1930s, economists studied macroeconomic issues under the heading of business cycle analysis, and here again the primary problem was the periodic bouts of unemployment that plagued the economy.[12] Early in the twentieth century, Ludwig von Mises, in his *Theory of Money and Credit*,[13] identified monetary disturbances as a cause of business cycles, and Mises's theory of business cycles was extensively developed by Friedrich Hayek in the 1930s,[14] and has continued being developed by Roger Garrison and others on into the twenty-first century.[15] The problem that leads to episodes of unemployment, following this line of reasoning, is inconsistent expectations among individuals in an economy. This theory relies heavily on monetary disturbances, but ultimately those disturbances create a situation where people make plans that cannot all be realized simultaneously. The monetary disturbances interfere with the coordination of individuals' economic plans. When the future arrives in which some plans cannot be realized, resources – both capital and labor – find themselves unemployed or underemployed as their owners search for ways to employ them more productively.

The relationship between Hayek's business cycle theory and Hayek's definition of equilibrium discussed in Chapter 4 should be apparent. Equilibrium exists when everyone's plans are mutually consistent. When people make plans that are inconsistent, ultimately some of those plans will not be able to be realized, creating a disruption that results in an economy out of equilibrium. Hayek focused on monetary causes of such disruptions, but Schumpeter, in his book, *Business Cycles*,[16] argued that the creative destruction of entrepreneurship created business cycles. Entrepreneurs introduce innovations into the economy, which at the same time creates new opportunities for a reallocation of resources and makes some existing methods of production and types of goods unprofitable. Dislocations caused by people reallocating their resources in response to the innovation lead to unemployment and business cycles.

Schumpeter's book on business cycles never got much of a hearing because it was swamped by the development of Keynesian economics, started by John Maynard Keynes's *General Theory* that was published three years before Schumpeter's book.[17] Hayek's work on business cycles was also pushed aside by Keynesian macroeconomics. In the Keynesian framework, aggregate output is determined by aggregate demand, and because the framework deals only in aggregates, the coordination problems that underlie Hayek's and Schumpeter's business cycle theories do not exist. Toward the end of the twentieth century, the Keynesian framework has also been pushed aside in favor of general equilibrium macro models.[18] In these models, the economy is always in equilibrium, so again the coordination problems that Hayek and Schumpeter envisioned underlying macroeconomic disturbances are assumed away.

While it may be a stretch to call the 25 percent unemployment rate in the depths of the Great Depression an equilibrium phenomenon, one can think of unemployment as the result of the choices of unemployed people to continue searching for a better opportunity rather than take the first (or second) job that comes along.

Even if unemployment is modeled as an equilibrium phenomenon in this way, it masks the coordination problem that gives rise to the choices of the unemployed to continue to search. In a situation of perfect information and perfect foresight, individuals would know what their best opportunities were and would immediately take them. This does not happen because of problems individuals have in coordinating their plans.

Part of the problem arises because of imperfect information, a subject analyzed in great detail by economists. But part of the problem is that even if everybody had perfect information about all current conditions, that still does not supply all information about the future conditions upon which today's decisions depend. This is due in part because people cannot foresee future changes, innovations, and shocks (to use current macroeconomic terminology) to the economy. It is also due to the fact that when disruptions occur in an economy, pushing the economy away from the current equilibrium, a new equilibrium is not immediately realized, so some trade will occur at disequilibrium prices, and nobody can know what the new equilibrium vector of prices will be until the market actually produces it. People can try to forecast future prices and markets, but the actual information people need to make fully informed decisions cannot be obtained, because it has not yet been produced.

In general equilibrium models, trade always takes place at equilibrium prices. A disruption to the economy creates a new equilibrium vector of prices which is immediately revealed to market participants. In the real world, disruptions do not create a new vector of prices; rather, individual exchanges at prices agreed upon by the trading parties tend to grope toward the new equilibrium prices. But in a world of heterogeneous capital, where old goods are traded alongside the new ones that will eventually replace them, it will take time for the market to produce those new prices. Sellers of old goods and producers using obsolete processes may not immediately shift their output or processes. Existing capital equipment might be made obsolete in the sense that it would cost more to replace it than its current market value, but if it has any residual value it will continue to be used, and old processes will survive even in the face of superior new alternatives, for some time. Similarly, buyers will not immediately shift their purchases from old goods to new – from typewriters to computers, for example – but rather will shift gradually, and while current information may reveal a direction of change, it will not reveal the new equilibrium vector of prices and quantities until the market actually ends up there. In addition, changes do not occur one at a time, waiting for the effects of the first to work themselves out before the next appears. As the economy is adjusting to one disruption, another is likely to appear. The challenge to the market system is to coordinate the plans of all individuals in an environment that is continually changing.

Thinking in this framework, one can see entrepreneurial foundations of macroeconomics, building on Schumpeter's idea that disruptions caused by entre-preneurial activity lead to business cycles. When economic adjustment cannot keep up with the disruptions, unemployment will result. The framework is well-described with reference to the Schumpeterian and Kirznerian entrepreneurship described earlier in the chapter. Schumpeterian entrepreneurship disrupts the economy, pushing the economy away from an existing equilibrium. People will respond by reallocating their resources, including their labor resources, to fit the new situation. Kirznerian entrepreneurs will spot profit opportunities resulting from the resulting disequilibrium allocation of resources and act on them to re-equilibrate the economy. As long as the Kirznerian entrepreneurs, in their equilibrating roles, can keep up with the disruptions caused by the Schumpeterian entrepreneurs, the economy will remain close to equilibrium. If the disruptions created by the Schumpeterian entrepreneurs are substantial enough to overwhelm the Kirznerian entrepreneurs, unemployment can result because the Kirznerian entrepreneurs are unable to reallocate resources rapidly enough to prevent some resources from being unemployed in the interim.

While this is far from being a complete macroeconomic framework, it shows how entrepreneurial activity can affect the macroeconomy, and it integrates macroeconomic fluctuations with economic growth. It is consistent with contemporary Austrian macroeconomics in that it emphasizes coordination problems and inconsistent plans as the underlying cause of macroeconomic fluctuations. Mises and Hayek cited monetary forces that can interfere with market coordination, and this is completely consistent with Schumpeterian entrepreneurship being another source of disruption. Regardless of the source of the disruption, policies that encourage entrepreneurship can help reequilibrate an economy and stabilize the business cycle, and policies that interfere with Kirznerian entrepreneurship – such as tax and regulatory policies – can slow the adjustment to an efficient reallocation of resources. This discussion of entrepreneurship has taken place mostly within the context of economic progress, but it is worth seeing that this entrepreneurial framework sits more generally within economic analysis and can provide some insight into macroeconomic fluctuations as well as economic progress.

Policy implications from equilibrium growth theory

Twentieth-century growth theory, based on the foundation of Solow's equilibrium growth model,[19] allows considerable development of the concept of growth by making assumptions about the production function. The production function approach to growth, where output is a function of capital and labor, or $Q = f(K, L)$, focuses on increasing the quality of capital and labor, and improving technology to produce more output from a given quantity of inputs, because there is nothing more to analyze within that framework. This model of growth has been taken seriously by both economists and policy makers. As Anne Kreuger notes,[20] it was at the foundation of world economic development policy for three decades after the Second World War, and application of this neoclassical approach to growth points out the advantages of central planning over market allocation, because planners are in a better position both to increase a nation's saving and investment rate, and to direct investment toward those sectors that can be most productive. Yet despite the advice of economic growth theorists, undeveloped economies remain undeveloped even though they have undertaken substantial investment initiatives. Furthermore, the data make clear that only a small part of economic growth can be explained by increases in investment. The answer must lie somewhere else.

Throughout much of the twentieth century, central planning was viewed as a better method of organizing an economy to produce economic growth than reliance on the market system. In his best-selling introductory textbook in 1973, Nobel Laureate Paul Samuelson argued that although per capita income in the Soviet Union was about half of per capita income in the United States, because of their centrally planned economy the Soviet Union would grow faster, and per capita income in the Soviet Union would catch up to that in the United States perhaps as early as 1990, but almost surely by 2010.[21] After the Berlin Wall fell in 1989 and the Soviet Union dissolved in 1991, almost everybody agrees that market economies are better suited to producing economic growth than centrally planned economies. However, policies regarding economic growth continue to be oriented toward increasing the quantity of output rather than fostering progress by advancing the type of output being produced.

The centrally planned economies of the twentieth century placed a big premium on the development of both human and physical capital, and on the production of advances in technology. Their collapse at the end of the twentieth century shows that it is not the advancement of human capital, physical capital, and technology by itself that leads to economic growth, but rather the environment within which these advances take place. The economic policies of those centrally planned economies fit the production function model of economic growth well, but that production function approach omits the key entrepreneurial foundations for economic progress. Centrally planned economies failed because central planning precludes entrepreneurship, which is necessarily decentralized in nature.

When one looks at the neoclassical growth theory that dominates the academic economic growth literature at the beginning of the twenty-first century, there are good reasons to doubt its general applicability, because it addresses growth rather than progress. When one looks at the policy implications of that theory, it is apparent that when it has been applied in a straightforward way, it has not led to progress nor to growth more narrowly defined. The entrepreneurial alternative, while less mathematically rigorous in its formulation, has the advantage that it addresses the fundamental causes underlying economic progress.

The entrepreneurial alternative

The most basic facts of economic progress weigh against focusing on the inputs into the production process, and point toward an examination of the process itself. Eugen Bohm-Bawerk[22] depicted a structure of production that would become more roundabout as more indirect methods of production were used. In contrast to the production function approach in which all capital is aggregated into a homogeneous commodity, Bohm-Bawerk's framework incorporates heterogeneous capital and more roundabout methods of production that have remained an integral part of Austrian capital theory,[23] and as noted earlier in the chapter, have been applied to explain business cycles[24] and economic growth.[25] This literature focuses on incentives for altering the production process, rather than focusing directly in the inputs used in production. As such, it looks at the incentives entrepreneurs have to discover new production processes, rather than looking at changes that occur to the production process after entrepreneurs have acted. The neoclassical framework argues in favor of enhancing human and physical capital, and improving production processes, but by focusing on inputs overlooks how market incentives lead entrepreneurs to invest and innovate.

Within a neoclassical framework, where things are produced by combining inputs in a production function, the most straightforward way to get technological change is to produce it. Research and development can be undertaken by combining land, labor, and capital, to produce technological change. The successes attributable to investment in research and development are indisputable, but R&D expenditures cannot be the whole story, because once the research is done, the results need to be applied to make production less costly, or even more mysteriously, to produce goods and services that have never been produced before. This is the role of entrepreneurship, which is barely treated in mainstream growth theory.[26]

Because entrepreneurship involves recognizing a profit opportunity what has previously gone unnoticed, it necessarily implies activity that is outside the previous routine. The novel nature of entrepreneurial opportunity means that it cannot be analyzed within an equilibrium framework where firms and individuals react to known parameters. For this reason, entrepreneurship excludes research and development activities, and the accumulation of human capital. These activities can augment factors of production, but by themselves do not provide the insights that lead to new goods and services, or new processes for producing existing goods and services. If this seems like an overly fine distinction, consider the policy implications. Centrally planned economies tried unsuccessfully for decades to produce growth through investment in research and education, but were missing the institutions that enabled entrepreneurship. If the incentives in an economy are right, individuals have an incentive to invest in human and physical capital, and to innovate and be entrepreneurial. If the incentives are wrong, investment and research and development will ultimately be unproductive.

Public policy toward research and development

Research and development is not entrepreneurship and does not necessarily lead to entrepreneurial insights. It can, however, produce an environment within which entrepreneurial opportunities are more likely to be discovered. As noted earlier, and as emphasized by David Harper,[27] the growth of entrepreneurial opportunities is intimately connected with the growth of knowledge, so generating new knowledge can increase the possibility of finding entrepreneurial opportunities.

Furthermore, if a firm has its own proprietary R&D activities, it can search an environment likely to have entrepreneurial opportunities to which nobody else has access. Entrepreneurship cannot be produced, but an environment within which entrepreneurial discoveries are more likely can.

The argument is sometimes made that research and development should be subsidized, because the resulting knowledge that is produced is a public good.[28] Thus, the argument goes, there will be underinvestment in the production of knowledge, and when knowledge is produced, it will be underutilized for two reasons. First, if it is covered by patents or copyrights, its availability will be restricted by the monopoly power conveyed by the producer of the knowledge. Second, if it is privately produced, those who have the knowledge have an incentive to withhold it from others who could use it profitably, in order to reap the benefits themselves. Thus, the optimal policy is to undertake R&D with public funds, and make the knowledge produced through R&D freely available to the public. These arguments apply to the products of research and development, once the research has been done, but treat research output as if it is a free good. However, there is a private incentive to engage in research activities to further the state of knowledge because it creates an environment that produces potential entrepreneurial opportunities. If the activity were subsidized, the researchers would have less incentive to undertake those research projects most likely to lead in the direction of welfare-enhancing innovation.

The argument against subsidization is that private activity provides the incentive to create an environment most likely to lead to profit opportunities, as opposed to merely engaging in the interests of the researchers themselves. The arguments favoring subsidization contain the implicit assumption that the same research activities would occur whether they were done privately and produced proprietary results, or whether the subsidized research results were available to all. But there is no reason to think that subsidized research and development will resemble privately financed R&D any more than the consumer products of the former Soviet Union resembled consumer products in the United States.

Subsidies to some research do not necessarily prevent others from engaging in their own independent research, but subsidies do take away from some of the profit potential of nonsubsidized research. If there is the chance that insights could be produced first by a subsidized operation, that reduces the incentive to engage in unsubsidized research, even if the unsubsidized research is likely to be more productive. Furthermore, if research in an area is subsidized, potential entrepreneurs might free ride off the subsidized research, waiting to see what the subsidized research produces rather than engaging in their own independent research. When one views research and development as an activity that creates an environment conducive to entrepreneurship, rather than an activity that produces technical advances, the argument for subsidization fares badly. Thus, the distinction between knowledge and entrepreneurship has important policy implications. A theory of economic growth based on technological advances will look upon subsidized research and development more favorably than a theory of economic growth based on entrepreneurship.

Implications for growth theory

While growth theory became far more formalized in the last half of the twentieth century, the fundamental ideas behind the engine of economic growth can be traced back to Adam Smith. As noted earlier, current mainstream theorists are focusing on the role of human capital, knowledge externalities, and increasing returns. These insights certainly are not wrong, but at the same time they do not go very far toward illuminating the process by which knowledge externalities produce growth, or by which increasing returns can be manifested in the production process. An entrepreneurial model of economic progress fills this gap. Knowledge externalities occur when the entrepreneurial insights of some produce entrepreneurial opportunities for others. Increasing returns occur because the more entrepreneurial activity an economy exhibits, the more new entrepreneurial opportunities it creates.

When one recognizes that entrepreneurship gives rise to knowledge externalities and increasing returns, it then becomes apparent that growth theory should focus less on the production function, where inputs are combined in a black box to produce outputs, and more on the process by which production processes are determined. Furthermore, growth should not be viewed as an increase in the amount of output, but as a change in the qualitative nature of output. The value of output is increased partly because more output is produced, but mostly because output undergoes qualitative changes. The engine of economic growth is not better inputs, but rather an environment in which entrepreneurial opportunities can be capitalized upon.

How did twentieth-century economics go so wrong?

In developing the relationship between entrepreneurship and economic progress, this analysis has been critical of the twentieth-century equilibrium approach to economic growth. One might wonder, then, how twentieth-century economics managed to go so wrong. In fact, twentieth-century economics did not go so wrong. Rather, it developed in a direction that was not very amenable to analyzing economic progress for two understandable – and maybe even good! – reasons. One reason has to do with the methodological framework of economics. The other has to do with the problems that preoccupied twentieth-century economists.

Twentieth-century economics began in 1890 with the publication of Alfred Marshall's *Principles of Economics*. Prior to Marshall's landmark book, the preeminent treatise in economics was John Stuart Mill's *Principles of Political Economy*, which was a development and extension of the ideas of David Ricardo. Following the publication of Mill's book, economic analysis underwent a substantial transformation as a result of what has been called the marginal revolution. The fundamental ideas underlying the marginal revolution were independently discovered in the 1870s by Carl Menger, William Stanley Jevons, and Leon Walras, yet while they provided an alternative to the classical economics of Ricardo and Mill, their ideas did not make it into the mainstream until Marshall presented them in a rigorous economic framework. Marshall answered many of the questions raised by classical economics, and did so in a rigorous framework of equilibrium models, which he presented in verbal, graphical, and mathematical form. Marshall's framework remained at the core of economic analysis throughout the twentieth century and into the beginning of the twenty-first.

The equilibrium framework depicted by Marshall provided an elegant understanding about the way that markets allocate resources, and was a tremendous advance over the economic analysis that had gone before. Marshall used the mathematical methods used by physics, both providing a readily understandable (for those versed in mathematics, anyway) rigorous framework for understanding the operation of a market economy, and also a framework which was ripe for the development of a more detailed mathematical description of economic phenomena.[29] As a result, economic theory advanced substantially in the twentieth century by providing a systematic mathematical description of the nature of economic equilibrium. By mid-century, Nobel laureate Paul Samuelson had laid out an even more rigorous mathematical foundation for economics that provided a framework for the further development of the mathematical analysis of economic equilibrium. Because the mathematical framework paralleled the use of math in physics to describe equilibrium states, the nature of economic methodology naturally pulled those working in economic theory to analyze the properties of economic equilibrium rather than the properties of economic progress. Entrepreneurship does not fit well within that economic framework, because it is not an equilibrium phenomenon.

This turn of economic theory toward the analysis of economic equilibrium was not a "wrong turn" in some sense, but rather an indication of the priorities of economic theorists. All models assume away some things in order to make others more clearly understandable, and equilibrium economics assumes away some of the key elements that allow for entrepreneurship. In order to answer some questions, the methodology made it more difficult to answer others, and the analysis of economic progress suffered as a result.

A second reason why twentieth-century economics focused on the nature of equilibrium rather than the nature of economic progress is that some major economic issues in the twentieth century fit neatly within the equilibrium framework. The neoclassical equilibrium economics built on Marshall suggested that all markets in an economy should rapidly equilibrate, leaving economists at somewhat of a loss to explain the major economic dislocations that came with the Great Depression in the 1930s. In particular, the labor market, characterized by massive unemployment, did not fit the neoclassical framework, and John Maynard Keynes revolutionized economics with his *General Theory of Employment, Interest, and Money* that explained how an economy could remain in equilibrium with substantial unemployment. For present purposes, the details of Keynes's analysis are of less interest than the fact that he developed his explanation within an equilibrium framework, and the Keynesian economics that followed, built on Keynes's *General Theory*, developed explicitly equilibrium models of macroeconomic phenomena.

From a policy standpoint, economic progress was not even an issue. The whole object of macroeconomic policy from the 1930s up through the 1980s (and perhaps further) was to design a set of policies that could lead an economy to an equilibrium characterized by full employment and low inflation. If the two goals of full employment and low inflation could be achieved, macroeconomic policy would be successful. Because of the policy issue economists wanted to address, the goal they sought was a static equilibrium result. The problems of inflation and unemployment were at the forefront of macroeconomics, and the nature of economic progress was not even subject to analysis in that framework.

A similar phenomenon occurred in microeconomic analysis. Microeconomists became increasingly focused on inefficiencies in the allocation of economic resources caused by externalities, public goods, and other "market failures." Market failure, as a technical economic term, means that markets are not allocating resources as efficiently as possible, and from a policy perspective, the solution is to design a policy to overcome the market failure and produce an efficient allocation of resources. Optimality is defined in a static equilibrium framework, and the analysis was complete after describing how a market failure could be corrected to allocate resources efficiently. The focus was on static efficiency in an equilibrium framework, not on the features of markets that would lead to economic progress.

Thus, the policy issues that economists focused on in the twentieth century reinforced the equilibrium orientation of economics. The goal of macroeconomic policy was to produce an equilibrium with full employment and low inflation, while the goal of microeconomic policy was to arrive at an efficient equilibrium allocation of resources. These policy questions that were amenable to equilibrium analysis, coupled with a theoretical framework that depicted an economy in equilibrium, led economics toward a framework that was not very amenable to answering questions about the causes of economic progress. Economics did make substantial advances in understanding the nature of economic equilibrium, and on the policy issues of how to produce stable macroeconomic equilibria and static efficiency in the microeconomic allocation of resources. But in doing so, the framework of economics assumed away features of the economy that were crucial to the understanding of economic progress. In a general sense, economics did not make a wrong turn, in that economic understanding advanced substantially in the twentieth century. But advances in some areas produced an economic framework that was not well-suited for analyzing other significant economic issues, and economic progress is one of those issues.

Conclusion

The combination of Schumpeter's and Kirzner's models of entrepreneurship into the framework of economic progress contributes to both growth theory and to the theory of entrepreneurship. The growth framework illuminates the theory of entrepreneurship by helping to illustrate where entrepreneurial opportunities originate, why more opportunities arise in some sectors of the economy than others, and what factors can provide incentives for entrepreneurs to more intensively search for new entrepreneurial insights. Entrepreneurial opportunities are not just exogenously delivered to an economy; in large part they are produced by entrepreneurial activities in the recent past. This aspect of entrepreneurship was not emphasized by either Schumpeter or Kirzner. This extension of this entrepreneurial framework explains the origins of entrepreneurial opportunities as well as the process of entrepreneurship.

Incorporating entrepreneurship into the framework of economic growth adds to growth theory by showing the nature of increasing returns to scale, knowledge externalities, and the role of human capital. These processes appear as a black box in mainstream growth theory, but when they are depicted as a part of the entrepreneurial process, it becomes apparent that the engine of economic growth is entrepreneurship, not technological advance or investment in human capital per se. It also becomes apparent that growth cannot be fully understood simply by looking at it as an increase in the level of income. This emphasis pushes growth theory in a Smithian direction that focuses on the institutional setting within which growth occurs, and away from a Ricardian direction that focuses on inputs into the production process. The incorporation of entrepreneurship into the framework of economic progress not only fills in these details to help make the growth process more understandable, but also points toward more promising economic policy recommendations for fostering economic progress.

In the latter half of the twentieth century, a production function approach to economic growth has led both growth theory and growth policy to conclude that increases in output could best be produced by increasing the inputs into the production process. Policies were aimed at increasing both the quantity and quality of inputs through investment, incorporation of modern technology, and education. In many less-developed economies, the results have been disappointing. This entrepreneurial framework for viewing economic growth shows that the key element in economic progress is the production of entrepreneurial opportunities. When such opportunities are available, individuals have the incentive to invest in human and physical capital without government intervention. Mainstream growth theory has seen the problems with the mechanistic application of the production function approach to economic growth, but has responded by incorporating increasing returns and knowledge externalities into formal models in a way that obscures the way in which these factors might actually manifest themselves in the real world. The straightforward prescription for economic growth is to create an institutional environment that encourages markets and rewards productive activity. Growth then occurs as a component of economic progress.

8 Institutions and entrepreneurship

Entrepreneurship generates economic progress, but a look around the world, and a look back through history, shows that some places are more entrepreneurial than others, and that some places are more prosperous than others. Obviously, the entrepreneurial process that produces prosperity is not automatic. History also shows that places with little entrepreneurship can be transformed to become entrepreneurial and more prosperous, so whether an economy is entrepreneurial is not determined by exogenous factors, and can be changed. Similarly, while some places in the world have enjoyed substantial economic progress, others have stagnated and even sunk into economic decline. If entrepreneurship is the key to economic progress, and if economies can be made more entrepreneurial, an important policy issue is how entrepreneurship can be encouraged. The answer is that institutions that create economic freedom by protecting property rights and removing impediments to market exchange encourage entrepreneurship and lead to economic progress.

This answer is at odds with the conclusions of much of the theory of economic growth as it stands at the beginning of the twenty-first century, not because mainstream growth theory concludes that institutions are not important but because mainstream growth theory does not even take institutions into account in its analysis. As the preceding chapters have noted, much of growth theory focuses on the growth of inputs – human and physical capital – and on technological change, and has ignored the institutional framework within which progress takes place.[1] This chapter argues that institutions are the crucial determinants of economic progress. With institutions conducive to economic progress, input and technology issues will take care of themselves; without appropriate institutions, improvements in inputs and technology will have little effect. If institutions conducive to entrepreneurship are in place, people will have the incentive to invest in human and physical capital, and will have an incentive to employ the best technology and to innovate to develop technological improvements. The argument is not that human and physical capital, and the use of the best technology, is unimportant. Rather, it is that individuals have the incentive to invest in these areas on their own, with the right institutional setting. Institutions, rather than inputs, should be the focus of public policy designed to promote economic progress.

The environment of entrepreneurship

Entrepreneurship begins with the observation of a previously unnoticed profit opportunity, but as the previous chapters have shown, profit opportunities are just not waiting for the ordinary person to observe and act upon. Once an opportunity is created, typically it is acted upon rapidly by those who are in the proximity of the opportunity. It makes sense, for example, that those working in the computer industry are the people most likely to observe an opportunity in that industry. As Hayek noted,[2] everyone has knowledge specific to their own activities, and the economy will be most productive when the economic system gives everyone an incentive to act on the specific knowledge they possess. A market economy allows individuals to act on their own specific knowledge of time and place, and also provides the incentive, in the form of entrepreneurial profits, to act entrepreneurially. Entrepreneurial activity depends to a large degree on an institutional structure that allows entrepreneurs to keep the profits from their entrepreneurial actions. This is well-recognized. Entrepreneurs also respond to the availability of entrepreneurial opportunities. The more opportunities available, the more alert entrepreneurs will be toward finding them.

William Baumol has argued that people in all societies are entrepreneurial; however, institutions tend to channel people's entrepreneurial impulses in different directions depending upon the institutional structure.[3] In societies that are structured so that people are able to keep the rewards from creating innovative goods and production processes, people have an incentive to innovate and economies in those societies will exhibit economic progress. Income will grow and people will have a greater quantity and quality of goods and services to consume. In other societies – the centrally planned economies of the twentieth century provide good examples – institutions prevent people from profiting by introducing new goods or better production processes. Even if there is private ownership of property, if the rewards to innovation are taxed or regulated away, or property rights are insufficiently protected so that predators make productive activities unprofitable, people have little incentive to take the risks involved in bringing improvements to market.[4] The way to get ahead in those societies is to become a member of the ruling elite, who have the ability to prosper by transferring wealth from other members of society to themselves. People then use their entrepreneurial abilities to plunder wealth from others rather than to generate new wealth and enhance the general economic welfare.[5]

The issue, then, is not how to make people more entrepreneurial. People in every society are looking for ways to modify their activities to enhance their incomes and increase their standards of living. The issue is how to direct the natural entrepreneurial impulses of people in productive rather than destructive directions.

Soviet-style central economic planning provides a model for how entrepreneurial impulses can be channeled in a destructive direction. Following the Marxist philosophy, "From each according to his ability; to each according to his needs," results in a society in which there is no personal return from being more productive, from producing better quality output, or from developing innovative goods and services for others to consume. The rewards to productive activity all go to others. The incentives for private productivity are even worse than at first they appear. "From each according to his ability" implies that those in charge know someone's ability, so if a person is too productive today, more will be expected from that person tomorrow. It is better to get by with the minimum effort so that one does not have to meet high future expectations. Furthermore, while some innovations work as planned, others are not successful for reasons that may not be easily foreseen. Business failures in market economies are evidence of this. Business people are willing to take the risk of failure in a market economy because they also reap the rewards of success, but with "from each according to his ability; to each according to his needs" as a philosophy, there is no personal reward for success. If one tries to innovate and fails, all the blame goes to the person attempting the innovation. If one tries to innovate and succeeds, all the rewards go to others. The best strategy is to simply do the minimum one needs to do to get by.

Actually, in the former Soviet Union and other centrally planned economies, there was a better strategy, which was to become a part of the political power structure. Despite the "from each according to his ability; to each according to his needs" slogan, people with political power had considerably higher standards of living than most citizens. They lived off of the (meager) productivity of the rest of the economy, producing nothing themselves, but getting a larger-than-average share of the productive activities of others. The best entrepreneurial strategy in the former Soviet Union was not to engage in economically productive activity but to find innovative ways of plundering those who were, and taking a share of their incomes. But whereas the market-oriented entrepreneurship that has been the subject of the book up to this point adds to the total productivity of a society and generates economic progress, this type of bureaucratic entrepreneurship is destructive because in the process of transferring wealth from others to themselves, these predatory entrepreneurs are removing incentives for productive behavior on the part of those others. Institutions channeled entrepreneurial incentives toward destructive rather than productive activity.

The productivity problems of centrally planned economies became so severe that eventually most of them collapsed. The Berlin Wall, separating the market economy of West Germany from the government-directed economy of East Germany, collapsed in 1989, beginning the transformation of Eastern Europe from a centrally planned economic system to a market economy. The Soviet Union imploded in 1991, a few years later. Prior to that time, it was a commonly held opinion, shared by many reputable economists, that central planning was a more rational way to run an economy than to leave economic activity to the uncertainties of the market system; after that time, the most commonly held opinion is that markets do a better job of allocating economic resources than government planning.

Plunder versus productivity

The problems of resource allocation in centrally planned economies were severe because the institutional structure of those economies channeled entrepreneurial effort toward plunder rather than productivity. A discussion of the inefficiencies of Soviet-style central planning may seem largely irrelevant in the twenty-first century when the failures of command economies are readily recognized, but market economies have built a substantial amount of the "from each according to his abilities; to each according to his needs" philosophy into their public policies. Progressive income taxation, generous income transfer programs, including those that support people because they are not working, labor and workplace regulations, all increase the incentives for predatory activities and blunt the incentives for productive activities.

One must recognize that those same incentive problems that plagued centrally planned economies are present to some degree in all government activities. Governments raise their revenues through compulsory taxation, so there is no need to satisfy consumers to get them to tender their money. Meanwhile, government employees do not share in any profit for satisfying those they provide services to, so there is no incentive for productivity. The challenge is to design institutions to channel people's entrepreneurial actions toward productive rather than predatory activities.

China provides an example to show that this can be done. As a dictatorship with a centrally planned economy through most of the last half of the twentieth century, China suffered the same lack of productivity as other centrally planned economies. At the beginning of the twenty-first century, China remains a dictatorship, but its economic system has become more market oriented and is among the fastest-growing economies in the world. China has become more entrepreneurial, in the sense that its citizens are channeling more of their energies into finding new and better ways to produce goods, and new goods to produce. It would be far-fetched to think that somehow, in the span of a decade, there has been some fundamental change in the Chinese people. The incentives changed, not the people. Under the old regime, entrepreneurial incentives led people toward predatory activities, and the best way to get ahead was by using government power to plunder the wealth of others. Under the new regime, entrepreneurial incentives lead people toward productive activities, because their rapidly developing market economy allows entrepreneurial individuals to profit from producing goods and services that provide benefits for others.

The productivity of Russia's economy is increasing too, but not as rapidly as China's. One obvious difference between the Russian and Chinese societies as both move out from under the umbrella of communism is that property rights are more secure in China. The Chinese government has retained a stronghold on society whereas in Russia, the government is more opportunistic and does less to protect individuals from plunder. In the vacuum, a Russian mafia has emerged that will offer protection to people doing business in Russia, for a price. People find themselves forced to pay protection money if they want to be in business, and even then they may not be safe. The incentives for entrepreneurial actions that add to the productivity of the economy are reduced, and the incentives to channel entrepreneurial activity toward predation are increased.

People everywhere have entrepreneurial instincts and work to engage in entrepreneurial activities that can provide them with profits. In some places, this means engaging in productive activity in the search for profits through the marketing of one's goods and services. In other places, this means gaining government power – or even predatory power outside of government, as with the mafia – in order to take from the productivity of other citizens. The challenge is to design institutions that channel people's entrepreneurial activities toward production and away from predation.

The economics of anarchy

If resource allocation through government channels entrepreneurial activities in nonproductive and predatory directions, whereas market allocation of resources channels entrepreneurial activities in productive directions, then it would appear that the less government there is, the better. Taken to its logical extreme, this argument would seem to suggest that a completely market economy with no government at all would maximize entrepreneurship and economic progress. To some readers, the idea that completely eliminating government would create greater prosperity is unthinkable. Society would devolve into anarchy, and with nobody to protect property rights there would be no incentive to engage in any productive activity. Yet some scholars would argue otherwise: that market institutions can not only replace everything government does, but can do a better job than government.

The argument against anarchy goes back to Thomas Hobbes who, in *Leviathan*, written in 1651, argued that in anarchy life would be "nasty, brutish, short, solitary, and poor," and that it would be a "war of all against all."[6] Hobbes's argument has survived essentially intact into modern times, and one prominent supporter is James M. Buchanan, whose book *The Limits of Liberty: Between Anarchy and Leviathan*, is titled to reveal just the issue being considered here.[7] Buchanan argues, like Hobbes, that without government predatory thugs would not respect anybody's rights, taking away any incentives for productivity. Nobody will produce more than they can immediately consume if they anticipate that what they produce will just be stolen from them. However, Buchanan also recognizes that governments are among the biggest threat to people's rights as well. Predatory governments also remove incentives to productivity, as the communist dictatorships of the twentieth century so clearly illustrated. Thus, Buchanan envisioned that the limits of liberty lay somewhere between anarchy and Leviathan, with a government empowered to protect its citizens' rights, but constrained in its power so that it cannot violate those rights.

Other scholars, such as Murray Rothbard and David Friedman, have argued that government is not necessary to protect people's rights, or to do anything else for that matter.[8] Market institutions can handle everything that government does, and do it better. For many of the things government does, this is obvious. The private sector already produces schools, health care, roads, and most of what government now produces.[9] The protection of rights is a more difficult issue, and is addressed well by this literature. At the beginning of the twenty-first century, there are more private police and private security guards in the United States than government police. It is easy to imagine that without public police, neighborhood associations, shopping centers, and other organizations would hire their own police.[10] Similarly, private arbitration is frequently used to resolve disputes in the United States, despite the fact that access to the courts is "free," whereas people must pay their arbitrators. The cost of having professional arbitrators devise a fair settlement obviously is worth the price for some people when compared to resolution through government courts.

In the orderly anarchy described by this literature, people's rights are protected by protection agencies they hire. If people have disputes with others – which can include such activities as robbery and murder – their protection agencies would defend them in arbitration proceedings, but would not prevent them from being punished if arbitration proceedings did find them guilty of violating the rights of others. Such protection would be too costly to provide, and all protection agencies would have an incentive to cooperate to protect the rights of their own clients and the clients of other agencies. In this way, private police and private courts could operate to maintain an orderly and productive anarchy.

Rothbard even explains that military functions of government would be unnecessary in such a setting, because, first, governments tend to attack other governments, not the people living under the rule of those governments, and second, it would be very difficult to militarily take over an area without a government. For one thing, there is no political leader to surrender, so each individual property owner would have to be taken over. For another, all property owners would be protected by protection firms anyway, and would be in a better position to protect themselves (e.g. with guns in their homes and businesses) than those in a society that relies on government police for protection.[11]

This only sketches the arguments of those who argue the feasibility of orderly anarchy. It is not intended to give a full exposition or defense of that position, but rather to suggest why some scholars argue that a complete elimination of government would produce the society most conducive to entrepreneurship and economic progress. In response to these advocates of orderly anarchy, others have argued that in the absence of government, even if things began as the anarchists described, with private protection and arbitration firms emerging to perform the functions of rights protection, those firms would tend to collude, and larger firms would have an advantage in the market, eventually putting smaller firms out of business, until one firm emerged as a monopoly protection firm and would be able to establish itself as a government.[12] Following this argument, government is inevitable, and the challenge is to try to design and constrain it to protect individual rights and to create a political environment that is conducive to entrepreneurship.

The purpose of this discussion in a book on entrepreneurship is not to debate whether government is necessary or desirable, but rather to recognize the arguments by some that government is unnecessary and that societies would be most productive under an orderly anarchy with no government. The issue does not have to be resolved here, because regardless of whether the argument is correct, it is irrelevant. There is no realistic prospect that government will be dissolved at any time in the foreseeable future in prosperous nations,[13] so the issue is not whether to have a government or not, even if one believes orderly anarchy would be superior to government, but rather how to design government policies to foster the entrepreneurship that leads to economic progress.

The advocates of orderly anarchy do make two good points that are directly relevant to entrepreneurship and economic progress. First, the private sector does produce most of the goods also produced by government, so in that sense government production is unnecessary. Reducing public sector activity would allow a shift of activities toward the private sector, reducing the incentives for predatory entrepreneurship and increasing the incentives for productive entrepreneurship. Second, government inherently produces incentives for predatory rather than productive behavior because government activity is backed by force rather than agreement (as in the case of market exchange).

Market-augmenting government

Mancur Olson has used the term market-augmenting government to describe government institutions that foster entrepreneurship and economic progress.[14] As Olson sees it, in some things government does hinder economic progress whereas in other things government does help foster economic progress. There is widespread agreement among economists that taxes create a disincentive to economic activity and that higher marginal tax rates create greater disincentives. There is widespread agreement among economists that many types of government regulation interfere with economic activity. There is widespread agreement among economists that trade barriers like tariffs and quotas hinder economic activity. Economists also agree that many government transfer programs hinder economic activity by creating a disincentive for people to work. In many ways government creates barriers to entrepreneurship and economic progress.

At the same time, many economists would also argue in favor of all those things. Taxes are necessary to finance government, regulation is necessary to channel people's activities toward the public interest, tariffs are appropriate policy to counter unfair trade, and transfer payments not only help those in need but also enable people to find better job matches for their skills, and perhaps even allow them to enhance their skills. The question, then, is what government activities hinder entrepreneurial activity and what activities enhance it.

Most people would agree that protection of private property rights enhances economic activity. Even if, as noted in the previous section, everyone does not agree that government is necessary to protect property rights, when government does protect property rights this augments market activity. In Some things, government does enhance market activity and foster entrepreneurship while in other things, government does hinder market activity and channel entrepreneurial actions away from productive toward nonproductive and destructive directions. The economic policy goal is to identify and encourage those government activities that are market augmenting while discouraging those policies that hinder market activity.

There is no doubt that market economies provide the environment for entrepreneurship and prosperity. In an extensive economic history of the world, David Landes shows that throughout history, those nations that established market economies grew and prospered while those that did not were left behind.[15] Technological advances certainly aid economic progress, but ancient China had the most advanced technology in the world a thousand years ago, but lagged behind the rest of the world in economic progress until the 1990s when it began economic reforms to move toward a market economy. The former Soviet Union invested heavily in education and research and development, but its economy lagged behind the West because it did not have market institutions.[16] Most dramatically, after the Second World War both Korea and Germany were divided into two countries, one part with a market economy and one part with a centrally planned economy. The market economy of West Germany was so superior to East Germany's centrally planned economy that East Germany's citizens (along with those of other Eastern European nations with centrally planned economies) rebelled so they could adopt market institutions and democratic governments. North Korea, as of this writing, is still suffering under their centrally planned economy, and while North Korea is one of the poorest nations in the world, South Korea, with its market economy, is one of the more prosperous nations with one of the more rapidly growing economies.

The evidence that market economies offer the institutional structure that leads to prosperity is overwhelming, and while in the mid-twentieth century many economists held the view that central planning will produce more economic growth than market economies,[17] after the collapse of the Berlin Wall in 1989 and the demise of the Soviet Union in 1991, nearly everyone would agree that market institutions lead to prosperity and that government planning of the economy is detrimental to economic progress.[18] However, that general conclusion still leaves open the question of what, exactly, constitutes market institutions, and how they might be implemented.

Institutions and entrepreneurship

Prior to the 1990s, the theory of economic growth was dominated by models that took a production function view of growth but ignored the institutional framework.[19] This began to change in the 1990s. Gerald Scully used measures of political freedom across countries to examine the relationship between freedom and economic growth, and found that those countries with the freest political institutions had higher rates of economic growth.[20] Empirically, this revealed a link between institutions and prosperity, but it is not entirely clear from what Scully had done, what specific institutional arrangements laid the foundations for prosperity. Scully had used an index of political freedom as his measure of institutional quality,[21] which would suggest that democratic governments that protect civil liberties would be more likely to rule over prosperous economies. The drawback of Scully's measure is that it looks at political institutions but not economic institutions, and so may not be measuring the same characteristics that lead to prosperity.

Robert Barro, in an empirical study, tried to capture both political and economic variables to see the effects of each, and found that once economic institutions are controlled for, political institutions do not have a significant impact on economic performance, and if anything, democratic governments may have a slightly negative impact on material well-being.[22] For particular examples along these lines, one can think of Singapore and Hong Kong as two countries that have had strong economic performance without much in the way of protection of civil liberties or democracy. Meanwhile, India has been democratic since its independence from Britain, but its economy performed poorly until it undertook reforms in the 1990s to embrace market institutions and lessen government control over the economy. Ireland provides another example of a democratic country that improved its economic performance through market reforms. Ireland was among the poorest of the EU countries until in the 1990s it lowered its tax rates and adopted more market-friendly institutions, after which it became the fastest growing of the western European economies.

This anecdotal evidence is suggestive, but it still leaves open the question of what, exactly, constitutes market-friendly institutions. One attempt to address this question has been made by James Gwartney and Robert Lawson who, with the cooperation of others, created an "index of economic freedom" to measure the degree to which institutions support market activity.[23] Their index was created by looking at the general arguments that economists have made about institutional features that support market activity to draw up a list of quantifiable characteristics to measure economic freedom. In its current incarnation, that list has 38 subcomponents divided into five general areas that measure different aspects of economic freedom.[24] Those aspects are (1) size of government, (2) legal structure and security of property rights, (3) access to sound money, (4) exchange with foreigners, and (5) regulation of capital, labor, and business. The 38 subcomponents are aggregated into these 5 primary components, which are in turn aggregated into a single index of economic freedom.

One virtue of this index is that it is composed of components that measure characteristics of economic institutions, leaving out other aspects of freedom such as political freedom, civil liberties, democratic government, and the like. A substantial empirical literature that has been developed using this index consistently shows a close correlation between economic freedoms and economic growth and level of income.[25] The literature shows that changes in economic freedom, as measured by changes in the index, are correlated with growth rates, and that levels of economic freedom are correlated with income levels. Thus, nations with the highest measured levels of economic freedom also have the highest incomes, and nations that increase their level of economic freedom tend to have higher economic growth rates while those that decrease their level of economic freedom tend to lower their growth rates. Investment is higher in nations with higher measured levels of economic freedom, and not only is it higher, it is also more productive.[26] Empirically, there is a close correlation between the quality of economic institutions as measured by the economic freedom index and economic prosperity across countries.

Measuring economic freedom

If nations with better economic institutions are more prosperous, there is good reason to identify those factors that produce an institutional structure conducive to prosperity. The components of Gwartney and Lawson's economic freedom index provide a good place to start, because their index is correlated with income growth and income levels.

Size of government

The first component is size of government, which Gwartney and Lawson measure by general government consumption spending as a percentage of GDP, transfers and subsidies as a percentage of GDP, government enterprises and investment as a percentage of total investment, and the top marginal income tax rate and the threshold to which it applies. Higher government spending and higher marginal tax rates lower economic freedom.[27]

The connection between these components of economic freedom and entrepreneurship is straightforward. The impact of marginal tax rates is perhaps most obvious. The greater the share of one's income the government takes, the lower is the incentive to earn income. Especially when one is engaging in risky economic activity, the government shares in entrepreneurial successes through its income taxation, but does not share in entrepreneurial losses, which tilts incentives away from entrepreneurial activity.

In the case of large business enterprises, losses in some areas can offset profits in others, so if a large firm takes entrepreneurial risks and suffers a loss, its tax burden can be lowered if it has other income to offset the loss. Smaller businesses and individual entrepreneurs are less likely to have sufficient income to offset any major losses they suffer due to entrepreneurial activity, which creates a bias toward large business enterprises. One need only look at the growth of the computer industry in the late twentieth century to see the significance of small entrepreneurial ventures to economic progress.

The level of government spending, and especially transfers and subsidies, also has an obvious negative impact on entrepreneurship. The greater the share of an economy's resources that are channeled through government, the smaller the share that is available for entrepreneurs to use to implement their plans. There is another effect that is at least as pernicious. As government takes a larger share of the economic pie, more opportunities open up for people to profit from government, either directly by working for the public sector or being a private contractor producing output for the public sector, or indirectly, by seeking government transfers to enhance one's wealth. The larger the government transfers are, the greater are the incentives to engage in predatory rather than productive activity.

When firms face competition in the marketplace, in a free market they have to find ways to increase their efficiency, lower their costs, and make their output more valuable to their consumers if they want to keep from losing market share, or even going out of business. But if those firms can obtain government subsidies or government contracts to add to their incomes, they do not have to be as entrepreneurial in the marketplace. As William Baumol has suggested, entrepreneurial activity exists in every type of society, but institutional structures in some push those entrepreneurial impulses in unproductive directions when people can profit from obtaining transfers from others rather then engaging in productive activity themselves.[28] Chapter 10 deals with this issue in more detail.

Legal structure and protection of property rights

The second area of the economic freedom index is the legal structure and protection of property rights. Here, Gwartney and Lawson look at judicial independence and impartial courts, protection of intellectual property rights, military interference with rule of law, and the integrity of the legal system. The security of property rights is indispensable to entrepreneurship, because nobody has an incentive to be entrepreneurial, or even productive, if when they succeed others are likely to take their gains away from them. Courts must be impartial, because if some people are favored in the legal system, then people have an incentive to steer their entrepreneurial impulses toward getting courts to side with them rather than engaging in socially productive activity. An economy cannot be entrepreneurial without strong protection of property rights.

Access to sound money

The third area of the index is access to sound money. Gwartney and Lawson look at inflation and at the ability of individuals to own foreign currency bank accounts. Inflation not only erodes the purchasing power of money, it reduces the informational content of prices. If monetary calculation becomes unreliable because of inflation, entrepreneurs will have more difficulty spotting true profit opportunities.[29] One way to get around some of the problems of unsound money is to hold bank deposits and transact business in another country's money. Thus, the ability to hold foreign-denominated bank accounts is important as a mechanism for avoiding domestic monetary instability as well as being a means of facilitating international transactions.

Freedom to trade internationally

The fourth area of the economic freedom index is freedom to trade internationally, measured by taxes on international trade and regulatory barriers to trade. If entrepreneurs face limited markets, their opportunities to profit from a larger market will suffer. Adam Smith, in his *Wealth of Nations*, attributed the wealth of nations to the division of labor, but said that the division of labor is limited by the extent of the market.[30] Trade barriers obviously limit the extent of the market, dampening entrepreneurial incentives.

Regulation

The fifth area of the economic freedom index is regulation. Gwartney and Lawson measure regulation in credit markets, in labor markets, and business regulations. If there are regulatory barriers to obtaining credit, some ideas entrepreneurs have may not be implemented because of lack of financing.[31] If labor market regulations prevent people from making employment arrangements they most prefer, this too will hinder entrepreneurial activity. Business regulations also stand in the way of entrepreneurial activity. If it is costly and cumbersome to comply with government regulations to start or run a business, some entrepreneurial ideas will not be implemented because of the regulations, and some business activities may be forced "underground," where they escape government regulation but also do not benefit from the legal protections of legitimate businesses.[32]

The point of discussing these components of the Gwartney and Lawson economic freedom index is two-fold. First, as the previous section noted, there is a well-documented correlation between countries that rate high in this index and economic growth and level of income. Empirical evidence indicates that if countries change their institutions so that they score higher in these areas, they will become more prosperous. Second, this shows that institutional differences can affect the way that entrepreneurship is channeled in an economy. An economy with sound institutions encourages individuals to engage in entrepreneurial activity that is productive and that enhances the well-being of everyone. An economy with unsound institutions encourages entrepreneurial individuals to engage in predatory activities and to try to enhance their well-being at the expense of others. Good institutions foster entrepreneurship and economic progress, and the components of the economic freedom index provide a good indication of what constitutes good institutions.

Rent-seeking versus profit-seeking

The term rent-seeking was coined by economist Anne Krueger, who observed that in India some of the best and brightest individuals were employed not doing anything to add to the productivity of the economy, but rather to deal with cumbersome government regulations and to try to produce some personal monetary gain by working those regulations to their advantage.[33] Rent-seeking has thus come to mean using the government to seek private benefits by transferring wealth away from others. If a company faces foreign competition, in a market economy it will have to increase its efficiency and make its products more attractive to its customers to keep from losing market share. But if it can convince the government to impose trade barriers in the form of tariffs or other regulations, then it can keep foreign competition at bay not by its own productive activity but by using the force of the state to give itself an advantage.

Opportunities for rent-seeking create the incentive for people to channel their entrepreneurial activities toward predation rather than production. The tariff in the previous example not only harms the foreign competitors, it also harms domestic consumers by raising the price of foreign goods, and by limiting competition so that domestic firms have less of an incentive to operate efficiently. But perhaps a bigger harm is that not only does it limit current competition, it also signals entrepreneurs that in the future, a good way to profit is through rent-seeking that will benefit some at the expense of others. In this way, such institutions provide an incentive for people to channel their entrepreneurial activities away from productive activity, toward activity that is on net harmful to the economy. An institutional environment that is conducive to productive entrepreneurship must reward productive activities and discourage rent-seeking.

Identification versus implementation

Simply having identified some policies that enhance entrepreneurship and encourage economic progress does not mean that these policies will be implemented. Policy makers have their own incentives, and when the incentives of policy makers are not consistent with policies that encourage prosperity, those policy makers are likely to place their own interests above the general public interest. Yet in a democratic society, policy makers are not dictators, and policies that are in the public interest can gain sufficient popular support to be implemented. Even in undemocratic societies, dictators can be unseated to pave the way for institutional change. Perhaps the most dramatic examples came in Eastern Europe along with and after the collapse of the Berlin Wall. Citizens in Eastern European countries understood that they were living under inferior institutional structures and took action to overthrow their existing institutions and replace them with institutions that were more conducive to entrepreneurship and economic progress. Citizens were not merely trying to replace one set of leaders with another; they were trying to replace one set of institutions with another.

Creating an environment conducive to entrepreneurship requires the set of institutions described earlier in this chapter. In the words of James Buchanan, it is a constitutional choice. Buchanan differentiates the typical subject matter of economics, which analyzes choice subject to constraints, with constitutional economics, which analyzes the choice of constraints.[34] One can discuss entrepreneurial behavior within a given institutional framework and analyze the effects, for example, of more research and development activity on entrepreneurship, but the arguments throughout this volume have pointed toward the conclusion that within a market economy people have an incentive to direct their entrepreneurial instincts toward increasing productivity and furthering economic progress. This chapter has indicated more specifically what institutional features constitute a market economy. To encourage entrepreneurship, then, one is more likely to have success by creating an institutional structure that fosters entrepreneurship than by trying to develop policies to get people to be more entrepreneurial within the existing institutional structure. Examples of potentially successful policies would be strengthening the protection of property rights and lowering regulatory and taxation barriers that create impediments to exchange. Examples of policies with dubious potential would be government-financed research and development and industrial policy that targets government aid to develop certain industries.

Certainly research and development, education, and investment aid economic progress. But if the appropriate institutional structure is in place, people have an incentive to undertake their own research and development, to obtain an education for their own personal benefit, and invest for their own personal gain. Implementation of policies to foster entrepreneurship requires what Buchanan would call a constitutional change: the creation of an environment with "rules of the game" that reward successful entrepreneurship.

Overcoming public choice problems

A substantial literature in public choice suggests that government policies are undertaken for the benefit of special interests rather than furthering the general public interest.[35] Because of the influence of special interests, it will always be difficult to implement the constitutional changes that enable societies to be more entrepreneurial. Business people have an incentive to be entrepreneurial because it helps them succeed in their enterprises. But it is a rare business person who would pass up the opportunity for some form of government protection to reduce the pressure he or she feels from competitors. Entrepreneurs are the heroes of this book's story, because they have to survive in the marketplace, and because the system rewards them for their entrepreneurial behavior. Entrepreneurs are responding to the incentives the institutional framework offers them. But if the system provides them with incentives to seek government protection for their businesses, if it rewards them for rent-seeking behavior, then their behavior will be turned from productive to unproductive entrepreneurship. The consequences of this are discussed further in Chapter 10.

Despite the influence of narrow special interests, many examples from the late twentieth century, ranging from the dramatic examples of the Eastern European countries and the former Soviet Union to China, to less dramatic but equally significant examples in New Zealand, Chile, and Ireland, show that when popular opinion comprehends the benefits of institutional reform, poorly performing institutions can be replaced by better institutions. Ideas do have consequences, and when they are able to be widely disbursed to the general public, popular opinion can overcome political interests.

John Maynard Keynes said, "the ideas of economists and political philosophers, both when they are right and when they are wrong, are more powerful than is commonly understood. Indeed, the world is ruled by little else."[36] Good ideas do not necessarily win in the short run. The transition to centrally planned socialism in many Eastern European countries after the Second World War shows that.[37] But ideas do not have to be as powerful as Keynes suggested to still make a difference. Ideas such as those discussed here in an academic setting lay the foundation for extension to the general public, and should they become a part of popular opinion, they can have a transforming effect. Implementing the institutional framework outlined in this chapter will not be easy, but there is hope that as evidence increasingly mounts showing the benefits of institutions conducive to entrepreneurship, popular opinion will lead them to be increasingly adopted, as has happened in China, in Eastern Europe, and elsewhere.

Institutions and entrepreneurship

When entrepreneurship is seen as the engine of economic progress, the emphasis in growth theory shifts toward the creation of an environment within which opportunities for entrepreneurial activity are created, and in which successful entrepreneurship is rewarded. Human and physical capital are important inputs into the production process, to be sure, but by themselves they do not create economic growth. Rather, an institutional environment that encourages entrepreneurship attracts human and physical capital, which is why investment and growth are correlated. The emphasis should be placed on market institutions rather than production function inputs. The importance of market institutions has now been generally recognized in practice, but has not been integrated into the mainstream theory of economic growth.

Work that focuses on human capital as the engine of economic growth is just as misleading as the growth theory of decades ago that focused on physical capital investment as providing a "golden rule" for economic growth. Human capital is correlated with economic growth because a growing economy provides a greater return to human capital. The direction of causation is from an environment conducive to growth to human capital, not the other way around. The existence of institutions conducive to entrepreneurship creates the profit opportunities which increase the return to education and lead to an increase in human capital. Human capital is important because it is a component of the production process, but entrepreneurship, not capital of any kind, is the underlying cause of growth.[38]

A substantial body of research has identified the general set of institutions that foster entrepreneurship and economic progress. The scope of government must be limited, in terms of expenditures, regulation, and taxation. Property rights must be protected, and a fair and impartial legal system is necessary. Monetary stability is important, and trade barriers must be minimal. In such an institutional environment, individuals have an incentive to channel their entrepreneurial activities in productive ways, leading to economic progress. Without this institutional foundation, entrepreneurship will be channeled in unproductive ways, preventing economic progress.

9   National income accounting and public policy

Entrepreneurship is the engine of economic progress, yet mainstream economics focuses on inputs such as human and physical capital, and technological advances, as causal factors. From a policy standpoint, the previous chapter argued, institutions should be the focus of analysis, rather than investment and education, as policies to promote economic progress. Yet institutions remain underappreciated both by economists and by policy makers. This chapter focuses on the impact of national income accounting on policies related to economic progress, in the context of public policy toward economic progress as it developed through the twentieth century.

The argument has already been made that policy should focus on a broader concept of progress rather than the narrow metric of income growth, yet both policy makers and economists almost always measure progress in terms of income growth. This is largely due to the fact that income growth is a well-established and reputable metric, because of the development of national income accounting. It is much easier to measure the growth of GDP than it is to evaluate the broader concept of progress. This chapter looks at the development of national income accounting, and considers the policy implications of having the measures of national income accounting to guide public policy. While economists have analyzed concepts of national income for centuries, modern national income accounting only began in the 1930s, and was developed specifically as a tool for managing the economy. Thus, it is not surprising that this tool has had a substantial effect on the way the economy has been managed.

Policy activism in the early twentieth century

The unprecedented worldwide economic progress in the nineteenth century was led by the United States, which began the century as an agrarian economy and ended it as the world's industrial leader. Nineteenth-century economic progress was not without its setbacks, however. Big economic issues toward the end of the nineteenth century included the growing concentration of economic power among a few individuals, monetary standards and bank credit, and banking panics and the increasingly severe economic downturns that periodically plagued the economy. By the early twentieth century, national economic policy had addressed these issues in several ways. Antitrust laws, beginning with the Sherman Act in 1890, were enacted and being enforced; various segments of the economy, from transportation to food and drugs, were being increasingly regulated; and the Federal Reserve Act, passed in 1913, created monetary institutions that began a substantial transformation of the nation's monetary system. Still, economists and government policy makers thought that more could be done to effectively manage the economy.

Economists were actively engaged in business cycle research with the hope of designing policies that could dampen the increasingly violent economic fluctuations, and principles of scientific management, which had spilled over from the private sector into government early in the twentieth century, suggested some promise that the macroeconomy could also be managed if effective policies could be designed. However, there was widespread agreement that more effective management of the economy would require better methods for measuring and assessing economic performance. Thus, a system of national income accounting was designed in the 1920s to better measure the performance of the economy, but with the significant secondary purpose of providing policy makers with performance indicators that they could use to better manage the national economy.

Modern national income accounting was developed through a cooperative venture among academics, the business community, and government. The National Bureau of Economic Research was established for the purpose of furthering business cycle research, which led to the development of a system of national income accounting that could monitor the performance of the economy so that policy makers would have good information on which to base their economic policy decisions. The result was the national income and product accounts that remain in use, largely unmodified, at the beginning of the twenty-first century. The challenge in measuring economic performance is formidable, because the economy produces a diverse array of goods and services that are difficult to aggregate. However, money serves as a natural common denominator. In the same way that individuals can aggregate their money incomes as a measure of the value of their production in terms of all goods and services, nations could do the same thing by measuring national income in dollar terms. Gross National Product (GNP), and later, GDP became the preferred measures of total national income. Along the lines of the way an individual's income would be measured, GNP is the market value of all final goods and services that are produced by an economy during a period of time (typically, a year).

When designing the national income accounts, many conventions for the measurement of income had to be devised, and every beginning student in economics learns that the compromises that went into the design of the national income accounts means that GDP cannot be accepted as a measure of the well-being of a nation. Many of the problems and shortcomings of national income accounting are well-understood by economists, and this chapter will not rehash them. The chapter will first describe the development of national income accounting in the United States to show how from the beginning its development was linked to public policy, and then will focus on two of the less-recognized problems of national income accounting.

One problem with national income accounting is the way that government is treated in the national income accounts. This has been discussed by others, and raises some obvious problems. The second problem is more subtle, but perhaps more important for purposes of economic policy. That problem is that by treating economic output as a homogeneous aggregate, economic policy focuses on increasing the quantity of goods and services and tends to ignore the changing nature of goods and services. Economic progress comes partly from increases in the amount of output, which GDP measures, albeit imperfectly, but economic progress mostly is the result of changes in the nature of the goods and services the economy produces. This is completely unmeasured by GDP, because GDP accounts for changes in the nature of goods merely by adjusting their value. For example, when computers routinely began being sold with hardware for internet access, this was accounted for by a price adjustment reflecting the fact that new computers were more valuable than old ones. New goods, even more problematic, are accounted for in the same way, through price adjustments. No measure of the changing nature of output is incorporated in the national income accounts, nor could one be as long as income is measured as a homogeneous dollar amount. Thus, this nearly universally used indicator of economic growth leaves out the most important element of progress. This, in turn, has had a substantial negative impact on the way that economic policy is undertaken.

This chapter begins by discussing the difficult problem of trying to measure national income. Then, the history of the development of the concept is recounted to show that national income accounting and public policy have been intimately related from the beginning. The chapter then considers appropriate goals of economic policy, and the way that the actual system of national income accounts affects these goals. After some analysis, it is apparent that the use of national income accounting has resulted in many types of public policy that have worked against the nation's best interest.

Measuring output and income

The ultimate goal for an economy is to produce value for those who inhabit it. There are many stories about problems in the economy of the former Soviet Union that arose because output was measured in physical terms rather than in terms of value. For example, a factory making nails was given a quota in terms of tons of nails produced, and produced only very large nails because it is cheaper to produce a ton of big nails than a ton of small nails. Planners, recognizing that there was a shortage of small nails, changed the factory's quota to produce a certain number of nails rather than a certain weight, with the result being that they produced lots of small nails but no large ones. A similar story recounts a Soviet factory producing roofing metal that had its output measured as the number of square yards of roofing metal produced. The resulting roofing metal was so thin that it could be damaged by a heavy rain. Again seeing their mistake, the planners changed their measure of output to tons of roofing metal, and the result was that roofs made with the output of that factory were so heavy that they caused structural damage to the buildings they were placed on. The lesson of stories like this is that a market economy, in which firms have an incentive to maximize profit, works better to produce output that enhances the well-being of people, because output in the market is judged by its market value, not its physical characteristics. In a market economy, factories have an incentive to produce output that adds as much value as possible to total output, rather than producing output that is as heavy as possible, or as big as possible.

This lesson extends only imperfectly to national income accounting. First, national income accounting measures the market value of output, not profit or total value to consumers. A better measure of the value of an economy's output would be total consumer surplus produced, but measurement of consumer surplus is not feasible, whereas measurement of the dollar value of output is.[1] Firms can increase their profits by raising the market value of their output or by lowering their costs, and lower costs are difficult to capture in national income accounts, even though they exert a substantial influence on economic well-being. If lower costs are manifested in higher output, that may partially capture the welfare enhancement from cost reduction, but if an increase in the supply of the good results in a lower price, the impact on the market value of output of higher output is offset – perhaps partially, perhaps fully or even more – by a lower price per unit. National income accounting attempts to adjust for this either through adjustments in the price level, which is an imprecise procedure, or in an even more *ad hoc* manner by directly trying to factor in changes in the quality of output.

Simply looking at the market value of output is problematic, because market prices are the result of the interaction between supply and demand. Assume, for example, that the demand for a product is inelastic. Last year, 100 units were sold at a price of $10, for a total contribution to GDP of $1,000. This year, a supply interruption resulted in only 60 units being produced, and the reduced supply caused the price to go up to $20 per unit, for a total contribution to GDP of $1,200. An accurate measure of an economy's output would show a reduction in output when the quantity falls like this, yet GDP, which measures the market value of output shows an increase. The price level could be adjusted to reflect this change, but if the resources that last year produced this good went into producing another good, how would one balance the 40 percent decrease in the output of this good with a 30 percent increase in the output of another good, which then may have seen its price fall? National income accounting actually does attempt to make these adjustments through price level adjustments, but to the degree it does, it no longer measures the market value of final goods and services (which, as argued, is not that good a measure anyway).

The real problem is that there is not a good aggregate measure of economic performance. The economy is a complex set of interactions among economic activities of a large number of individuals. Any attempt to reduce the performance of the economy to a single number must leave out a great deal. Within that context, the next section considers the political and economic environment within which national income accounting was presented, to see how those designing the national income accounts were able to grapple with these problems.

The creation of national income accounting

National income accounting was created for the purpose of producing a more scientific measure of the performance of the economy. The concept is an old one, having been originated by William Petty (1623–1687) and refined continually since. The way in which national income is measured has always had policy implications. Petty's conception of national income included the total production of goods and services, but the mercantilist idea developed in the seventeenth century displaced Petty's ideas, and viewed a nation's wealth as embodied in its stock of gold. In contrast, physiocrat Francois Quesnay's (1694–1774) development of his "Tableau Economique" depicted agriculture and mining as productive activities, but not manufacturing. Adam Smith partially accepted Quesnay's vision, but included manufacturing as a part of productive labor. Smith called labor used in the production of services, which did not increase the stock of national wealth, unproductive labor. From a policy standpoint, one can see that a mercantilist vision of national income would focus on increasing a nation's gold stock, whereas a physiocratic vision would focus on developing agriculture. Using Smith's concept, one can enhance the wealth of nations by channeling labor into productive (agriculture and manufacturing) rather than unproductive (service) activities.[2]

Modern national income accounting has overcome many of the shortcomings of these early attempts from centuries ago, but although these specific shortcomings have been remedied, the same types of shortcomings remain. Some of the problems were mentioned in the previous section, but two other problems will be considered in more detail here. One is the accounting for government output at cost, which is an obvious problem, and the other is treating aggregate output as a homogeneous quantity, which has more subtle policy implications. But while national income accounting has a long history, it was not closely integrated into economic policy until the 1930s. One reason is that statistics on national income were not very comprehensive until that time, and another is that in the early twentieth century, governments became much more interested in taking an active role in managing the economy.

Toward the end of the nineteenth century, the Progressive idea that government should expand its role beyond simply protecting the rights of citizens to looking out for their economic welfare became increasingly accepted among the American public.[3] Meanwhile around the beginning of the twentieth century, scientific principles of business management began to be developed, and progressives promoted the idea that scientific principles of business management could be adapted to government. Early in the twentieth century, universities began creating business schools that developed and taught scientific principles of management. Academic influences spread beyond colleges of businesses as the social sciences began developing, with economics, political science, and social work all laying claim as academic disciplines that could be drawn on to improve government policy. Stephen Skowronek describes a push by those in government to adapt those academic principles of social science and scientific management to more effectively run the government.[4] Thus, there was a general shift in popular ideology toward more government control of the economy, coupled with an academic movement toward the development of principles that could allow government policy to be carried out more effectively.

The result was what Guy Alchon calls technocratic Progressivism, which was developed through a joint effort of government, academic institutions, and private philanthropic organizations.[5] While the benefits of scientific management had the potential to improve all of government policy, the promise of technocratic Progressivism appeared especially great with regard to the government's management of economic policy. The problems were generally agreed upon, and ranged from persistent problems like poverty to newly emerging problems related to the new industrial economy. The increasing concentration of economic power was viewed as a problem with the rise of industry, as was the periodic problem of recessions, which appeared to be increasing in severity over time. Yet, if there was general agreement on the problems, and widespread popular support for increased government involvement in the management of the economy, there was not a corresponding body of economic knowledge that gave clear guidance about the way that economic policy could be used to improve the economy.

In 1914, two conferences were held on the problem of unemployment that were attended by leading economists of the day, including John Commons of the University of Wisconsin and Edwin F. Gay, the first Dean of the Harvard Business School. One of the recommendations from that conference was the "Keynesian" idea that the government should engage in countercyclical fiscal policy, increasing public works spending during recessions to help boost the economy.[6] Indeed, as J. Ronnie Davis notes, Keynesian fiscal policy was widely accepted among US academic economists as appropriate macroeconomic policy well before the publication of Keynes' *General Theory* in 1936.[7] Yet one problem with implementing countercyclical macroeconomic policy was that there were not good measures of economic performance. Employment and unemployment might prove to be adequate measures for some purposes, but they are measures of economic input rather than economic output. The concept of national income had been well-known for centuries,[8] but there were not good estimates of national income for the United States, nor was there an agreed-upon methodology for measuring national income.

The First World War created great demands for scientific management in government to oversee the war effort, and as Robert Higgs notes,[9] to oversee the economy that became increasingly government controlled. Wesley C. Mitchell, already well-known for his 1913 book on business cycles, argued that problems that surfaced when trying to manage the war effort showed that the government needed a much stronger apparatus for collecting statistics on the performance of the economy and inventorying national resources,[10] and in 1918 a Division of Planning and Statistics was created, headed by Wesley Mitchell and Edwin Gay. Mitchell and Gay were not alone in arguing that better statistics could produce better government economic planning, and their wartime organization laid the foundation for the collection of economic statistics after the war. There was much debate about how the statistical efforts begun during the war should be continued, and after the war there was public pressure for government retrenchment, weighing in against the continuation of wartime programs such as Mitchell's and Gay's. The result was the creation of the National Bureau of Economic Research (NBER) in 1920.

The NBER was created out of a cooperative effort among academic institutions, government, and private organizations. The intellectual foundations for the NBER were laid by Gay and Mitchell, with the cooperation of John Commons, who was president of the American Economic Association, and Allyn Young, president of the American Statistical Association. It had the support of those in government, for obvious reasons, but while it was designed to provide statistics that could be used for government policy, it was also designed to be independent of government. The NBER got its initial funding from the Carnegie and Commonwealth foundations, which not only made it financially independent of government but started the organization as an academic research organization rather than a product of politics. Private funding of NBER as a nongovernmental organization was purposefully done with the hope that politics would not set the NBER's agenda or distract from its research mission. Once established, Wesley Mitchell took the lead in setting the NBER's agenda.

This background on the founding of the NBER is crucial to understanding the nature of the NBER's activities, and the nature of national income accounting that was developed by the NBER. Because it was privately funded, the NBER was independent of both academic and governmental institutions, but it was staffed by academic economists who had a desire to make economics more scientific, along the lines of the natural sciences, and who believed that economic policy could be used to improve the performance of the economy. Further, it was supported by those in government who believed that principles of scientific management could be used to manage the macroeconomy. One thing that was lacking for precise management of the economy was good measures of economic performance. The goal of developing an improved method of national income accounting was to create better measures of economic performance so that government could be more aggressive in its management of the economy.

Among the questions that national income accounting was supposed to address were measuring the aggregate money income of the nation, and generating a time series so that its performance could be tracked over time; developing a method for determining how much of the changes in aggregate income were caused by fluctuations in prices and how much were due to fluctuations in output; determining how income was distributed among individuals, and what proportion went to labor; determining how output and wages varied across industries, and how these variations changed over time; and developing a method for comparing income in the United States with income in other nations.[11] By generating this data, government would be in a better position to accurately assess the performance of the economy, thus giving them a better opportunity to undertake policies that could improve its performance. From the standpoint of the academic economists who were instrumental in creating the NBER, and who did the NBER's work once it was created, their motivations were to elevate economics to be a more scientific discipline, and to enable the government's economic policy be more active and more effective.

Government supporters had much the same motivation, but came from the perspective of engineering rather than social science. The greatest supporter in government was Herbert Hoover, an engineer by training who worked in President Wilson's administration during the First World War, and was Secretary of Commerce throughout the eight years of the Coolidge and Harding administrations in the 1920s, before being elected president himself in 1928. Hoover saw the potential of extending engineering principles to the management of the economy, and supported the NBER as an organization that could provide support for more active and precise government economic policies. As Alchon notes,[12] engineers looked at this as a great opportunity for them to allow their education and experience to be used to improve social conditions.

All parties who were cooperating to develop the national income accounts had consistent goals. Private sector businesses looked at this as an opportunity to create a better business environment by extending the same principles of scientific management that they had been integrating into their businesses, and private sector foundations were willing to fund the endeavor because of its potential to enhance the public welfare. Those in government saw an opportunity to apply engineering principles to the management of the economy, and economists saw the opportunity to make their discipline more scientific, and to be more influential in the determination of public policy. Alchon refers to this cooperation as "a bargain between technocratic social science and managerial capitalism,"[13] and notes that while everyone had worthy motives, they were also motivated by the enhanced power and prestige that would come to participants. Economists could not only become full-fledged scientists, but could have a hand in the management of the economy, while those in government would gain more power over economic affairs.

The desirability of this activity was reinforced when a severe recession hit the economy in 1920. Prices plummeted, and unemployment stood at about 12 percent. When Herbert Hoover began his tenure as Secretary of Commerce in 1921, he was given considerable influence over economic policy, and pushed the idea of Keynesian-style countercyclical fiscal policy a decade and a half before the publication of *The General Theory*. Hoover asked Wesley Mitchell to join him in the Department of Commerce, but while Mitchell declined, he worked closely with Hoover through the NBER to advise the government on macroeconomic policy. The economy recovered from the 1920 recession and the remainder of the decade was prosperous, giving Hoover further reason to see the merits in his engineering approach to managing the economy. When the economy again turned down in 1929, Hoover again thought that active government intervention could smooth the recovery, and by that time, a decade's worth of work had been done toward better understanding the economy.

The crowning achievement of the research at the NBER was the development of the national income and product accounts in cooperation with the Department of Commerce. After the nation plunged into the Great Depression, it became apparent to those who wanted to engineer the economy back to health that the existing statistics on economic performance were woefully inadequate. In 1932 the Department of Commerce began cooperating with the NBER to develop a comprehensive set of national income and product accounts. By this time the NBER's work was being directed by Simon Kuznets, and the result of this cooperative venture between the federal government and the NBER was the first official statistics on national income, published in 1934, which gave measures of national income back to 1929.[14] While the concepts have been updated periodically, the current national income accounts used to direct macroeconomic policy go back to this work done by the NBER, and the fundamental underlying principles have not changed.

Modern national income accounting began in the 1930s as a cooperative venture among academicians, government officials, and private sector organizations, as a way of developing better measures of economic performance so that the government could more actively involve itself in managing the economy. Thus, it is entirely reasonable to examine national income accounting in terms of the impact that it has had on public policy. The concept of national income was refined so that it could be used as an indicator of the economic health of the nation, and economic policy has been designed to produce GDP growth. As the examples discussed earlier in this chapter have illustrated, the way in which economic output is measured can have real and substantial impacts on the nature of that economic output. The remainder of the chapter considers two specific issues regarding the measurement of national income: the way in which government expenditures are accounted for, and the implications of measuring national income as a single homogeneous quantity.

Government expenditures and national income

GDP is defined as the market value of all final goods and services produced in an economy during a time period (usually, one year). However, government expenditures are included in GDP at cost, rather than at market value. The justification for this is that public sector output is part of the nation's output just like private sector output, but typically it is not sold on the market, so in contrast to private sector output, there are no market prices at which it can be evaluated. Therefore, it is added in at cost. However, following the conventions of national income accounting, Francesco Forte and James Buchanan argue that there are at least two reasons why government output should not be included in GDP at all.[15] The first reason is that national income accounting conventions value private sector output at its market value, and if government output is valued using the same standard, it should also be included at its market value, which is zero, because government does not sell its output. The second reason is that government output is almost always an intermediate good, and intermediate goods are not included in GDP. As a result, GDP is overstated, but from a policy standpoint, there are more significant problems with the way that government expenditures are included in national income. Before considering the policy problems, the arguments against including government expenditures in GDP should be reviewed.

Most government output consists of intermediate goods. If the total output of steel were to be added to the total output of automobiles in accounting for income, the steel would be double-counted. It would be counted once when the steel was originally produced, and again when the value of the steel in the automobiles was added in. In the same way, adding the cost of government services that are intermediate goods double-counts income. If a store hires a security guard, that is included in the store's cost of production and not as a part of final output. The same should be true when a community hires a police officer. The police services are valuable, as are other intermediate goods, but intermediate goods are not counted in total GDP, and for consistency, governmentally produced intermediate goods should be treated the same as private sector intermediate goods. Most of what government produces is intermediate goods and services, not final output, so government output should be excluded from GDP.

A second wholly different reason for excluding most government output is that it is typically given away rather than sold. One might argue, for example, that as public sector investments, government-owned highways should be included in any accounting of national income. Even if highways have some value to those who use them, the market price of the highway is zero, unless a toll is charged, so the highway should be included at its market price of zero. Some government output, such as toll roads, water sold by government waterworks, and so forth, should be included in GDP because those goods do have a market price,[16] but most government output does not fall into this category. Because it is given away, its market value is zero and it should not be included in GDP. This would treat government output consistently with the way that private sector output is treated in the national income accounts.

Whether government output has any value to those who receive it is completely irrelevant to the arguments just given. GDP is not a measure of the value of output to those who consume it. GDP is not a measure of consumer surplus, or some related concept of consumption value, and when applied to the private sector, is specifically designed not to be a measure of the cost of output. Much final output in an economy has value but is excluded from GDP because it is not sold. Household production is probably the most significant example. Highways may have value, but like personal home repair projects and home cooking, that output is not sold on the market. For consistency, highways, police and fire services, and national defense should not be included in GDP for the same reason home production is excluded: they are not sold in the market.[17]

Policy implications of government expenditures in the national income accounts

One implication of including government production in GDP is that the level of income is overstated, but a larger problem is that changes in government expenditures result in changes in measured national income under the current system. Thus, if government grows, this government growth is added to the income statistics measuring income growth. If an economy shifts resources from the private sector into the public sector to increase its military forces, the increase in military expenditures is added to national income. If, unrealistically assuming away the excess burden of taxation, the dollar decline in the production of final private sector goods is just offset by the same dollar increase in military expenditures, it appears that the nation's income has remained unchanged. More realistically, the excess burden of taxation will cause private output to fall by more than the increase in military expenditures, but even here the decline in national income will be understated due to faulty national income accounting conventions.

In some European nations – Sweden is a good example – government expenditures as a share of GDP soared between 1960 and 1990, and much of the increase was government provision of social services such as pre-school care for children and nursing home care for elders. Prior to the increase, families would have cared for their own children and their own elders at home; after the increase, what was once home production became government production. Big government reduces an economy's productivity and slows its measured GDP growth rate,[18] and because of the increase in the size of the public sector, economic growth as measured by GDP declined in Sweden and other nations with substantial government growth. However, that slower measured GDP growth actually understates the decline in national income because as GDP is currently measured, the substitution of government expenditures to produce what once was home production counts as an increase in income.

The problem is that government growth is mistakenly accounted for as real economic growth. Thus, if growth in measured GDP according to national income accounting conventions is a goal of economic policy, one way to accomplish this goal of GDP growth is to increase the size of the public sector. While it should be obvious that shifting child care from home production to government production does not increase anybody's income (although it does transfer resources from taxpayers to daycare workers, who may be the same people in many cases), or that buying more military hardware does not increase aggregate income (although it does transfer resources from taxpayers to military contractors), or that it does not increase anybody's income to hire ten bureaucrats to do the job that one used to do, in all these cases measured GDP will rise. Thus, if a nation judges its economic health by its measured GDP, the inclusion of government expenditures in GDP can have severely distorting effects. More significantly, if a nation pursues a policy of trying to increase its measured GDP, this leads policy makers to devote excessive resources to the public sector, and makes it look like they are succeeding in increasing income when, if income were properly measured, it would be apparent that they are not.

The way that income is measured has serious policy implications. Because GDP is used as the measure of the productiveness of the economy, and because increasing measured GDP is a public policy goal, public policy is biased toward devoting an excessive share of resources to the public sector. In the same way that when, in the former Soviet Union, the output of roofing metal was measured in terms of square feet of output, too many square feet of output (that was inefficiently thin) was produced, measuring the output of government as its dollar cost results in too many resources being channeled into government. Nations like Sweden that experimented with democratic socialism in past decades are now seeing the problems that result from excessive government and are reversing some of their policies, but the problems were masked to a substantial degree by the methodology of national income accounting. Because government expenditures are included in measured GDP, the increase in government spending to provide things that people once provided for themselves hid the decline in actual income that was produced by their turn toward socialism.

GDP as a measure of aggregate output

A more subtle problem with the use of GDP as an indicator of the economy's performance is that for policy purposes, GDP is equated with real output, and maintaining growth in real output, as measured by GDP, is adopted as a policy goal. The subtle aspect of this problem is that GDP is an aggregate measure, which makes aggregate output appear as a homogeneous commodity. Twentieth-century economic theory adds to this impression. In a macroeconomic setting that analyzes aggregate demand, GDP is the sum of consumption plus investment plus government spending, or as economics professors tell their introductory students, $Y = C + I + G$. If Y is too low, macroeconomic policy suggests several ways that monetary or fiscal policy can be used to stimulate C or I, or offers the option of increasing G directly through more government spending. In this simple macroeconomic framework, the idea that there is an optimal mix among these components of Y is rarely considered, let alone the idea that C, I, and G are not homogeneous themselves.

A supply-side emphasis suggests that the way to increase income is to increase productivity, either through an enhancement to the inputs into production or through technological advances that can enable an economy to produce more output with the same inputs. More formally, using a simple production function, f, where output is produced by capital and labor, $Y = f(K, L)$. Within this framework, more output can be produced either by increasing inputs K and L, or by altering the functional form, f, so that the same inputs generate more output. Economists tend to think of changing the functional form as technological progress, and tend to look at increasing inputs both as increasing the quantity of inputs, and increasing their quality, such as enhancing labor through education. Of course, national income accounting recognizes that the production process is more complicated than this, and the national income accounts include both inputs and outputs for hundreds of sectors of the economy, which can be analyzed in an input–output model in which outputs from all sectors can serve as inputs in all others. These quantities of inputs and outputs are measured in detail for the national income accounts. Even though the production relationships may be more complicated, the basic production function approach still holds, where inputs are combined to produce outputs in each sector, and national income is the aggregate of the production of all sectors in the economy. More significantly, changes in the quality of output, or the production of new types of output, show up only in an increasing quantity in some sector.

The problem with using this framework as a foundation for economic policy, as Mitchell, Kuznets, and the other developers of national income accounting envisioned it to be used, is that the framework makes no allowance for changes in the nature of inputs and outputs. A key theme of this volume is that the essential feature of economic progress is not that larger and larger amounts of output are being produced – although that is indeed a good thing – but rather that the nature of both inputs and outputs are changing over time in ways that are not easy to anticipate. When one compares the standard of living in 1900 with the standard of living in 2000, while it is true that the economy produces more output, the biggest difference is the changing nature of output. The change in the qualitative nature of output is not easily captured using the production function approach to modeling the economy, where the long-run goal is increasing homogeneously measured GDP.

Models allow the economy to be depicted as having an infinite number of sectors, so one could model an economy with n different goods, and could make provisions in the model for new goods $n + 1, n + 2, \ldots, n + n$, to be developed, but the modeling of the economy does not capture how these new goods come into being. Within this context, one can envision growth as the production of more of what the economy is already producing, or producing additional new goods, but nothing in the model addresses how innovation can take place to bring new goods into production. One way, economists know, is for research and development to produce new goods. How is R&D undertaken? In economic models, it is undertaken in the same way as any other productive activity, by using inputs of K and L to generate R&D output. Modeling economic progress in this way, however, leaves out the process by which economic progress actually takes place. In this type of model, economic progress means increasing K and L to produce more Y, or devoting some K and L to R&D to improve the functional form f so more Y can be produced with a given amount of K and L. The fact that models can incorporate an infinite number of goods does not change the conclusion that national income accounting conventions point policy toward producing a bigger quantity of output rather than changing the qualitative nature of that output. In this framework, improving the performance of the economy means producing more Y, or producing more GDP.

The national income accounts do include hundreds of sectors in the economy, and input–output models show the interrelationships among all these sectors. Nevertheless, when innovations change the qualitative nature of output in a sector, they show up as an increase in the quantity of output. In the 1980s, computers moved from character-based user interfaces to graphical user interfaces, but the only way this is reflected in the national income accounts is in the dollar amount of output in that sector. Despite the complexities, from a policy standpoint national income accounting ultimately says that GDP $= f(K, L)$, and that increasing income means producing more GDP by using more K and L inputs, or improving the functional form f to get more output from those inputs. Even if new sectors are added to the national income accounts to include new types of goods, this does not affect the bottom line. National income accounting cannot measure changes in the character of the economy's output. It only measures the amount of output, denominated in dollars.

National income accounting and public policy

At first glance it might appear that national income accounting could not have had much of an effect on public policy. It is, after all, only a set of conventions for measuring the nation's output and converting it into dollar terms. However, the way people measure their goals affects the ways that they try to achieve them. National income accounting looks at the production of income in a particular way, and steers public policy toward a specific vision of how income can be increased. National income accounting conceives of income as homogeneous, and conceives of economic growth as an increase in the quantity of that homogeneous output. The goal of growth is to increase GDP, and GDP $= f(K, L)$, so public policy should be geared toward increasing human and physical capital, and developing better technology. Furthermore, because government expenditures are included in GDP at cost, increases in the size of government make GDP appear to go up, creating an incentive for policy makers to divert resources from the private sector to the public sector. Ideologically, the United States has remained a market economy, but the conception of growth and progress in terms of national income has had a substantial impact even in a primarily market-oriented economy.

The most obvious impact is in the heavy government investment in education and research and development. In the United States, 78 percent of all college students and 89 percent of all elementary and secondary students attend government schools, and 32 percent of total research and development expenditures in the nation are made by government. Interestingly enough, government R&D expenditures have been declining substantially as a percentage of the total over the years; in 1960 government R&D expenditures made up 66 percent of the total.[19] While the declining percentage of government R&D expenditures (due largely to a decline in military and space-related R&D) offers some reason to believe that policy is turning toward market allocation of resources rather than government planning, government still spends about one-third of the total R&D expenditures in the United States, and government investment in education shows no signs of letting up.

Government in the United States has not had as heavy an involvement in directing investment in physical capital as in most nations, but the regulatory environment of business is designed with the production function approach to income in mind rather than being geared toward encouraging innovation. The regulation of medicine and medicinal drugs has been geared toward maintaining the status quo and producing more of the same type of output rather than innovating and changing the nature of the output, despite the fact that so much innovation has taken place in the industry.[20] Similarly, antitrust policy has been geared toward holding back and penalizing those firms that were able to gain an edge in the market through entrepreneurship and innovation.[21] This was especially apparent in the 1990s when several firms on the cutting edge of technology (e.g. Intel, Microsoft) found themselves facing antitrust enforcement because of the market share their technological advances had given them.

The clear orientation in antitrust and regulation policy in the United States is that welfare is enhanced by ensuring competitive markets to produce more output at the lowest cost. The notion that welfare is enhanced by continual improvement in products, and that market share is a reward for entrepreneurship and innovation, appears to have no impact on policy. This production function approach to policy is readily apparent in the computer and medical industries, which are two industries that have seen the greatest amounts of progress as a result of entrepreneurship and innovation. Yet even here, where one would think that policies encouraging entrepreneurship would win out over policies designed to encourage greater production of "output," the production function approach to policy has dominated. The way that one measures progress does matter, and the use of national income accounting to measure the health of the economy has pushed policy toward focusing on the production of more of the same output, rather than on improving the quality of output and producing new types of output.

The first step in solving any problem is recognizing that the problem exists. Without some analysis, it may not be apparent that the way in which a nation accounts for its national income affects the type of economic policy the nation pursues. This analysis shows that the way in which national income is measured in the national income and product accounts makes income appear as a homogeneous product of inputs into a productive process. This biases public policy toward trying to increase income by producing a greater quantity of income rather than focusing on qualitative changes in output, even though the qualitative changes are more important for advancing economic well-being than the quantitative changes. Furthermore, public policy is biased toward trying to enhance the inputs into the productive process and produce technical advances, rather than focusing on the development of an institutional structure that fosters entrepreneurial activity, even though entrepreneurship is more important for advancing economic well-being than attempting to enlarge the nation's productive capacity. In addition, the way in which government expenditures are accounted for biases policy toward the diversion of resources from the private sector toward the public sector.

The bias in public policy is even more apparent when one compares economic policy in the nineteenth century with economic policy in the twentieth. Based on the ideas of Adam Smith and David Ricardo, nineteenth century economic policy focused on reducing trade barriers, limiting government regulation, and creating an environment where entrepreneurship could thrive.[22] The role of government was to protect property rights and provide stable institutions, and the concept of laissez-faire described what policy makers pursued as the most appropriate economic policy. Toward the end of the nineteenth century, public policy began turning away from the concept of laissez-faire in favor of the idea that enlightened government economic policy can be used to engineer the economy to enhance prosperity. But this required a way to measure prosperity, which led to twentieth-century national income accounting, and measurement of prosperity in those terms led to policies that have stifled entrepreneurship – the true engine of prosperity.

10 The political environment and entrepreneurship

Political entrepreneurship occurs when an individual observes and acts on a political profit opportunity. As with market entrepreneurship, entrepreneurial actions require, first, that a profit opportunity exists; second, that someone is alert enough to spot the opportunity and recognize the opportunity for profit; and third, that the individual is willing to act on the opportunity once it is spotted. Each of these three requirements are common elements of political and market entrepreneurship, yet in each of these requirements there are both subtle and substantial differences between entrepreneurship in markets and in politics. The fundamental differences arise from the fact that market exchange is based on voluntary agreement, whereas political action always has an element of compulsion behind it. The fact that force can be used to generate political outcomes produces two key differences in the nature of political versus market entrepreneurship. First, opportunities for political entrepreneurship will always exist. One might imagine an economy in complete general equilibrium, implying that there are no unexploited profit opportunities in the market, but there will always be opportunities for political profit from the forced transfer of resources from some to others. Second, whereas successful entrepreneurial acts are welfare-enhancing in markets, that may not be true in politics, because the costs forced on the losers may be greater than the gains to the gainers.

To examine the welfare implications of political entrepreneurship, this chapter first presents a framework that shows how entrepreneurial opportunities are generated in politics. That framework clearly shows that acting on some entrepreneurial opportunities will enhance welfare, whereas acting on other opportunities will reduce welfare. This comparison shows that entrepreneurial opportunities in politics and markets arise in different ways, and demonstrates why there always must be opportunities for political entrepreneurship. As a result, there are important differences in the ways that political and market opportunities are noticed and acted upon.

Market exchange can occur between two individuals, whereas political agreement typically involves a large number of participants. Similarly, acting on an entrepreneurial opportunity in a market often can be done by a single entrepreneur who observes a profit opportunity and acts on it through market exchange. In the market, nobody else need be involved in the entrepreneurial action; others simply buy and sell their goods and services on the market and the entrepreneur can limit her involvement with others only to market transactions. Acting on an entrepreneurial opportunity in politics requires collective action. The political entrepreneur cannot simply rely on market data, because the entrepreneurial action requires anticipating whether the entrepreneur can entice a sufficient number of others to cooperate in collective action.[1]

If the entrepreneurial opportunity is a Pareto improvement, then enlisting the cooperation of others should be relatively easy for the entrepreneur, because nobody has a strong reason to object to the change. If, however, the opportunity creates gains for some but losses to others, as is almost always the case in politics, lining up the support of others is crucial to the success of the entrepreneurial action. Given the problems of coordinating collective action, one might at first think that entrepreneurs should be biased toward productive actions that avoid these problems, but this chapter shows that there is a significant bias in the other direction. The incentive structure in politics leads political entrepreneurs toward actions that benefit some at the expense of others rather than toward actions that benefit everyone, and leads entrepreneurs toward an inefficient allocation of resources rather than toward an efficient allocation. There is a subset of the public choice literature that argues otherwise,[2] so one of the main goals of this chapter is to show why the incentive structure in democratic politics entices entrepreneurs to act on opportunities for inefficient resource allocation and to bypass opportunities for efficient resource allocation.

The fundamental difference between the invisible hand of the market and the coercive hand of government is that government allows some to impose their preferences on others by force. The reallocation of resources through coercion is not an anomaly that sometimes arises in politics, but is inherent in the way that the democratic political system was designed. What follows is an examination of the implications of democratic decision making on the opportunities for political entrepreneurship, and in turn the implications of political entrepreneurship on the political allocation of economic resources.

After examining the concept of entrepreneurship in more detail in the next section, the chapter then shows what causes entrepreneurial opportunities to arise in politics. Entrepreneurial opportunities in politics are tied closely to both the efficiency and stability of the political system. When the political system is inefficient (in the Paretian sense that there are potential changes that could benefit some without harming others), entrepreneurial opportunities arise in politics for many of the same reasons that they appear in markets – to reduce the inefficiency. However, entrepreneurial opportunities arise regardless of the efficiency of resource allocation, and acting on many of these opportunities can result in a less efficient allocation of resources. An important conclusion of this analysis is that the incentives to act on opportunities that reduce the efficiency of the system are likely to overwhelm the incentives for efficient entrepreneurship. If the political system is unstable (in the sense that the status quo is always dominated politically by some alternative), then change is more likely, and entrepreneurs can profit from leading the way toward political change. Political instability creates entrepreneurial opportunities.[3] The model shows that inefficiency and instability are more closely linked than the literature on the topic typically has recognized. The introduction of political entrepreneurship provides a crucial link between political efficiency and political stability, and thus sheds light on some long-standing questions in public choice theory.

Entrepreneurship in markets and politics

In both markets and politics, entrepreneurship can be defined as the observing and acting upon a profit opportunity.[4] In the neoclassical model of competitive equilibrium, entrepreneurial opportunities are ruled out by the assumptions of no transaction costs and perfect information on the part of all market participants. As Ronald Coase noted, in a zero transaction cost world, there would be no reason for government to aid in the allocation of resources, because all potential Pareto improvements would be made through market exchange.[5] In the real world, transaction costs are significant, giving a justification for government intervention, but there is a substantial literature arguing that transaction costs and agency costs are higher in politics than in markets.[6] This is partly due to the fact that government can act without the explicit consent of its constituents, requiring constituents to have to actively seek out information about the behavior of principals in this principal–agent relationship, coupled with the rational ignorance of constituents noted by Anthony Downs,[7] and the monopoly power that political institutions give to those in government.

The informational differences between private markets and political markets have not been sufficiently recognized by those who argue the efficiency of political institutions. As Friedrich Hayek emphasized,[8] the market serves as a mechanism that coordinates all of the decentralized knowledge shared by market participants that could not be effectively shared or communicated directly. Hayek persuasively argues that any one person can comprehend only a small fraction of the total amount of available information. The marketplace allows people to take advantage of the information they acquire, but the market process does not actively harm people for the information they do not acquire. In private markets, people can act in areas where they are informed, but only through voluntary exchange, and ignore areas in which they have limited information. In political markets, predatory politics causes people to be harmed unless they find it worthwhile to actively prevent that harm. Because of the coercive nature of government action, the informational requirements for the Coase theorem to imply the efficient allocation of resources in the public sector are much greater than to achieve the efficient allocation of resources in the private sector.

People cannot be informed about every market and every exchange, in either private markets or in politics. The information costs are too high, and the opportunity cost of gaining more information about some potential exchanges is a reduction in resources available to gain information about other potential exchanges. In private markets, people gather information about those exchanges where they see potential profit opportunities, but do not have costs imposed on them by ignoring activities in other markets. In politics, people also become informed about potential exchanges where they perceive the potential costs to exceed the potential benefits. As in private markets, this means focusing one's attention narrowly, and specializing in a particular area of the market, forgoing activity in areas outside one's specialization. The idea of rational ignorance in politics is exactly parallel to people's acquiring of information in markets. People profit by specializing, so they know a lot about the narrow area in which they specialize, and know relatively little about other areas, because it would not pay to become very informed in areas where others are specializing. But in markets people do not have costs imposed on them by force in areas where they do not specialize. In politics, the coercive nature of government action means that costs can be imposed on those who are relatively uninformed. The opportunity cost of becoming informed guarantees that most people will be uninformed about most political decisions, opening up the opportunity for predatory politics.

The fact that most people are relatively uninformed about most markets and most potential exchanges does not impede the efficiency of market exchange because the voluntary nature of exchange guarantees that people will engage in exchange only when they believe they will receive net benefits, and people cannot have resources transferred away from them without their consent. In politics, the lack of information creates the opportunity for predatory politics, precisely because resources can be transferred from those who are uninformed without their consent. Thus, with the same level of information, conditions that lead to efficient exchange in markets create predatory entrepreneurial opportunities in politics, resulting in inefficiencies. When one recognizes the differences in informational requirements, it becomes apparent that the analogy between efficient market exchange and efficient political exchange is, at best, incomplete.

Market institutions are relatively transparent by design. Their role is to facilitate voluntary exchange when parties have an incentive to trade for their mutual benefit. Political institutions must be more structured and less transparent because they are used to produce outcomes that would not be generated by voluntary action, and where all participants may not agree with the government's action.

Government action might be undertaken for several reasons. The literature on market failure argues that resource allocation can be improved through government intervention, but the fact that government can coercively reallocate resources opens the possibility that government intervention is demanded by those who have political power, for the purpose of transferring resources from others to themselves. Regardless of the reason for government intervention, all government action makes people interact in ways that they would not choose to voluntarily, for if that were not true, there would be no reason for the government to intervene. This coercive aspect to political institutions creates the key difference between political and market entrepreneurship. It creates the possibility that a political profit can be generated by giving some people benefits at the expense of others.

The market failure explanation for government intervention is fundamentally incomplete, because it does not explain who has the incentive to rectify the inefficiency. From a Coasian perspective, it might appear self-evident that any inefficiency generates a profit opportunity for the entrepreneur who allocates resources more efficiently, but political institutions stand in the way of a political entrepreneur who wants to be a residual claimant in such a situation. Thus, one must look at political institutions and political incentives to see where the opportunities for political entrepreneurship lie, and what those opportunities imply for the democratic allocation of economic resources.

Two sources of political profits

Entrepreneurial opportunities in politics originate in two ways. The first way is through the removal of inefficiencies, or the discovery of potential opportunities for gains from trade through the political process. This process of political exchange has been analyzed extensively, and the concept of the political marketplace based on efficiency-enhancing political exchange tends to be associated with the Chicago school.[9] The basic idea behind this approach to political entrepreneurship is that if political goals are not being implemented in the least-cost way, then there is a profit opportunity from restructuring the nature of the government activity so that the goals are achieved at least cost. The cost savings are a political profit that the entrepreneur can then apply toward the satisfaction of other goals.[10] Following this line of reasoning to its logical conclusion, the political allocation of resources can be just as efficient as the economic allocation of resources.

The second way that entrepreneurial opportunities are created in politics is by forcibly transferring wealth from one group of people to another. If the political support lost from those who pay for the transfer is less than the political gain in support from the recipients, then the political entrepreneur can profit from such a forced transfer. A simple way to contrast these two sources of entrepreneurial opportunities in politics is to note that people can enhance their incomes in two ways: production and predation.[11] Production uses resources in a more efficient and economical way to produce a profit for the political entrepreneur. Predation is the taking of resources from some for the benefit of others.[12] Of course, these same two methods of income enhancement are available in the private sector too. However, private sector predation is discouraged and viewed as unethical and illegal. People take actions to prevent themselves from becoming victims of private sector predators, and governments universally view as one of their missions the prevention of nongovernmental predation.[13] Government predation, on the other hand, is often viewed as one of the core functions of the state. For example, Richard Musgrave's classic textbook on public finance conceptually divides the government into three branches: the allocation branch, the distribution branch, and the stabilization branch.[14] Thus, through redistribution, Musgrave legitimizes political predation, and raises predation to the level of one of the three core functions of government.

One feature of the profit opportunities presented through political predation is that such opportunities are always present in a democratic political system. This point deserves some emphasis because of the way that it contrasts with entrepreneurial opportunities in the market. In economic equilibrium, all profit opportunities are competed away.[15] In politics, an equilibrium will also eliminate profit opportunities from productive political activities, because inefficiencies will be eliminated.[16] However, potential profits from political predation always remain in a democracy. Thus, as Fred McChesney notes,[17] under many circumstances people must devote resources to protecting themselves from political predation, or they become easy targets.

This does not imply that an equilibrium condition will ever be attained, either in markets or in politics, or that all productive entrepreneurial opportunities will be exhausted. Rather, it implies that should an equilibrium be attained, that would eliminate profit opportunities from the market, and it would eliminate profit opportunities from political production, but profit opportunities from political predation remain in equilibrium in a democracy. The reason is that there is always a way to construct a majority coalition in a distributive setting that will favor an alternative over the status quo.

A simple example can illustrate this point. Assume that a dollar is to be divided up among three individuals, who will determine the distribution of the division by majority rule. One possibility would be for two individuals to form a coalition against the third, dividing the dollar in the proportions (1/2, 1/2, 0). The third individual, who has nothing in this division, could propose an alternative, which can be labeled alternative A, (0, 2/3, 1/3). Alternative A would be favored over the original division by both persons two and three, who could outvote the first person by majority rule. Now the first person could propose alternative B, (1/3, 0, 2/3), which would be favored by individuals one and three over A. Similarly, person two could propose alternative C, (2/3, 1/3, 0), which would be preferred to B by both one and two, making C dominate B by majority rule. But alternative A could now defeat C by majority rule, so B defeats A, C defeats B, and A defeats C, setting up the classic cyclical majority. The possibility of a cyclical majority is widely known, but the thing to note here is that this cyclical majority exists only because the status quo can be changed by the approval of a simple majority.

If unanimous approval were required to change the status quo, so that like in the market, a person would have to agree to give up some of his share, then any outcome in this distributive game would be a stable equilibrium. Once a distribution became the status quo, it would then require the approval of all voters to change it, and because this example is purely distributional, any benefit to one person must come at a cost to someone else. Every outcome is, in that sense, Pareto optimal, and there would be no profit opportunities lying in wait for potential political entrepreneurs. This is analogous to the market setting, in which a Pareto optimal allocation of resources implies the absence of entrepreneurial opportunities. However, with simple majority rule, the political entrepreneur does not need to provide benefits to every individual, but just to a majority, and because resources can be taken away from a minority to enrich a majority, there are always predatory (distributional) entrepreneurial opportunities available in a democracy.

Predatory entrepreneurship and efficiency

Productive entrepreneurship leads resources to be allocated more efficiently. The same is not true for predatory entrepreneurship. Returning to the three person example, a majority would favor a program that provides $1 in benefits for two people while imposing a cost of $2.50 on the third. An outcome with a payoff of ($1, $1, −$2.50) would win the approval of a majority. This example makes it clear that under majority rule, predatory entrepreneurship does not have to be efficient. Of course, a numerical example could be constructed where the total benefits exceeded the total cost, but political institutions tend to create situations in which redistributional entrepreneurial opportunities generate total costs that exceed the total benefits. For one thing, all purely redistributive programs have the feature that, because of the cost involved in implementing the transfer, the dollar costs exceed the dollar benefits. Another factor leaning toward the political demand for distributive programs is that people enter the political process to try to produce benefits for themselves, and it is easier to devise a scheme for doing so that takes resources from others than it is to devise a scheme that results in efficiency enhancements. On top of that, in simple majoritarian politics, where each vote is weighted equally, there is less incentive to consider total costs and total benefits. Political support, not economic efficiency, is the criterion for success in a democratic environment. As a result, political entrepreneurs can always find opportunities for predatory entrepreneurship.

The predatory nature of political proposals is never revealed in their packaging. Rather, potential beneficiaries will lobby for the program that gives them $1 in benefits based on the argument that it is in the public interest, and will either ignore the $2.50 in costs or claim that either the benefits are really greater than $1 or the costs are really less than $2.50, or both. Sometimes costs are even presented as if they are benefits.[18] For example, a program might bring jobs to an area, increasing the local payroll by $1 million. In the private sector, this labor cost of a project is correctly considered as a cost of the project, but in the public sector the labor cost is tallied as a benefit. Thus, proponents often overstate the benefits of a proposal by listing its costs as one of its benefits. Sometimes costs and benefits are simply budgetary matters, as with jobs or cash transfers, but often they are not. When the costs and benefits are the result of regulation, it is easy to overstate the benefits and understate the costs. The major point, however, is that with democratic decision making, opportunities for political profit often imply a less efficient use of resources, and successful political entrepreneurship does not necessarily lead toward efficiency or equilibrium. It does not necessarily lead toward efficiency because changes are based on weighing political support and opposition rather than dollar benefits and dollar costs. It does not necessarily lead toward equilibrium because no matter what the status quo, there is always some purely distributional change that could win the support of a majority.[19]

Productive versus predatory entrepreneurship

The efficiency question, addressed in the previous section, has not been completely answered. Predatory entrepreneurship has the potential for inefficiency, but productive entrepreneurship is efficiency enhancing. As Becker notes,[20] distributional goals are a part of the political system, but there is an incentive to achieve all political goals, including redistributional goals, as efficiently as possible. Two questions suggest themselves. First, why would political entrepreneurs engage in predatory politics, which amount to a negative sum game, when productive opportunities are available to them? The productive opportunities are a positive sum game, increasing political benefits which then can be added to the entrepreneur's profit. Second, even if predatory entrepreneurship does take place, that creates a productive profit opportunity, allowing a political entrepreneur to later remedy any inefficiency, which can then result in efficient redistribution and more political profit. Thus, why does productive entrepreneurship not eliminate any inefficiencies caused by predatory entrepreneurship? The answers to both questions lie in the nature of the political marketplace. This section answers the first question, while the following section covers the second.

The tautological answer to the first question is that predatory entrepreneurial opportunities offer greater profit to the political entrepreneur, so political entrepreneurs act on those more profitable opportunities even though they result in a less efficient allocation of resources. Gary Becker, who emphasizes the efficiency-enhancing aspects of political exchange, depicts the legislature as a marketplace where interest groups express their demands for and against political programs and policies, and the legislature clears the market by passing legislation up to the point where the marginal political benefits of legislation just equal the marginal political costs. If the Coase theorem applies, so that transactions costs do not keep anyone from registering their political demands, then the legislative market should clear efficiently. However, most people have very limited access to political markets because the opportunity cost of expressing political demands on most issues is so high relative to the benefit. Legislators do have an incentive to pay attention to the preferences of unorganized constituents,[21] because unorganized but informed constituents will vote in upcoming elections, and interest groups have an incentive to provide information to uninformed constituents who would be likely to side with them.[22] Still, any individual opposition to legislation that spreads costs across a large number of citizens is a public good. The individual opponent bears the costs personally, but if successful must share the benefits with all of the citizens who would have borne the cost. Thus, while in the aggregate, the benefits of opposing inefficient legislation exceed the costs, the public good nature of this opposition means it is not worthwhile for any one opponent to do so, allowing inefficient legislation to be passed.[23]

A straightforward analysis of the nature of the political marketplace shows that individuals do not have an incentive to register their demands against political predation. A comparison with the private sector emphasizes this point. Those who champion the efficiency of political markets argue that there are the same incentives to reduce inefficiencies in the political marketplace as there are in private markets. A careful analysis shows that this is not true, because people are coerced into being participants in the political process whether they consent or not, whereas in private markets people participate only in those exchanges that they anticipate will benefit them. In private markets, just as in political markets, individuals do not have the incentive to become informed and to register their demands in most markets. Thus, in both cases, most people choose not to participate in most markets. The crucial difference is that in private markets where individuals choose not to participate, people on the other side of those markets cannot coerce transfers from the nonparticipants. In contrast, democratic politics allows those who choose not to participate to be the victims of political predation.

The reason why political entrepreneurs pursue predatory opportunities is that they tend to be more profitable. Lobbyists and special interests come to legislators seeking predatory policies that provide them with transfers, tax breaks, or favorable regulations, but only rarely approach legislators with productive policies, because predatory policies tend to provide concentrated benefits to those seeking them whereas productive policies tend to produce public goods that benefit a wider group, so have a weaker constituency. Because information on pending legislation is costly to obtain, and even with information in hand, action against legislation is costly to undertake, most people passively accept most legislation, creating a set of victims who can always be raided to pay for predatory policies. Again, it is worth emphasizing that the profitability of predatory policies comes from the fact that the costs of such policies can be coercively imposed by government.

Why do productive opportunities remain?

The answer to the second question, about why productive policies do not eliminate the inefficiencies of predatory policies, lies in the opportunity cost of political entrepreneurship. Yes, after inefficiencies are created there is an entrepreneurial opportunity to reallocate resources more efficiently, but political entrepreneurs are limited in the number of issues they can pursue, and so choose the options that are most profitable. The passage of legislation requires a majority of votes in the legislature, and the legislative process involves logrolling. While at first it might appear that political exchange is inefficient and vulnerable to bad-faith promises, that is less true in an environment where there are a small number of people, where they all know each other, and where future support is necessary for professional success. If legislators do not make good on their IOUs, they will not be able to trade in the future; thus, legislators have an incentive to reciprocate when they have been helped by others, and they have an incentive to be careful about when they ask for support.

Just as consumers must be careful not to charge too much on a credit card and accumulate too much debt, legislators must be careful not to accumulate too much political debt, and skillful legislators must discipline themselves to ask for support only when the benefits of passing legislation (or maybe just bringing it to a vote) exceed the future costs of having to reciprocate and support those with whom they exchange. In short, legislators have a budget constraint that limits the policies they can actively pursue. This limits their ability to pursue productive policies even when they would be in everybody's interest.

The free rider problem applies again, because a policy that provides efficiency gains to everyone imposes a cost on the legislator who sponsors it, because votes must be traded to get it passed, but the gains are more widely shared. Meanwhile, the effort spent to provide this type of public good takes away from the effort that the legislator could be devoting to producing predatory legislation that will garner special interest support and provide a higher private payoff. Without the budget constraint it would be feasible for legislators to pursue both predatory and productive policies, but when the legislator's budget constraint is factored in – the legislator has only a certain number of votes he or she can trade away – it causes legislators to favor predatory policies over productive ones. One might be tempted to think that legislators could pursue both productive and predatory profit opportunities, but just as in the market, where buying one thing precludes buying another, any productive opportunity that a political entrepreneur chooses to seek support for displaces a predatory opportunity that the entrepreneur could have pursued. And as the analysis has shown, unlike productive political opportunities, predatory profit opportunities never run out, and are always available.

Political stability and political entrepreneurship

Theorists studying the democratic political process have long observed that under many circumstances, majority rule voting has no unique stable outcome, yet the democratic decision-making process does appear to be stable in most cases. Understanding why that is the case lends insight into the process of political entrepreneurship.[24] To be successful in politics, political entrepreneurs need political support. To gain the support of constituents, elected representatives must provide them with benefits, and such benefits might come in the form of efficiency gains that are a public good shared with the constituents of all representatives, or might come as programs targeted toward that representative's constituents and paid for by others. Pork barrel projects and transfers targeted to constituents provide a surer route to political support than the benefits from productive activity for a number of reasons. First, the magnitude of the potential benefits from forcibly transferring resources from some to others is much greater. Efficiency gains are limited by the degree of inefficiency, but there is no limit to the magnitude of transfers that could garner majority support. Second, constituents tend to reward legislators more for bringing programs and dollars to them than for the production of public goods. Constituents prefer to let other people's representatives enhance the efficiency of the system, so that their own representative can concentrate on diverting as many programs and expenditures toward the home district as possible.

All representatives find themselves in a similar situation, and in a democracy, representatives cannot carry out their goals without the cooperation of other representatives. Thus, representatives must form coalitions and engage in political exchange in order to succeed in transferring resources from the general treasury to their constituents. One way to do this would be for a group of legislators to form a minimum winning coalition, and for those in the coalition to use their political power to transfer resources from others to themselves.[25] A minimum winning coalition creates an entrepreneurial opportunity for those not in the winning coalition to conspire with a subset of those in the coalition, offering them an even larger payoff if they break ranks. Thus, it may be cheaper to form a larger coalition to prevent such defections,[26] which Carrubba and Volden refer to as the minimum necessary coalition.[27] The minimum necessary coalition is the smallest necessary to maintain a stable winning coalition. But any coalition that does not include everyone always opens up some opportunity for political entrepreneneurship within the minority to disrupt the majority coalition.

There are always incentives for those out of power to destabilize the political system, which gives insiders an incentive to bargain with everyone, in order to maintain stability, and thereby to maintain their power.[28] The entrepreneurial incentives for instability are always present, because predatory politics always pits some against others, but the entrepreneurial incentives to promote stability have an important advantage. The incumbents, who already have political power, have the incentive to stabilize the political system, and the incumbents also have the greatest amount of political power to change the political environment. One implication of this is that unless those with political power miscalculate, political change should be evolutionary, to maintain the power of those in power, rather than revolutionary. This creates incentives for a more universal coalition in which all interests enter the bargaining process to some degree, and with everyone having a chance to benefit from political exchange, political entrepreneurship tends to create political stability.[29]

Entrepreneurial opportunities in politics

An analysis of democratic political institutions shows that while there are entrepreneurial opportunities that can lead toward an improved allocation of resources, the institutions of democracy tend to pull political entrepreneurs toward predatory opportunities rather than toward productive ones. The potential profits are greater through predation, and the gains are more appropriable: productive opportunities too often are non-appropriable because the benefits are spread throughout the population rather than concentrated on the entrepreneur's constituents. The nature of political budget constraints also implies that potentially profitable productive opportunities may go unexploited even if they are noticed, because there will be more profit in predatory opportunities, and predatory opportunities always exist. Because democratic politics always allows some people to coercively obtain resources from others, elected representatives have the incentive to pursue those opportunities for their own political benefit.

Legislators can act on these opportunities only by cooperating with other legislators, because they need the support of a majority to get their legislation passed. Thus, legislators cooperate with each other in order to obtain their political goals. Part of being an effective legislator means being a good bargainer, so that the legislator can obtain as much as possible in exchange for supporting the programs of other legislators. The result is that legislative exchange takes place as legislators cooperate with each other, and in the process that enhances the opportunities for all legislators. Legislators have an incentive to enhance their ability to create effective exchanges, to enforce those exchanges, and to enhance the security of their positions as legislators. In this sense, democratic institutions provide the incentive for all legislators to cooperate with each other to further their collective goals.

The mechanisms by which legislators enhance their security and ability to cooperate with each other through predatory democracy have been discussed in detail in the literature. Legislators have an incentive to form a universal political coalition in which they all cooperate to share the benefits of resources obtained through political predation.[30] This gets them the votes they need to support their own interests, and prevents minority coalitions from disrupting the logrolling process. The way in which political jurisdictions are delineated divides the political marketplace among incumbents for their benefit, and keeps challengers from unseating incumbents.[31] The committee system acts as a method of establishing clear property rights to areas of the legislative agenda to enhance the ability of the legislature to produce benefits for special interests.[32] There are wide varieties of barriers to entry that provide incumbent advantages, including the franking privilege, the staff and expenses paid for with tax dollars, and the use of single-member districts and staggered senate election terms to prevent incumbents from competing with each other.[33] These political institutions, often designed by the legislature itself, are created to enhance the ability of legislators to produce special interest benefits through predatory politics, and to protect legislators from the challenges of incumbents.

The nature of political entrepreneurship in a democracy, then, is that a group of representatives work together to systematically transfer resources by force from some groups of citizens in order to provide benefits for other groups. Because each legislator has an agenda, many transfers occur from many groups to many groups. The typical citizen will be on the receiving end of some transfers and on the paying end of others. Legislators initiate these transfers for their own benefit, because the political cost to them of taking resources from the groups that are preyed upon is less than the political benefit they receive from the groups that get the transfers.

Two dimensions of political competition

This view of the political marketplace contains within it an important insight about the nature of political competition. As the political marketplace has been depicted earlier, incumbent legislators have the incentive to maintain stability by forming a coalition among all incumbents to prevent themselves from being displaced. Thus, the critical dimension of political competition is not along ideological or party lines, as it is typically depicted, but between incumbents and nonincumbents. When an election is held in the United States, typically a Republican candidate will run against a Democrat, and one will be the incumbent while the other will be the challenger. In this situation, political competition is commonly viewed as competition between parties: Republicans versus Democrats. This view of political competition obscures the fact that the more significant dimension of political competition is not between parties, but rather is between those who hold political power (incumbents) and those who want to take that power away from them (challengers). In fact, legislators in one party have more interests in common with their fellow legislators in the other party than they have in common with challengers in their own party.

Looking at the interests of an incumbent legislator, that legislator's primary political goal is to maintain power, which automatically puts the incumbent in an adversarial relationship with all nonincumbents. In most cases, measures that would help legislators elect more members of their own party will weaken the benefits of incumbency, and an incumbent would rather strengthen the benefits of incumbency than undertake measures that could help challengers. All incumbents share the same interests in this regard, in opposition to all challengers. Furthermore, incumbents must cooperate with each other to gain majority support in the legislature to pass the legislation they favor. Through cooperation among themselves, incumbents use their political power to coercively transfer resources from some citizens to others in order to further the goals of the representatives. When one examines the incentives of the political system, it is apparent that the primary dimension of political competition is not between parties or ideologies, but rather between incumbents of all parties against challengers of all parties. While an election that pits an incumbent of one party against a challenger of another at first appears to be primarily a competition among individuals of different parties, upon closer examination, the party affiliation is secondary, and the competition is primarily between an incumbent who wants to retain political power and a challenger who wants to take it away.[34]

The different impressions conveyed by these two different dimensions of political competition have significant implications for the nature of political resource allocation. If political competition is primarily among parties to claim the benefits of incumbency, then from an industrial organization standpoint, it might be viewed as competition among various firms for the right to be a temporary monopolist. This competition for the right to monopoly power can lead to an efficient allocation of resources as monopoly profits are bid down to zero.[35] Party competition is analogous to economic competition in the marketplace. If political competition is primarily between those who have political power and those who do not, a different picture emerges. Incumbents erect barriers to entry to provide profits to those who have political power, and the source of the profits is the coercive power of government.

One factor that casts doubt on the competitive view of politics is that people are willing to invest so much to win the political competition. If once victory is attained, the winners must follow the dictates of the voters to retain their power,[36] and all profits are competed away, there is little benefit to gaining political power, and the distribution of benefits to the general population will be roughly the same no matter who wins. If political competition instead is between incumbents who erect barriers to entry in order to keep the profits of political power for themselves, and this power is used to produce benefits to the interest groups that support them at the expense of others, then there is a substantial potential reward for political victory, and there is a good reason to devote a considerable amount of resources toward trying to win this competition.

The mere fact that there is such heated competition for elected office, and that people are willing to spend so much money to try to influence the outcomes of elections, suggests that there are substantial profits to be gained by the victors. This, in turn, suggests that democratic politics is not like a competitive marketplace where there are no above-normal profits to be reaped, but rather that barriers to entry have created a profitable monopoly for incumbents, who use their power to keep challengers out and to channel benefits toward themselves and their supporters. The competition is always stacked in favor of incumbents, because if a challenger does win, the challenger then becomes a member of the incumbent coalition. This is yet another factor that works for the benefit of those who already hold political power.

When reviewing the advantages that favor incumbents over challengers, the amount of money that people invest to attain political power, and the barriers to entry that enhance the profitability of political power, it is apparent that the essence of political competition is that those who have political power are competing with those who are trying to get it. Incumbents of different parties have more interests in common than incumbents of one party have with challengers in their own party. Parties do compete with each other, just as sales people from the same company may compete with each other to see who can generate the most sales. This competition is incidental to the fundamental competition, which in politics is not parties competing with each other but incumbents competing with nonincumbents.

Political entrepreneurship

Political entrepreneurs, like those in the market, discover and act on unexploited profit opportunities. In many ways, there are parallels between political exchange and market exchange, and the political marketplace is, indeed, a market. Democratic political institutions are different from market institutions, however, and this chapter shows that there are two significant institutional differences that result in resources being allocated differently through democratic governments than they are through markets. One crucial difference is that governments use coercion to obtain resources, so those who pay for government decisions do not do so voluntarily. This is true even for those who completely support government intervention: even the strongest supporter of government action still has no choice but to abide by the government's conditions. The second crucial difference is that in a democracy, a majority has the power to take collective action for the whole group. This means that those with political power have the potential to exploit those who do not, but it also means that elected representatives need the cooperation of other elected representatives in order to accomplish their political goals.

Some scholars have made the argument that political markets tend to allocate resources efficiently, as do economic markets, because there is always the incentive to attain any goal as efficiently as possible, leaving the largest possible surplus to be divided among the participants. That argument might be viewed as a tautology: if there was a more efficient way of doing things, all things considered, people would be doing things that way. If it is interpreted as more than a tautology, the analysis in this chapter shows that the characteristics of democratic politics create inefficiencies that do not exist in markets, and that democratic governments systematically allocate resources inefficiently.

The biggest reason for inefficiencies in government resource allocation is that people are forced to participate. In private markets, people can choose to participate in a market or not, based upon their expectations of the benefits. With government resource allocation, people are forced to pay taxes regardless of whether they expect a net benefit, and are forced to comply with regulations the same way. This opens the door for coerced transfers, but when taking account of Hayek's insightful analysis of knowledge,[37] it does much more. It means that unlike private markets, government action forces people to participate in activities in which they are uninformed, and in which they are unequipped to make cost-benefit calculations. In the private sector, people trade in those markets where they believe they have sufficient information to make exchanges to enhance their well-being. In areas where they lack sufficient information, they do not trade. As Hayek notes, each individual can know only a small fraction of the total amount of information available. In the public sector, people are forced through coercive taxation and regulation to participate in activities in which they have no information, and have no incentive to become informed. The result is that those who are informed can use the political process to prey on those who are not. This is a significant and overlooked characteristic of government resource allocation, and because of the informational differences, political resource allocation can not be as efficient as resource allocation through markets.

This is more than just a matter of transactions costs or information costs. In markets, people choose to transact, and choose to become informed up to the degree where they view that the marginal benefits of more information are equated with the marginal costs. In government, people know that in some areas it does not pay them to become informed, but they are forced to participate anyway through coercive taxation and regulation. Those situations always produce potential victims of predatory programs. In markets, predation is illegal, but in government, predation is the standard mode of operation. Because of the limited information that anyone can possess, this necessarily means that many people are going to be victims of government predation because they have no option not to participate in those activities where they are likely to be victims of predation. The inefficiency in democratic politics is more than just saying the information requirements are greater, so political resource allocation will not be as efficient. In markets, the incentive structure is such that people have the incentive to seek out opportunities for more efficient resource allocation, whereas in democratic politics, the institutions give political entrepreneurs the incentive to seek out opportunities for predatory and inefficient policies. It is not just that the invisible hand does not pull quite as hard toward efficiency in politics, but rather that in politics the incentives pull toward inefficient resource allocation.

The political marketplace does present entrepreneurial opportunities for more efficient resource allocation which, once exploited, disappear, but predatory entrepreneurial opportunities are always present in government, because it is always possible to come up with a transfer of resources that can receive majority support. Predatory entrepreneurial opportunities are more readily available and are potentially more profitable than productive entrepreneurial opportunities in politics. In democratic politics, all political action requires cooperation from others, and the result is the formation of very inclusive political coalitions that cooperate to engage in predatory transfers from one group to another.

In both politics and markets, entrepreneurship consists of discovering and acting upon unexploited profit opportunities. In markets, the invisible hand leads entrepreneurial acts to enhance the productivity of the economy, but in politics entrepreneurship in the main leads to inefficient transfer activity. This should not be surprising, considering the coercive nature of political institutions. Centuries ago, Thomas Hobbes described a situation of anarchy as a war of all against all, where life would be nasty, brutish, short, solitary, and poor.[38] The problem with anarchy, as Hobbes saw it, was that without clearly defined and enforced property rights, people would engage in predation rather than production, to the detriment of everyone. The same lessons should apply to government. When an institution is established that allows people to profit from predation, inefficiency results for the reasons Hobbes articulated so long ago. The American Founders were well aware of this, and tried to design a government insulated from democratic pressures, dedicated to protecting the rights of individuals. Over the next two centuries, American government has become increasingly democratic, and because of this, increasingly predatory. Under these institutions, predation is where the bulk of opportunities for political entrepreneurship lie.

Institutions, again

William Baumol has made the insightful conjecture that people in all societies have roughly the same propensities for entrepreneurship, but that in some societies people's entrepreneurial impulses are channeled in a productive direction, while in others institutions steer their entrepreneurial impulses in a destructive direction.[39] This chapter has examined the nature of political entrepreneurship to show how even in the most democratic of governments, the incentive structure leads people's entrepreneurial impulses toward economic predation, and that entrepreneurship steered this way reduces people's overall economic well-being. Politics is predatory by its very nature.

Chapter 9 looked at the impact on entrepreneurship of public policy that results from the way in which economic goals are measured, and again showed that public policy often hinders entrepreneurship and economic progress. Chapter 8 showed that under certain institutional arrangements, people's entrepreneurial impulses would be channeled in a productive direction, leading to economic progress. The analysis of the present chapter reinforces how important the institutional structure discussed in Chapter 8 is for the advancement of economic well-being. If the institutional setting protects and encourages market exchange, if government taxation and regulation impose minimal constraints on economic exchange, if property rights are protected, and if rule of law allows everyone to be treated equally within the legal system, then entrepreneurship will lead to the spectacular type of economic progress that the United States and Western Europe have enjoyed over the past two centuries. In the absence of these institutions, economic progress will not occur and people will be mired in poverty. Regardless of how well-meaning people in government are, the incentive structure that is produced by government allocation of resources leads to the predatory entrepreneurship that this chapter has described. The difference between progress and poverty lies in the institutional structure within which people operate.

11 Conclusion

Anyone looking at the state of the world in the twenty-first century should be struck by the remarkable prosperity that nearly everyone in developed nations enjoys. However, it is easy to take that remarkable prosperity for granted because it is so much a part of everyday life for so many people. Even people of modest means (in developed economies) take it for granted that if they are watching television and want a snack, they can just go to get something from the refrigerator, and it is a bit of an aggravation if that particular something the person might want is not in the refrigerator and the person has to get in the car and drive to the store to get it (taking for granted, meanwhile, the television, the refrigerator, the car, and the store with its substantial inventory). Two centuries ago, everyone except for the wealthy had to struggle just to obtain enough calories to survive, and that remains true in less-developed economies today.

The remarkable transformation of the world economy since the beginning of the industrial revolution around 1750 poses a fascinating set of questions. How did it happen that there was so little economic progress for so long – from, perhaps, AD 500 until the 1700s, and then the world economy began the transformation that is still occurring today? While this prosperity and progress is familiar enough to those who live in developed economies for them to take it for granted, the fact that it is not universal, and that some economies that are already poor suffer declining incomes, shows that prosperity and progress are not automatic. The evidence shows that prosperity can be produced. By adopting productive institutions, poor economies have become prosperous, and by abandoning productive institutions, prosperous economies have become poorer. The prosperity of the developed world is fragile enough that it is important to understand its underlying causes so that it can be nurtured. Although many parts of the world have not shared in that prosperity, even in the most developed economies there appears to be limitless potential for further development.

There are two good policy reasons for understanding the underlying phenomena that have generated this prosperity: to try to extend that prosperity to less prosperous places, and to try to continue that economic progress in already prosperous economies. Of these two motivations, the former has received the most attention from economists. Perhaps that is because the issue there is more obvious. It is easy to compare existing less-developed economies with developed economies and to look for ways to try to extend the prosperity of developed economies to those that are lagging behind. It is more difficult to imagine, in a world so prosperous, the changes that can occur over decades or centuries that can make the world even more prosperous. Perhaps because of this, economists have focused on income growth rather than on the qualitative changes that generate prosperity. When comparing developed with less-developed economies, if people in less-developed economies had more income, they could consume more, and if the quantity of output in those economies approached that of developed economies, the standards of living of people in those economies would approach that of people in developed economies. In this comparison of developed and less-developed economies, the focus naturally turns toward how economies can produce more output and generate more income for their citizens. Extending the same idea, people in developed economies could also increase their standards of living if their economies continued to produce more output and generate more income. It is at this point that the analysis of economic growth and economic progress begins to diverge.

Growth versus progress

Chapter 2 considered in detail the differences between progress and growth. Merely to look at increases in the quantity of output, or to look at income growth, ignores the essential qualitative differences in the nature of output that constitute the essence of economic progress. The issue is not simply that to look only at growth leaves out some of the details, but rather that it looks at the wrong thing altogether. Focusing on growth rather than progress is misleading for three reasons. First, much of the increased prosperity that people enjoy comes not from more income, but rather from the ability to consume new goods and services not available before. Second, growth could not occur without progress, so progress is really the phenomenon that must be understood, even if one is interested in income growth more narrowly defined. Third, from a policy perspective, a focus on growth rather than progress points toward policies that at their most benign are not the most effective at increasing prosperity, and often can even be counterproductive. Consider each of these three issues to see their significance.

On the first point, much of Chapter 2 was devoted to describing the aspects of economic progress that go beyond economic growth. The example that opened this chapter, about the individual who drives to the store to buy a snack that was not in the individual's refrigerator illustrates the point well. The main benefits of progress come from the improved quality and variety of goods and services people can consume, not just a greater quantity of the same things. The example of consumer goods represented by the snacks, cars, refrigerators, and televisions will resonate with most readers, but progress in less obvious areas, such as medical technology and health care, financial services, and information technology, are equally remarkable. People are better off not just because their incomes have risen, but because people of average means can now take advantage of things that nobody could have a few decades before.

Goods such as automobiles, microwave ovens, air conditioning, and mobile telephones were first introduced as luxury goods affordable only to very few, but within a few decades of their introduction they were available to the masses. Nobody could watch television broadcasts prior to the 1940s, the interstate highway system began construction in the 1950s, the fist coronary bypass surgery was performed in 1968, and the World Wide Web was introduced on the internet in 1992. These are examples of the qualitative changes that are components of economic progress, and that are not reflected in a simple measure of output growth or income growth.

On the second point, the remarkable growth in output would not be possible without these underlying qualitative changes in output. In the United States, per capita income at the end of the twentieth century was about seven times as high as it was at the beginning. People today would have little use for seven times as much food, seven times as many horses, or seven times as many wood stoves as the typical American had at the beginning of the twentieth century. As a result, there would be little incentive to generate increases in output if the characteristics of output remained unchanged. The qualitative changes in output are what have driven the quantitative changes. While people consumed more food on average at the end of the twentieth century than at the beginning, they did not consume seven times as much. But they consumed a greater variety of food, and they consumed food that was processed and packaged more conveniently. Horses, sailboats, and bicycles, once routine methods of transportation, became recreational goods, replaced by airplanes, automobiles, and motorboats. The average size of homes increased over the twentieth century, but more significantly, homes got electricity, indoor plumbing, and central air conditioning. Innovations like these led to the demand for more output because the new output was qualitatively different from the old output.

Without these qualitative changes in economic output, the quantitative changes would not have occurred, so focusing on the growth in levels of income or output leaves out that dimension of progress that is ultimately responsible for the income growth. The point is not simply that there is more to progress than just income growth – even though that is true – it is that the income growth itself cannot be understood independently of the qualitative changes in output that cause the income growth. This essential aspect of economic progress is not accounted for in the mainstream models that represent economic growth theory, so those models can never fully capture the fundamental causes of income growth.

This leads to the third point. Economic policy designed to foster prosperity has focused on income growth, not progress more generally. The result has been a policy orientation that is not always the most conducive toward the creation of progress and prosperity. Policies that focus on increasing the quantity of output tend to look toward ways of increasing inputs, such as investment and education, and on ways of producing output more efficiently. While these are good things, they overlook the crucial issue of economic progress, which is how policies can foster the innovation that leads to qualitative changes in the economy's output. Those innovations are created through entrepreneurship, so the analysis should focus on entrepreneurship as an economic activity before considering policy more directly.

Innovation, not investment in human and physical capital and technological development, is what drives economic progress. Of course human and physical capital are important to economic progress, as is technological development. From a policy perspective, however, in an innovative and entrepreneurial economy people have the incentive to invest in human and physical capital, and to develop and use technological advances, without any government policy directing or encouraging them. Conversely, as the former Soviet Union and other failed centrally planned economies in the twentieth century showed, government policies that produce investments in human and physical capital and encourage technological advances will not produce prosperity in the absence of an institutional structure that encourages people to act entrepreneurially. To produce prosperity, economic policy must focus on producing an economic environment conducive to entrepreneurship, and the other factors needed for economic progress will be brought forth by market forces.

Entrepreneurship and management

The nature of entrepreneurship was examined in depth in Chapter 3. Entrepreneurship introduces innovations into the economy, which can be new or improved goods or services, or better production processes. Management means implementing a given production process to produce a given output as efficiently as possible. Within the neoclassical theory of the firm that forms the foundation for the neoclassical growth models that dominate the literature in the early twenty-first century, firms are run by managers and there is no room for entrepreneurship. In the real world, good management is not enough, and firms must be entrepreneurial to survive. In an economy characterized by economic progress, firms can get by with mediocre management if they are innovative and entrepreneurial. Entrepreneurship can keep them a step ahead of their rivals. However, a firm that is well-managed and efficient will fall further and further behind its rivals if it is not innovative. Firms cannot succeed in the long run by finding a successful formula and sticking with it, because other firms can imitate a successful formula, but more significantly, because a formula that is successful today will become obsolete in the future as economic progress brings with it changes in both the characteristics of output and innovations in production processes. Entrepreneurship is essential to a firm's success.

Entrepreneurial activities can be broken down into three components that lead to entrepreneurial innovation. First, entrepreneurs can undertake activities like research and development that create an environment that may generate profit opportunities. Second, entrepreneurs can build their stock of knowledge so that when a profit opportunity does appear, they will be in a position to recognize it. Third, there is that elusive characteristic of alertness that enables an entrepreneur to spot what others have not recognized. This third step is the crucial and necessary step – the actual entrepreneurial act – and the first two merely enable the entrepreneur to be in a better position to actually spot a profit opportunity.

The entrepreneurship that is essential to the success of individual firms is also the engine that drives economy-wide economic progress. Firms that are acting entrepreneurially, because they have to in order to survive, introduce new products and new production processes, creating economic progress. Economic growth – the growth in output and income – is a by-product of this economic progress. Because of this, the growth in output and income cannot be fully understood outside of the broader framework of economic progress, and economic progress cannot be understood without understanding the entrepreneurial activities that create it.

Equilibrium and progress

One characteristic of the literature that focuses more on growth than progress, and more on management than entrepreneurship, is that it takes an equilibrium view of the economy. The neoclassical framework is at its foundation a static equilibrium model of the economy, and neoclassical growth theory has added a dynamic element to the neoclassical model while maintaining its equilibrium orientation. The equilibrium orientation of that framework leaves out the entrepreneurial process that drives economic progress.

In neoclassical growth theory, innovations like new goods and new production processes are treated as "shocks" to the economy, as are natural disasters, strikes, and so forth. As such, they are exogenous to the growth process the model is trying to explain. Yet those innovations are the cause of growth. A model that depicts fundamental causes of the process being studied as exogenous to the model will have obvious problems trying to illuminate that process.

The twentieth-century preoccupation with equilibrium in economic models has led economic policies toward correcting inefficiencies rather than toward creating an environment for economic progress. In the end, one can see that this preoccupation with the concept of equilibrium has stood in the way of the operation of the invisible hand. Of course, if resources are allocated inefficiently, there is a potential for improvement, and this potential is the preoccupation of equilibrium economics. If resources are unemployed, they can be put to work to produce more for everybody. If externalities, monopolies, public goods, or other market failures keep resources from being allocated Pareto optimally, policies can be designed to mitigate the market failure, moving the economy closer to Pareto optimality. Equilibrium theories of growth add a time dimension to the process, producing an equilibrium growth path; deviations from that equilibrium growth path are inefficient. While efficiency is a desirable goal, it is apparent that the remarkable economic progress of the past two centuries is not a result of the economy reducing inefficiencies and moving closer to a Pareto optimal allocation of resources. Rather, it is the result of innovations that have produced new goods and improved old ones, and that have enhanced production processes.

The economic engine of entrepreneurship

Entrepreneurial economies generate an environment within which entrepreneurship generates more entrepreneurship. There are several reasons why entrepreneurial actions stimulate additional entrepreneurship. To see why, consider the entrepreneurial role of spotting and acting on an unexploited profit opportunity. In an economy described by neoclassical equilibrium, all profit opportunities have been exploited and there is no innovation. People's economic activities continue as they have in the past. Now imagine an entrepreneur who believes he has spotted an unexploited profit opportunity. While there is the incentive to act on it and reap the profits, the entrepreneur must also recognize the possibility that what at first appears to be a profit opportunity will in fact turn out to produce losses once all the costs and benefits are realized. Entrepreneurship involves taking a risk by doing what has not been done before. Should the entrepreneur take a chance? If this really is a profit opportunity, why has someone not acted on it already? The entrepreneur would have to act in contrast to the experience of others in a non-entrepreneurial environment.

In this example, where the initial assumption was that the economy is in neoclassical equilibrium, by assumption all profit opportunities have already been competed away, and what appears to be a profit opportunity is not, once all the relevant costs are taken into account. In a real-world economy with little entrepreneurial activity being undertaken, the situation may appear to the potential entrepreneur to be like the neoclassical general equilibrium. Nobody else is earning entrepreneurial profits, so the likelihood of this potential entrepreneur spotting one will be slim. The entrepreneur may weigh the risks and not act, even if the profit opportunity is real. Contrast this situation with one in an economy that has a substantial amount of entrepreneurial activity. In an entrepreneurial economy, the potential entrepreneur can see that others are taking entrepreneurial chances and profiting, and the actions of others can provide visible evidence of the potential returns to entrepreneurship. Others are profiting from entrepreneurial actions, demonstrating that profit opportunities exist and encouraging the potential entrepreneur to follow the successful examples of those others.

A related reason that an entrepreneurial economy generates entrepreneurship is that institutions to support entrepreneurship will develop and support entrepreneurial actions. Banks will be accustomed to lending for entrepreneurial ventures and not just to proven businesses, suppliers will be accustomed to dealing with innovative ventures, and equity funding will be more readily available.[1] Also, consumers will be more ready to embrace innovations in output and to deal with new firms in an environment where these things are a part of their routine rather than an unusual occurrence.

While these factors are important, the major reason why entrepreneurship generates more entrepreneurship is that an entrepreneurial innovation by one entrepreneur creates new entrepreneurial opportunities that can be harvested by others. There are more profit opportunities in an entrepreneurial economy, and new opportunities are continually being generated. When famous bank robber

Willie Sutton was asked why he robbed banks, he replied, "Because that's where the money is."[2] Similarly, entrepreneurs gravitate toward more entrepreneurial economies because that's where the profit opportunities are.

That observation holds true for countries, because some countries have legal systems, tax policies, and regulatory environments that are more conducive to entrepreneurship. As Chapter 8 argued, countries that adopt policies that provide better institutional environments will generate more entrepreneurship. The observation also holds for geographic areas and industries independent of government policies. The Silicon Valley area of California illustrates both cases. In that area, there is a concentration of people working in high-tech electronics industries, which allows the fertile interchange of ideas, and even employees. Some things are easier to perceive firsthand; other things are impossible to perceive or convey to others any other way. Austin, Texas, the North Carolina research triangle, and Boston's high-tech corridor are other examples of agglomeration economies that spur entrepreneurship because of geographical proximity. Geographic areas that are entrepreneurial foster more entrepreneurship because entrepreneurial opportunities are more visible to those in close geographic proximity.

Similarly, some industries are more entrepreneurial, and again the electronics industry provides a good example. Innovations by one entrepreneur produce opportunities for others, leading to the hope that if entrepreneurial innovations begin in an industry, that will set the foundation for additional entrepreneurship, leading to more economic progress.[3] There are many examples outside the electronics industry. Innovations and improvements in running shoes by Nike, Reebok, and other companies have opened further entrepreneurial opportunities in athletic wear that have spilled over into fashion; financial services have seen similar rates of entrepreneurial innovation; and the entertainment and vacation industry around Orlando, Florida, is another example where the agglomeration economies are related to both geographical proximity and to a specific industry.

The key point is that for many reasons, entrepreneurship leads to more entrepreneurship, which produces economic progress. To generate prosperity, public policy must therefore focus on creating a fertile environment for entrepreneurship.

Entrepreneurship in a transfer economy

William Baumol has made the insightful observation that people in all societies have similar amounts of entrepreneurial initiative, but in some societies institutions give people the incentive to channel their entrepreneurial activities in a productive way while in others institutions push entrepreneurial individuals toward unproductive and counterproductive activities.[4] Individuals can increase their material well-being in two ways: they can engage in productive activities, or they can enhance their own well-being by taking assets and income from others. As Chapter 8 argued, when institutions protect private property rights, enforce rule of law, and establish low tax and regulatory costs on productive activity, individuals have an incentive to channel their entrepreneurial activities to add value to an economy. By producing valuable output in a market economy, individuals benefit themselves at the same time that they produce benefits that add to the general welfare. Entrepreneurship generates economic progress.

When institutions prevent individuals from reaping the benefits of productive activity, entrepreneurial individuals have an incentive to channel their entrepreneurial proclivities into predatory activities, and increase their well-being by receiving transfers from others. One way to do this, in a society where property rights are poorly protected, is through theft. However, in more developed societies, the same type of activity comes through the actions of government. Governments provide benefits for some at the expense of others in many ways. Most obviously, they can tax some and redistribute the proceeds to others. Regulation can serve the same purpose, by requiring that some individuals incur costs that generate benefits for others.[5] Government activities that result in the transfer resources from some to others redirect entrepreneurship from productive to unproductive activities for two reasons. First, transfers reduce the benefits to productive activities, and so reduce the incentives to productive entrepreneurship. Second, such policies allow individuals to benefit from using government to obtain transfers, creating an incentive for unproductive entrepreneurship. The more actively government undertakes these activities, the greater is the incentive for people to devote their entrepreneurial activities toward the seeking of government transfers rather than production. Such government activities undermine the foundations of economic progress.

The most obvious examples of such policies are direct transfers, where government taxes some to provide benefits for others, but protective tariffs, regulatory barriers to entry, tax breaks, and other policies are often provided to businesses. The mere possibility of such benefits gives entrepreneurs the incentives to rechannel their entrepreneurial efforts away from productive activity toward the seeking of transfers.

Similarly, rule of law, where everybody is treated the same under the law, is crucial to productive rather than predatory entrepreneurship. If some people are favored under the law, it diminishes the incentives for productive entrepreneurship, because the product of a person's efforts can be vulnerable to predation by those who are favored by a corrupt legal system. If people must pay bribes to those favored by a corrupt legal system, or are subject to arbitrary fines or other legal actions, or risk having their resources become the victim of corrupt courts, the incentive for productive activity is reduced. At the same time, entrepreneurial individuals have the incentive to work the system so they are favored by the law and can be recipients of such transfers. Rule of law is essential for productive entrepreneurship, and the absence of rule of law pushes entrepreneurial individuals to become predators rather than producers.

This line of analysis leads to substantial and significant policy implications. Chapter 8 explained the institutional structure that lays the foundation for economic progress. Without an institutional structure conducive to entrepreneurship, other policies intended to generate economic progress will often have counterproductive results. For example, government investment to develop industries is likely to result in industries that will not be competitive on world markets, and will therefore be a continuing drain on a nation's resources that could be used for other purposes. In an entrepreneurial economy, people will have the incentive to invest without government policies to support them – but only if government policies do not hinder them. Similarly, foreign aid to less-developed economies has often been counterproductive, because the money goes to support corrupt governments. Without the aid, governments would have to rely on the productivity of their economies to extract resources, providing some incentive for those governments to foster productive entrepreneurship. Foreign aid has given corrupt governments resources regardless of the productivities of their economies, and has created incentives for predatory government policies because it creates the expectation that foreign aid will continue as long as the economy struggles.

Economic progress requires an institutional structure that provides incentives to productive entrepreneurship, and that does not give people an incentive to substitute predatory for productive activities. Government transfers of resources create perverse incentives. Neoclassical growth theory would encourage such transfers to less-developed economies as a way of increasing human and physical capital, while a more entrepreneurial approach to development policy recognizes the incentive problems that such policies create.

How vulnerable is the modern growth miracle?

This chapter started with the observation that people tend to take for granted the remarkable progress and prosperity enjoyed by modern market economies. One consequence of that attitude is that popular opinion often supports policies that are at odds with the very foundation of the market economy. After the Second World War, Joseph Schumpeter was concerned that people living in market economies had such a low commitment to the institutions of capitalism that they were unwilling to resist the pressures of others more committed to their movement to push the economy toward socialism.[6] It may appear, after the collapse of the Berlin Wall in 1989, that Schumpeter's fears were unfounded, but even though the advocacy of complete socialism has fallen, there is still a widespread support for policies that reduce entrepreneurial incentives and threaten the goose that lays the golden eggs.[7]

While the modern market economy with its massive corporations, its huge capital structure, and its regimented labor relations augmented by government policies, seems solid and enduring, it may be more fragile than is readily recognized. Argentina, among the world's more prosperous nations early in the twentieth century, found itself among the poorer nations by the end of the century. It appears that with the right institutions, economic progress has no limits, but if the incentives for entrepreneurial activity are sufficiently dampened, the world's prosperous economies could stagnate and collapse. The economic progress that underlaid the development of the Roman Empire lasted far longer than the brief 250 years of progress the developed world has experienced since the beginning of the Industrial Revolution, but it came to an end and economic progress slowed to an imperceptible crawl for a thousand years. Then, when conditions were right, the Industrial Revolution began in Britain around 1750 and spread throughout much of the world. Nations that adopted the institutions described in Chapter 8 have prospered, while those that did not have languished and fallen behind.

Those solid market institutions people take for granted today are not very old by the standards of world history, and it may be difficult in the short run to perceive the effects of regulation, progressive taxation, and the transfer economy on entrepreneurship and progress. Would the citizens of East Germany have recognized how their economic system was holding them back had they not been able to compare their situation with that of their brothers in West Germany? With much of the developed world adopting regulatory, tax, and expenditure policies that hinder entrepreneurship, it may be difficult to see how much progress is being sacrificed in the process, or how close the economy is to slowing to the point where progress ends. More than two centuries of unprecedented progress have made people comfortable enough that they do not have a strong commitment to the system that gave them that comfort, and some even argue that we are comfortable enough already.[8] Without an ideological commitment to the system that has generated such prosperity, it is vulnerable to those who argue that the incentives for entrepreneurship should be eviscerated to spread wealth around from those who have it to those who do not.

For the past two centuries, the market economy has proven itself resilient to attack, but it is clear from the experiences of nations that have weakened their institutional structures that unless an institutional structure conducive to entre-preneurship is maintained, progress will cease and perhaps reverse. Experience also suggests that if nations do go too far in their anti-entrepreneurial policies, it will only be apparent in hindsight, perhaps half a century after those policies have been implemented. Remember, up into the 1980s reputable economists were arguing that central economic planning following the model of the Soviet Union was a more productive way to run an economy than to rely on the uncertainties of the market.

Understanding economic progress

Sometimes economic analysis provides insights because it draws conclusions that are surprising and counterintuitive, and therefore enlightening. Other times, economic analysis reaffirms conclusions that accord with common sense. The discussion of economic progress in this volume is not counterintuitive, but it does run counter to some well-established ideas in the mainstream theory of economic growth. It is worth focusing on the differences between this analysis and other analyses of growth, both to gain a better understanding of what produces economic progress and because understanding the fundamentals of economic progress provides insights into the operation of a market economy.

Mainstream economic growth theory focuses on income growth, and this analysis has shown that economic progress, more broadly defined, is what produces income growth. Income growth cannot take place outside of a broader economic progress characterized by improvements in goods and services and improvements in production processes. Progress is the fundamental cause of income growth, so growth cannot be understood outside of this framework of economic progress. Entrepreneurship generates economic progress, but mainstream models of growth theory neglect this entrepreneurial foundation.

Economic analysis at the beginning of the twenty-first century has offered two alternative conceptions of economic growth.[9] One is based on entrepreneurship, as described in this volume. The other is based on inputs into the production process, and technology. The two theories are not necessarily inconsistent, but often the policy implications drawn by analysts are. The entrepreneurial explanation presented here recognizes that growth in output requires enhanced inputs – enhancements to human and physical capital. It also recognizes the importance of technological improvements. But from a policy standpoint, the entrepreneurial explanation for growth suggests that with the right institutional environment, people have an incentive to invest in human and physical capital and to incorporate technological advances in an institutional structure that is conducive to entrepreneurship. Thus, policies should focus on institutions, not inputs.

Similarly, the approach to growth that focuses on inputs and technology readily acknowledges the contribution of entrepreneurship to growth. While the approaches do not conflict in theory, the different focus shifts the policy analysis to the development of inputs and technology, and neglects institutions. The development of inputs and technology without the right institutional structure will not result in economic growth; conversely, the right institutional structure will generate the economic progress that causes economic growth.

Understanding economic progress points toward a broader understanding of economic activity in general. At one time, growth and development were central topics of economic analysis. Indeed, the title of Adam Smith's 1776 masterpiece, *The Wealth of Nations*, shows that Smith was interested in understanding the factors that caused nations to prosper. But throughout most of the twentieth century, the focus of economic analysis was on the properties of economic equilibrium, and growth and development were relegated to the fringe of economic analysis. The focus was on efficiency rather than on prosperity. That began to change toward the end of the twentieth century, and particularly in macroeconomics, growth has again become an integral part of economic analysis. While the analysis in this volume has taken issue with the way that mainstream economics has characterized growth, the characterization of growth as a normal and ongoing part of a market economy is a welcome development.

Because of the way that economic analysis developed in the twentieth century, it often appears that a static equilibrium is a desirable – and normal – state of affairs in a market economy, that economies can be characterized as either developed or less developed, and that the goal of development policy is to turn less-developed economies into developed economies. In fact, economic progress is an integral part of a market economy at all levels of development, and the entrepreneurial activities that generate progress are descriptive of the normal ongoing operation of a market economy.[10] Thus, while the focus of this volume has been on issues of progress and growth, the economic activities described here are the essence of normal operations in a market economy. It is worth noting, then, that the entrepreneurial activities that are essential to understanding the actual operation of the economy are so rarely incorporated into mainstream models of the economy. At the very least, this suggests a promising direction for the further development of economic analysis.

Notes

1 Progress and entrepreneurship

1 Prior to Smith, the mercantilists were interested in this same question and thought that a nation's accumulation of gold and silver increased its wealth; and the physiocrats argued that wealth is the product of the land, and so encouraged agriculture. So the issue was raised before Smith's monumental treatise was published, and one of Smith's motives for writing *The Wealth of Nations* was to try to correct what he perceived as errors on this subject in the views of these earlier economists.

2 Thomas Robert Malthus, *An Essay on Population*. New York: E.P. Dutton, 1914 (orig. 1798).

3 David Ricardo, *The Principles of Political Economy*, third edn. London: J.M. Dent, 1912 (orig. 1821).

4 The language became somewhat more obscure when it became fashionable to refer to less-developed economies as developing economies. Political correctness seems to affect even the language of economic science, and seems to be behind this linguistic change. But many less-developed economies are not developing, and in fact some of the poorest nations in the world have seen decades in which their per capita incomes have fallen. Thus, it seems factually correct to refer to many nations as less developed and not developing.

5 Robert E. Lucas, Jr, "On the Mechanics of Economic Development," *Journal of Monetary Economics*, 22 (1988), pp. 3–42.

6 John Maynard Keynes, *The General Theory of Employment, Interest, and Money*. New York: Harcourt Brace and Company, 1936.

7 Robert M. Solow, "A Contribution to the Theory of Economic Growth," *Quarterly Journal of Economics*, 70 (1956), pp. 65–94.

8 This welfare economics was developed along with the mathematical framework of economics in the mid-twentieth century. See Francis M. Bator, "The Simple Analytics of Welfare Maximization," *American Economic Review*, 67 (1957), pp. 22–59, and J. de V. Graaf, *Theoretical Welfare Economics*. Cambridge: Cambridge University Press, 1957 for expositions of this welfare economics framework.

9 Joseph A. Schumpeter, *The Theory of Economic Development*. Cambridge, MA: Harvard University Press, 1934.

10 Joseph A. Schumpeter, *Business Cycles: A Theoretical, Historical, and Statistical Analysis of the Capitalist Process*. New York: McGraw-Hill, 1939.

11 General equilibrium macro models would incorporate such disruptions as exogenous shocks to the system, and the fact that such shocks are exogenous shows that they are not a part of the process that is incorporated within the model.

12 One distinguished and well-known economist who has devoted considerable attention to entrepreneurship is William J. Baumol, who has written *Entrepreneurship, Management, and the Structure of Payoffs*. Cambridge, MA: MIT Press, 1993 and

The Free-Market Innovation Machine: Analyzing the Growth Miracle of Capitalism. Princeton, NJ: Princeton University Press, 2002, among other works, on the subject.

13 See, for examples, Lucas, "On the Mechanics of Economic Development," cited earlier, and Paul M. Romer, "Increasing Returns and Long-Run Growth," *Journal of Political Economy*, 94 (1986), pp. 1002–1037, which laid the foundation for this literature. This literature has become less fashionable in the twenty-first century, perhaps because it was unable to make much headway into understanding the underlying causes of economic growth.

14 C.E. Ferguson, *Microeconomic Theory*, rev. edn. Homewood, IL: Richard D. Irwin, 1969.

15 Hal R. Varian, *Intermediate Microeconomics: A Modern Approach*, sixth edn. New York: W.W. Norton, 2003, and David Besanko and Ronald R. Braeutigam, *Microeconomics*, second edn. Hoboken, NJ: John Wiley & Sons, 2005.

16 Carl Shapiro and Hal R. Varian, *Information Rules: A Strategic Guide to the Network Economy*. Boston, MA: Harvard Business School Press, 1999.

17 David Besanko, David Dranove, Mark Shanley, and Scott Schaefer, *Economics of Strategy*, third edn. Hoboken, NJ: John Wiley & Sons, 2004.

18 The use of simplifying assumptions in models, and a more detailed discussion of maps as models, is found in Randall G. Holcombe, *Economic Models and Methodology*. New York: Greenwood, 1989.

2 Growth versus progress

1 See Oded Galor and David N. Weil, "Population, Technology, and Growth: From Malthusian Stagnation to the Demographic Transition and Beyond," *American Economic Review*, 90, No. 4 (September 2000), p. 808, for estimates that per capita economic growth began only after 1500, and was very modest until about 1820.

2 This comment is not meant in any way to minimize the problems associated with poverty in the United States. Rather, it is meant to illustrate that despite the real problems associated with poverty, some problems that have chronically been associated with poverty – like hunger – have all but disappeared as a result of economic progress.

3 See Robert L. Heilbroner, *The Economic Problem*, second edn. Englewood Cliffs, NJ: Prentice-Hall, 1970, for a persuasive discussion about the importance of the development of factor markets in the industrial revolution. David S. Landes, *The Wealth and Poverty of Nations: Why Some Are So Rich and Some So Poor*. New York: W.W. Norton, 1998, also takes an interesting look at the institutional foundations of modern prosperity.

4 This conjecture about future progress is based on the idea that entrepreneurial actions generate additional entrepreneurial opportunities, as described in Randall G. Holcombe, "Entrepreneurship and Economic Growth," *Quarterly Review of Austrian Economics*, 1, No. 2 (Summer 1998), pp. 45–62. There is the threat that a growing government could stifle economic growth. For an analysis of this issue, see Sanford Ikeda, *Dynamics of the Mixed Economy: Toward a Theory of Interventionism*. London: Routledge, 1997.

5 Data in this and the following paragraphs are from Stephen Moore and Julian L. Simon, "The Greatest Century That Ever Was: 25 Miraculous Trends of the Past 100 Years," Cato Institute Policy Analysis no. 364 (December 15, 1999), p. 6. See also W. Michael Cox and Richard Alm, *The Right Stuff: America's Move to Mass Customization*, Annual Report, Federal Reserve Bank of Dallas, 1998, and Cox and Alm, *Myths of Rich and Poor: Why We're Better Off Than We Think*. New York: Basic Books, 1999, who show measures of economic progress beyond just income growth.

6 For a discussion, see Holcombe, "Entrepreneurship and Economic Growth," pp. 45–62.

7 D. Gale Johnson, "Population, Food, and Knowledge," *American Economic Review*, 90, No. 1 (March 2000), pp. 1–14, gives a good account of the progress made in

agriculture over a period of centuries, but still couches economic progress in terms of increases in per capita income rather than changes in the types of goods produced and consumed. Similarly, Galor and Weil, "Population, Technology, and Growth," pp. 806–828, discuss the substantial economic progress after 1700 made possible by technological innovation, but depict that progress as income growth rather than qualitative changes in output. Both of these articles appeared in the *American Economic Review*, typically considered the top academic economics journal, suggesting mainstream economic thinking on the topic.

8 Moore and Simon, "The Greatest Century That Ever Was," p. 6.
9 Cox and Alm, *Myths of Rich and Poor*, p. 15.
10 Cox and Alm, *The Right Stuff*, p. 12.
11 This is the opening sentence of Adam Smith's *An Inquiry into the Nature and Causes of the Wealth of Nations*. New York: Random House, Modern Library, 1937, originally published in 1776.
12 Smith, *The Wealth of Nations*, p. 4.
13 Pin factories at the beginning of the twenty-first century are highly automated, with each worker overseeing six to eight machines that turn out 50,000 straight pins per minute!
14 Smith, *The Wealth of Nations*, p. 9.
15 Friedrich A. Hayek, "The Use of Knowledge in Society," *American Economic Review*, 35 (1945), pp. 519–530.
16 This is a key feature of the analysis in Baumol, *The Free-Market Innovation Machine*.
17 See Heilbroner, *The Economic Problem*, pp. 48–71, for an insightful discussion of the emergence of market society.
18 It is interesting to note the increasing tendency of modern governments to reinstate some of those obligations to employees on employers. Governments want employers to extend health care benefits, maternity leave, pay and hours of work conditions, and many workplace amenities to employees, complicating the exchange of labor for wages and imposing additional costs on employers.
19 Landes, *The Wealth and Poverty of Nations*, notes the importance of these cultural, and especially institutional, conditions to set the stage for increasing wealth.
20 Scientific progress in Britain also began around this time. Isaac Newton (1643–1727) was a professor at Cambridge, for example. But the scientific advances in Britain produced knowledge that was available outside Britain, and one could argue that the cultural and institutional factors that laid the foundation for economic progress also provided a foundation for scientific inquiry.
21 These seemingly minor innovations and their contributions to economic progress are noted by Landes, *The Wealth and Poverty of Nations*.
22 But agricultural productivity grew for the same reasons manufacturing productivity did: changes in production methods that were the result of entrepreneurial insight. See Johnson, "Population, Food, and Knowledge," cited earlier.
23 Joel Mokyr, *The Gifts of Athena: Historical Origins of the Knowledge Economy*. Princeton, NJ: Princeton University Press, 2002, p. 31.
24 *The Gifts of Athena*, p. 31.
25 Mokyr, *The Gifts of Athena*, p. 278. See Mancur Olson's *The Rise and Decline of Nations*. New Haven, CT: Yale University Press, 1982 for a development of this idea.
26 Joseph A. Schumpeter, *Capitalism, Socialism, and Democracy* second edn. London: George Allen & Unwin, 1947; see, for example, p. 143.
27 See Ricardo, *The Principles of Political Economy*.
28 See Malthus, *An Essay on Population*, for his ideas. Malthus's original ideas predated Ricardo's and inspired Ricardo. The two were good friends and had a lengthy correspondence over these issues. Although they did not agree on everything, they did share this view that in the face of limited resources, population growth would keep most people's incomes at the subsistence level.

29 As one observer has said, "When the only tool you have is a hammer, everything looks like a nail." The economics profession's approach to economic growth reminds one of the old joke about the man who is standing under a streetlight looking for his keys when another man offers to help him. "Where did you drop them," the helper asks. "Across the street," the man answers. "Then why are you looking here?" "The light is better." This book heads where the light is not as good, but where the answer is more likely to be found.

30 This model is introduced in Solow, "A Contribution to the Theory of Economic Growth," pp. 65–94.

31 Robert J. Barro and Xavier Sala-i-Martin, *Economic Growth*. New York: McGraw-Hill, 1995, give a good exposition of the ways that the Solow model has been developed, and the implications that have arisen from the model. Barro and Sala-i-Martin use a slightly different variant of the production function given here to depict the Solow model, allowing time to enter explicitly, so $Q(t) = f[K(t), L(t)]$. The implications remain the same regardless of some variation in the mathematical formulation.

32 Danny T. Quah, "Convergence Empirics Across Economies with (Some) Capital Mobility," *Journal of Economic Growth*, 1, No. 1 (March 1996), pp. 95–124, presents empirical evidence showing that national incomes are becoming bimodal, with some nations converging at high levels of income while others stagnate at low levels. Quah suggests, based on the evidence, that under the right conditions nations can converge as the Solow model suggests, but that low-income nations do not exhibit the right conditions.

33 Of course, in the general functional form, dividing by L may not eliminate it from the right side of the equation, but it would eliminate population growth per se as a factor in income growth.

34 Anne O. Krueger, *The Political Economy of Policy Reform in Developing Countries*. Cambridge, MA: MIT Press, 1993.

35 Larry E. Jones and Rodolfo Manuelli, "A Convex Model of Equilibrium Growth: Theory and Policy Implications," *Journal of Political Economy*, 98, No. 5, Part 1 (October 1990), pp. 1008–1038.

36 Lucas, "On the Mechanics of Economic Development," pp. 3–42.

37 Allyn, Young, "Increasing Returns and Economic Progress," *Economic Journal*, 38 (December 1928), pp. 527–542.

38 Nicholas, Kaldor, "The Irrelevance of Equilibrium Economics," *Economic Journal*, 82 (December 1972), pp. 1237–1255.

39 Romer, "Increasing Returns and Long-Run Growth," pp. 1002–1037, looks at increasing returns, and human capital is featured in his "Endogenous Technological Change," *Journal of Political Economy*, 98, No. 5, Part 2 (October 1990) pp. S71–S102.

40 Oliver Jean Blanchard and Stanley Fischer, *Lectures on Macroeconomics*. Cambridge, MA: MIT Press, 1989, pp. 1–2.

3 Entrepreneurship versus management

1 Israel M. Kirzner, *Competition and Entrepreneurship*. Chicago, IL: University of Chicago Press, 1973.

2 See, however, Baumol, *The Free-Market Innovation Machine*, who argues that innovation is increasingly becoming a routine part of the production process.

3 This idea is explained in Armen A. Alchian and Harold Demsetz, "Production, Information Costs, and Economic Organization," *American Economic Review*, 62 (1972), pp. 777–795.

4 These contrasting theories of firm activities are discussed in Donald J. Boudreaux and Randall G. Holcombe, "The Coasian and Knightian Theories of the Firm," *Managerial and Decision Economics*, 10 (1989), pp. 147–154.

5 Hayek, "The Use of Knowledge in Society," pp. 519–530.

6 See Randall G. Holcombe, "Information, Entrepreneurship, and Economic Progress," in Roger Koppl, ed., *Advances in Austrian Economics: Austrian Economics and Entrepreneurial Studies*, vol. 6. Amsterdam: JAI, 2003, pp. 173–195.

7 Pierre Desrochers, "Geographical Proximity and the Transmission of Tacit Knowledge," *Review of Austrian Economics*, 14, No. 1 (2001), pp. 25–46.

8 See Richard L. Collins, "On Top," *Flying*, 129, No. 7 (July 2002), pp. 20–27.

9 Smith, *The Wealth of Nations*, p. 9.

10 Clayton M. Christensen, *The Innovator's Dilemma*. Boston, MA: Harvard Business School Press, 1997.

11 Schumpeter describes his entrepreneurial theory of growth in *The Theory of Economic Development*, and introduces the term "creative destruction" in *Capitalism, Socialism, and Democracy*.

12 Kirzner, *Competition and Entrepreneurship*, and Baumol, *The Free-Market Innovation Machine*, both cited earlier. Romer, "Endogenous Technological Change," pp. S71–S102, is another example of innovation being depicted as a result of profit-maximizing investment decisions rather than entrepreneurship. While Baumol does refer to entrepreneurship, Romer never even mentions the term.

13 Schumpeter, *The Theory of Economic Development*, cited earlier.

14 David A. Harper, *Entrepreneurship and the Market Process: An Enquiry into the Growth of Knowledge*. London and New York: Routledge, 1996, discusses entrepreneurial activity within a growth-of-knowledge framework and recognizes that entrepreneurs create an environment within which entrepreneurial discoveries are more likely.

15 Desrochers, "Geographical Proximity and the Transmission of Tacit Knowledge," cited earlier.

16 Holcombe, "Entrepreneurship and Economic Growth," pp. 45–62.

17 Frank H. Knight, *Risk, Uncertainty, and Profit*. New York: Harper & Row, 1965 (orig. 1921).

18 Israel M. Kirzner, *The Meaning of Market Process*. London and New York: Routledge, 1992, pp. 39–42.

19 These differences are discussed in Randall G. Holcombe, "Progress and Entrepreneurship," *Quarterly Journal of Austrian Economics*, 6, No. 3 (Fall 2003), pp. 3–26.

20 Cox and Alm, *The Right Stuff*. See, in particular, p. 4.

21 This in itself is desirable, because it allows people to better find goods and services that satisfy their own particular desires rather than having to accept a product that is aimed at the middle of the market.

22 The standard theory does allow for a "normal profit," which is just sufficient to keep the business from leaving the market, but this is a return to a factor of production, not profit as the term is ordinarily used. See Bator, "The Simple Analytics of Welfare Maximization," pp. 22–59 and Graaf, *Theoretical Welfare Economics* for expositions of the competitive outcome as a benchmark for efficiency.

23 This assumes a competitive general equilibrium. It is possible that some firms would have monopoly power in equilibrium, allowing for monopoly profit, but this profit would not serve the same role as profits in a market process view, because the profits would remain permanently as a part of the equilibrium condition.

24 For a critique of government policy toward monopoly, which is based on an equilibrium approach to markets, see Dominick T. Armentano, *The Myths of Antitrust: Economic Theory and Legal Cases*. New Rochelle, NY: Arlington House, 1972, *Antitrust and Monopoly: Anatomy of a Policy Failure*. New York: Wiley, 1982, and *Antitrust Policy: The Case for Repeal*. Washington, DC: Cato Institute, 1986.

25 This methodological issue was discussed in more detail in Chapter 1. Holcombe, *Economic Models and Methodology*, notes that all models are built on simplifying assumptions, and that simplifying assumptions are a virtue because they enable people

to see the essential features of a process by assuming away irrelevant or unimportant features. However, there is a danger that some things may be assumed away that are essential for understanding the issue at hand, in which case the model will be misleading. This is the case with growth theory at the beginning of the twenty-first century.

26 Pareto optimality could be redefined so that it means that nobody's lifetime welfare could be increased without reducing someone else's, but this would really be a different concept. To see this, consider the conclusion that monopolies allocate resources suboptimally as Pareto optimality is applied. If monopoly profits are the result of entrepreneurial activity, those profits are the reward that produces progress, not a deadweight loss as they are represented to be in the Paretian framework.

27 Murray N. Rothbard, "Toward a Reconstruction of Utility and Welfare Economics," in Mary Sennholz, ed., *On Freedom and Free Enterprise: Essays in Honor of Ludwig von Mises*. Princeton, NJ: Van Nostrand, 1956, pp. 224–262, offers a different and more general critique of neoclassical welfare economics.

28 Examples from a public policy standpoint include antitrust policy, laws that dictate product standards and specifications, and product quality laws such as those set by the Food and Drug Administration. All of these types of regulations are designed to make the allocation of resources more closely approximate a Pareto optimal allocation.

4 Equilibrium versus the invisible hand

1 Alfred Marshall, *Principles of Economics*. London: Macmillan, 1890. The works in which the widely acknowledged co-discoverers of the concept of marginal utility presented their ideas are Carl Menger, *Principles of Economics*. New York: New York University Press, 1976 (orig. 1871), William Stanley Jevons, *The Theory of Political Economy*, fourth edn. London: Macmillan, 1931 (first edn. 1871), and Leon Walras, *Elements of Pure Economics; or The Theory of Social Wealth*. Homewood, IL: R.D. Irwin, 1954 (orig. 1874).

2 Keynes, *The General Theory of Employment, Interest, and Money*.

3 Bator, "The Simple Analytics of Welfare Maximization," pp. 22–59, and Graaf, *Theoretical Welfare Economics*, give good expositions of the welfare economics framework upon which a theory of market failure was developed.

4 Solow, "A Contribution to the Theory of Economic Growth," pp. 65–94.

5 Ludwig von Mises, *Human Action*, third rev. edn. Chicago, IL: Henry Regnery Company, 1966, and Murray N. Rothbard, *Man, Economy, and State*. Los Angeles, CA: Nash, 1962. Ludwig von Mises, "Monopoly Prices," *Quarterly Journal of Austrian Economics*, 1 (1998), p. 13, says, "...the state of equilibrium is a hypothetical concept only, although a concept indispensable for every economic analysis."

6 See Kaldor, "The Irrelevance of Equilibrium Economics," pp. 1237–1255, for a critique of equilibrium economics along similar lines. Kaldor develops his argument from Young, "Increasing Returns and Economic Progress," pp. 527–542, who in turn finds his inspiration in Smith's *The Wealth of Nations*.

7 Ferguson, *Microeconomic Theory*, pp. 226–227. Ferguson's book is a good presentation of neoclassical microeconomics, and the neoclassical model as described in this chapter conforms with Ferguson's depiction. As noted in Chapter 1, there is a close correspondence between the microeconomic theory Ferguson presented and what appears in contemporary microeconomics books.

8 "Consumers, producers, and resource owners must possess perfect knowledge if a market is to be perfectly competitive." Ferguson, *Microeconomic Theory*, p. 224.

9 Of course, this means that immediate action must be possible, which is where the assumption of perfect mobility of resources comes into play. "A third precondition for perfect competition is that *all* resources are perfectly mobile." Ferguson, *Microeconomic Theory*, p. 224.

10 Following Milton Friedman, "The Methodology of Positive Economics," Chapter 1 in *Essays in Positive Economics*. Chicago, IL: University of Chicago Press, 1953, however, one might argue that the assumptions of a model should be tested by the model's predictions, not by casual observation. Pursuing that argument would lead the chapter off track, but the argument is critiqued in Holcombe, *Economic Models and Methodology*, ch. 5.

11 See the following section for quotations from each of these authors that express this view.

12 Joseph E. Stiglitz, "The Causes and Consequences of the Dependence of Quality on Price," *Journal of Economic Literature*, 25 (1987), pp. 1–48.

13 Israel Kirzner, *Perception, Opportunity, and Profit: Studies in the Theory of Entrepreneurship*. Chicago, IL: University of Chicago Press, 1979, p. 110.

14 Joseph E. Stiglitz, *Whither Socialism?* Cambridge: MIT Press, 1994, notes that in his previous work he has emphasized information problems that interfere with efficient allocation, suggesting that he would want to retain the possibility of imperfect information when discussing market equilibrium.

15 Harper, *Entrepreneurship and the Market Process*.

16 Prior to his work on entrepreneurship, Israel M. Kirzner, *Market Theory and the Price System*. Princeton, NJ: Van Nostrand, 1963, p. 258n, states "From this point of view a market system might be described as always in a state of disequilibrium, with respect to the infinity of knowledge that is beyond human reach." If one considers unobserved profit opportunities to be beyond human reach (until they are observed), this further reinforces the idea that a steady-state evenly rotating economy (to use Mises' phrase) would not be in equilibrium as Kirzner defines it when there are unnoticed profit opportunities.

17 Hayek, "The Use of Knowledge in Society," pp. 519–530.

18 An earlier note addresses Stiglitz's views, and Peter Lewin, "Hayekian Equilibrium and Change," *Journal of Economic Methodology*, 4: 245–266 (1997), argues that this is what Hayek means by equilibrium, and gives an insightful analysis of the concept. In addition to Kirzner's published work (see the previous note, for example), personal correspondence with Professor Kirzner confirms that this is Kirzner's vision of equilibrium.

19 These characterizations are from Kirzner's *Competition and Entrepreneurship* and Schumpeter's *The Theory of Economic Development*. In later work, Kirzner's views appear more consistent with Schumpeter's.

20 Friedrich A. Hayek, "Economics and Knowledge," in Friedrich A. Hayek, *Individualism and Economic Order*. London: Routledge & Kegan Paul, 1949, p. 41.

21 Frank A. Hahn, *Equilibrium and Macroeconomics*. Cambridge, MA: MIT Press, 1984, p. 44.

22 Lewin, "Hayekian Equilibrium and Change," p. 245.

23 Mises, *Human Action*, and Rothbard, *Man, Economy, and State*, both cited earlier.

24 Kirzner, *The Meaning of Market Process*, p. 169.

25 Holcombe, "Entrepreneurship and Economic Growth," pp. 45–62.

26 A caveat must be added. If entrepreneurial acts themselves generate more profit opportunities, it could be that the act of eliminating one profit opportunity creates many more, as discussed in Holcombe, "Entrepreneurship and Economic Growth." Even here, however, one might reply that all the later profit opportunities were always lying in wait, contingent upon someone acting upon the first opportunity.

27 This is recognized in the new classical macroeconomics in which model economies always remain in general equilibrium by assumption.

28 Ronald H. Coase, "The Nature of the Firm," *Economica*, 4 (1937), pp. 386–405, and Alchian and Demsetz, "Production, Information Costs, and Economic Organization," pp. 777–795, provide examples of this type of management in economic models.

29 Henry George, *Progress and Poverty: An Inquiry into the Cause of Industrial Depressions, and of Increase of Want with Increase of Wealth – The Remedy*. London: Kegan Paul, Trench, 1889.

30 Paul A. Samuelson and Robert M. Solow "Analytical Aspects of Antiinflation Policy," *American Economic Review*, 50 (1960), pp. 177–194, is a clear statement of this Keynesian approach by two Nobel laureates in economics.

31 For examples, see Romer, "Endogenous Technological Change," pp. S71–S102; Romer, "Increasing Returns and Long-Run Growth," pp. 1002–1037, and Lucas, "On the Mechanics of Economic Development," pp. 3–42.

32 Romer, "Endogenous Technological Change."

33 For a dissenting view, see Baumol, *The Free-Market Innovation Machine*.

34 Krueger, *The Political Economy of Policy Reform in Developing Countries*.

35 See, for examples, Gerald W. Scully, "The Institutional Framework and Economic Development," *Journal of Political Economy*, 96 (1988), pp. 652–662, Robert J. Barro, "Democracy and Growth," *Journal of Economic Growth*, 1 (1996), pp. 1–27, Steve Knack, "Institutions and the Convergence Hypothesis: The Cross-National Evidence," *Public Choice*, 87, Nos. 3–4 (June 1996), pp. 207–228, James Gwartney and Robert Lawson, *Economic Freedom of the World: 1997 Report*. Vancouver, BC: Faser Institute, 1997, and Mancur Olson, *Power and Prosperity: Outgrowing Communist and Capitalist Dictatorships*. New York: Basic Books, 2000.

36 Armentano, *The Myths of Antitrust, Antitrust and Monopoly*, and *Antitrust Policy*, offers insightful criticism and policy analysis on these issues.

37 See Ferguson, *Microeconomic Theory*, ch. 10, for an explanation.

38 See Harper, *Entrepreneurship and the Market Process*.

5 Entrepreneurship and knowledge

1 Baumol, *Entrepreneurship, Management, and the Structure of Payoffs*, p. 15, italics in the original.

2 Baumol, *The Free-Market Innovation Machine*, conjectures that most of the advance in market economies is due to this routinized innovation that falls under the heading of management, as opposed to entrepreneurial acts.

3 Kirzner, *Competition and Entrepreneurship*.

4 This idea about specific knowledge of time and place is found in Hayek, "The Use of Knowledge in Society," pp. 519–530.

5 Peter J. Boettke, "Information and Knowledge: Austrian Economics in Search of its Uniqueness," *Review of Austrian Economics*, 15 (2002), pp. 263–274.

6 Boettke, "Information and Knowledge," p. 268.

7 Boettke, "Information and Knowledge," p. 269.

8 Kirzner, *Competition and Entrepreneurship*, p. 67, emphasis in original.

9 This is a key idea in James M. Buchanan, *Cost and Choice: An Inquiry in Economic Theory*. Chicago, IL: Markham, 1969.

10 I do not know the origin of this slogan, but first saw it painted on the wall of the football locker room at my high school. At the time, it appeared to apply to winning sports contests, and with each passing decade it seems to me more generally applicable to all aspects of life.

11 See Christensen, *The Innovator's Dilemma* for many examples of this idea.

12 Schumpeter, *The Theory of Economic Development*.

13 Xerox did try to market products based on their graphical user interface, but none that succeeded in earning them profits.

14 See Christensen, *The Innovator's Dilemma*.

15 Schumpeter, *The Theory of Economic Development*, p. 154.

16 This type of economy is described by Robert L. Heilbroner, *The Making of Economic Society*. New York: Prentice-Hall, 1962.

17 See Mancur, Olson, Jr, "Big Bills Left on the Sidewalk: Why Some Nations are Rich, Others Poor," *Journal of Economic Perspectives*, 10, No. 2 (Spring 1996), pp. 3–24, for an interesting analysis of this example.

18 Alwyn Young, "Invention and Bounded Learning by Doing," *Journal of Political Economy*, 101, No. 3 (June 1993), pp. 443–472, develops a model along these lines. Joel Mokyr, *The Lever of Riches*. Oxford: Oxford University Press, 1990 classifies technological advances as "macroinventions" and "microinventions." The idea is that major inventions like the steam engine and the microprocessor create entrepreneurial opportunities for microinventions that further drive economic growth.

19 See Eugen von Bohm-Bawerk, *Capital and Interest*, 3 vols. Spring Hills, PA: Libertarian Press, 1959, orig. 1884, 1889, 1909.

20 See, especially, the first few pages of Adam Smith's *The Wealth of Nations*.

21 Young, "Increasing Returns and Economic Progress," pp. 527–542, and Kaldor, "The Irrelevance of Equilibrium Economics," pp. 1237–1255.

22 W. Brian Arthur, "Competing Technologies, Increasing Returns, and Lock-In by Historical Events," *Economic Journal*, 99 (March 1989), pp. 116–131, presents a model showing how increasing returns can lock an economy into an inferior technology. Perhaps the most famous (but questionable) example is related by Paul A. David, "Clio and the Economics of QWERTY," *American Economic Review*, 75, No. 2 (May 1985), pp. 332–337. See also Paul A. David, *Technical Choice, Innovation, and Economic Growth*. Cambridge: Cambridge University Press, 1975, for a clear recognition of the importance of increasing returns to economic progress.

23 Romer, "Endogenous Technological Change," pp. S71–S102, and "Increasing Returns and Long-Run Growth," pp. 1002–1037

24 Paul Krugman, "Increasing Returns and Economic Geography," *Journal of Political Economy*, 99, No. 3 (June 1991), pp. 483–499, and David B. Audretsch and Maryann P. Feldman, "R&D Spillovers and the Geography of Innovation and Production," *American Economic Review*, 86, No. 3 (June 1996), pp. 630–640.

25 Desrochers, "Geographical Proximity and the Transmission of Tacit Knowledge," pp. 25–46, building on the ideas of Hayek, "The Use of Knowledge in Society."

26 This section draws on Hayek's "The Use of Knowledge in Society," cited earlier.

27 Hayek, "The Use of Knowledge in Society," p. 528.

28 For a discussion of their discovery and attempts to patent and develop it, see Lane Wallace, "December 18, 1903: The Morning and Era After," *Flying*, 130, No. 12 (December 2003), pp. 64–68.

29 In 2003 the Experimental Aircraft Association built a replica of the original Wright flyer and attempted to recreate the Wright brothers' first flight a century after their flight at the exact same location in North Carolina. Despite the accumulation of 100 years of knowledge about the technical aspects of flight, they were unable to get their replica to fly. While the weather conditions were not as favorable on the day of the recreation of that first flight, one wonders whether, if the Wright brothers could have been brought back, their specific knowledge of time and place would have enabled them to have flown the aircraft.

30 Michael R. Darby and Lynne G. Zucker, "Growing by Leaps and Inches: Creative Destruction, Real Cost Reduction, and Inching Up," *Economic Inquiry*, 41, No. 1 (January 2003), p. 11.

6 The origins of entrepreneurial opportunities

1 While equilibrium models do dominate economics, there has been an increased interest in institutions and market processes in the last decades of the twentieth century. For an interesting discussion and taxonomy, see Oliver E. Williamson, "A Comparison of Alternative Approaches to Economic Methodology," *Journal of Institutional and Theoretical Economics*, 146, No. 1 (1990), pp. 61–71.

2 This taxonomy comes from Randall G. Holcombe, "The Origins of Entrepreneurial Opportunities," *Review of Austrian Economics*, 16, No. 1 (2003), pp. 25–43.

3 George J. Stigler and Gary S. Becker, "De Gustibus Non Est Desputandum," *American Economic Review*, 67, No. 2 (1977): 76–90, question any economic analysis that is based on preference changes, and with good reason, because what appear to be preference changes are likely to be a response to changes in the environment, relative prices, wealth, or some other observable factor.

4 Kirzner, *Competition and Entrepreneurship*, pp. 72–75.

5 Kirzner, *Competition and Entrepreneurship*, pp. 72–73, emphasis in original.

6 Kirzner, *Competition and Entrepreneurship*, p. 73, emphasis in original.

7 Kirzner, *Competition and Entrepreneurship*, pp. 73–74. Kirzner argues in chapter 7 that there are important differences between his and Schumpeter's ideas. In *Discovery and the Capitalist Process*, ch. 4, however, Kirzner develops the idea of entrepreneurship in a manner that encompasses the spirit of Schumpeter's ideas, and their ideas on entrepreneurship clearly can be reconciled.

8 Lewin, "Hayekian Equilibrium and Change," pp. 245–266, discusses change within the context of economic equilibrium, and explores the notion that equilibrium can be defined as a situation in which everybody's plans are compatible.

9 G.B. Richardson, "Adam Smith on Competition and Increasing Returns," in Andrew S. Skinner and Thomas Wilson, eds, *Essays on Adam Smith*. Oxford: Clarendon Press, 1975, p. 351. Young, "Increasing Returns and Economic Progress," pp. 527–542, and Kaldor, "The Irrelevance of Equilibrium Economics," pp. 1237–1255, also emphasize Smith's principle of the division of labor as an important and underappreciated engine of economic progress.

10 Originally introduced into the market as Palm Pilots, the Palm handheld computers are no longer called Pilots because of a lawsuit brought by the Pilot Pen Corporation.

11 The Palm Pilot was developed by the 3Com Corporation, which later spun Palm off into a separate company.

12 Olson, "Big Bills Left on the Sidewalk," pp. 3–24.

13 William Bygrave and Maria Minniti, "The Social Dynamics of Entrepreneurship," *Entrepreneurship: Theory and Practice*, 24, No. 3 (2000), pp. 25–36, depict entrepreneurship this way.

14 For an analysis of such factors in the mainstream literature, see, Krugman, "Increasing Returns and Economic Geography," pp. 483–499.

15 Kirzner, *Competition and Entrepreneurship*, is the work in which he is most critical with Schumpeter, and in which his ideas are most at odds with Schumpeter's.

16 Ferguson, *Microeconomic Theory*, a good reference for the neoclassical framework, outlines the assumptions for the competitive model, saying on page 224, "Consumers, producers, and resource owners must possess perfect knowledge if a market is to be perfectly competitive." There is some ambiguity here, because Ferguson appears to be using the term knowledge to refer to information (as the terms were used in the previous chapter), and is suggesting that competition requires that any information known by some people must be known to everyone. Knowledge might also refer to the expertise that allows some people to gain from information that is available to all. This section uses this broader concept of knowledge.

17 Lucas, "On the Mechanics of Economic Development," pp. 3–42, and Romer, "Endogenous Technological Change," pp. S71–S102.

18 See Baumol, *The Free-Market Innovation Machine* for an explanation of this view.

19 Kirzner, *Competition and Entrepreneurship*.

20 Harper, *Entrepreneurship and the Market Process*.

7 Markets, entrepreneurship, and progress

1 Smith, *The Wealth of Nations*, p. 423.

2 Smith, *The Wealth of Nations*, pp. 4–5.

3 Kirzner, *Competition and Entrepreneurship*, pp. 72–73, emphasis in original.

4 Kirzner, *Competition and Entrepreneurship*, p. 73, emphasis in original.

5 Kirzner, *Competition and Entrepreneurship*, pp. 73–74.

6 Kirzner, *Competition and Entrepreneurship*, p. 71, emphasis in original.

7 Israel M. Kirzner, *Perception, Opportunity, and Profit: Studies in the Theory of Entrepreneurship*. Chicago, IL: University of Chicago Press, 1979, ch. 7, argues that there are important differences between his and Schumpeter's ideas, and takes Schumpeter to task for not discussing the equilibrating role of entrepreneurship. Elsewhere, however, Kirzner, *Discovery and the Capitalist Process*, ch. 4, develops the idea of entrepreneurship in a manner that encompasses the spirit of Schumpeter's ideas, and in private correspondence Kirzner has told me that he believes Schumpeter's ideas on entrepreneurship are important, and that they can be reconciled with his ideas.

8 Young, "Invention and Bounded Learning by Doing," pp. 443–472, develops a model along these lines. Mokyr, *The Lever of Riches*, classifies technological advances as "macroinventions" and "microinventions." The idea is that major inventions like the steam engine and the microprocessor create entrepreneurial opportunities for microinventions that further drive economic growth. See also Maria Minniti, "Entrepreneurship and Economic Growth," *Global Business and Economic Review*, 11, No. 1 (1999), pp. 31–42.

9 Schumpeter, *The Theory of Economic Development*, p. 63, discusses the revolutionary nature of economic growth, and later (p. 65) describes the motive forces as "spontaneous and discontinuous."

10 Kirzner would include only the discovery of the unnoticed opportunity as entrepreneurial, with the follow-up as an employment of other factors of production, but the key idea remains that Kirzner's and Schumpeter's entrepreneurs are doing the same thing – going after a profit opportunity.

11 Recall from Chapter 4 that a Hayekian equilibrium may be a disequilibrium situation as Kirzner describes it, but that is unimportant for present purposes.

12 The classic work from this period is Wesley C. Mitchell, *Business Cycles*. Berkley, CA: University of California Press, 1913.

13 Ludwig von Mises, *The Theory of Money and Credit*. New Haven, CT: Yale University Press, 1953 (orig. in German, 1912).

14 See, for examples, Freidrich A. Hayek, *Monetary Theory and the Trade Cycle*. New York: Augustus M. Kelley, 1966 (orig. 1933), and *Prices and Production*, second edn. New York: Augustus M. Kelley, 1935.

15 Roger W. Garrison, *Time and Money: The Macroeconomics of Capital Structure*, London: Routledge, 2001.

16 Schumpeter, *Business Cycles: A Theoretical, Historical, and Statistical Analysis of the Capitalist Process*.

17 Keynes, *The General Theory of Employment, Interest, and Money*.

18 A seminal article in this literature is Robert E. Lucas, Jr, "An Equilibrium Model of the Business Cycle," *Journal of Political Economy*, 83, No. 6 (December 1975), pp. 1113–1144.

19 Solow, "A Contribution to the Theory of Economic Growth," pp. 65–94.

20 Krueger, *The Political Economy of Policy Reform in Developing Countries*.

21 Paul A. Samuelson, *Economics*, ninth edn. New York: McGraw-Hill, 1973, p. 883.

22 Bohm-Bawerk, *Capital and Interest*.

23 Friedrich A. Hayek, *The Pure Theory of Capital*. Chicago, IL: University of Chicago Press, 1941.

24 Hayek, *Monetary Theory and the Trade Cycle*, and Hayek, *Prices and Production*.

25 Israel M. Kirzner, "Roundaboutness, Opportunity, and Austrian Economics," in Martin J. Anderson, ed., *The Unfinished Agenda*. London: Institute of Economic Affairs, 1986, pp. 93–103.

26 Baumol, *Entrepreneurship, Management, and the Structure of Payoffs*, offers a good analysis of the effects of entrepreneurship and the importance of institutions, but in a later work, Baumol, *The Free-Market Innovation Machine*, suggests that entrepreneurship is a minor factor in the production of innovation. Instead, it is the routinized and bureaucratized corporate R&D that is responsible for most economic progress. Needless to say, this book's analysis is at odds with Baumol's 2002 book (but not with the analysis of his 1993 book).

27 Harper, *Entrepreneurship and the Market Process*.

28 However, Randall G. Holcombe, "A Theory of the Theory of Public Goods," *Review of Austrian Economics*, 10, No. 1 (1997), pp. 1–22, questions the idea that the existence of public goods, as defined by neoclassical economics, results in any economic inefficiencies that can be overcome by government intervention.

29 Marshall only used mathematics in the footnotes of his treatise, at least partly so readers not well-versed in mathematics could follow along with his arguments without having to stumble over the mathematics. However, the development of Marshall's ideas tended to be focused on the mathematical formulations in the footnotes rather than the arguments in the text.

8 Institutions and entrepreneurship

1 In the 1990s a strand of the literature on economic growth did focus on the importance of institutions, yet mainstream growth theory still found its main focus on the inputs of human and physical capital, and on technological advances.

2 Hayek, "The Use of Knowledge in Society," pp. 519–530.

3 See William J. Baumol, "Entrepreneurship: Productive, Unproductive, and Destructive," *Journal of Political Economy*, 98, No. 5, Part 1 (October 1990), pp. 893–921. Baumol's book, *Entrepreneurship, Management, and the Structure of Payoffs* extends the same theme. For additional evidence, see Bradley R. Schiller and P.E. Crewson, "Entrepreneurial Origins: A Longitudinal Inquiry," *Economic Inquiry*, 35, No. 3 (1997), pp. 523–531.

4 See, for example, Gordon Tullock, "The Welfare Cost of Tariffs, Monopolies, and Theft," *Western Economic Journal*, 5 (June 1967), pp. 224–232, who explains how the possibility of predation from theft imposes costs on producers and on the economy more generally.

5 Dan Usher, *The Welfare Economics of Markets, Voting, and Predation*. Ann Arbor, MI: University of Michigan Press, 1992, develops a detailed model that describes the inefficiencies that result from this type of social organization.

6 Thomas Hobbes, *Leviathan*. New York: E.P. Dutton, 1950 (orig. 1651).

7 James M. Buchanan, *The Limits of Liberty: Between Anarchy and Leviathan*. Chicago, IL: University of Chicago Press, 1975. Along these same lines, see Usher, *The Welfare Economics of Markets, Voting, and Predation*, cited earlier.

8 Murray N. Rothbard, *For a New Liberty*. New York: Macmillan, 1973, and David Friedman, *The Machinery of Freedom: A Guide to Radical Capitalism*, second edn. La Salle, IL: Open Court Press, 1989.

9 For a detailed discussion about how contractual arrangements can efficiently produce public goods, see Fred Foldvary, *Public Goods and Private Communities: The Market Provision of Social Services*. Brookfield, VT: Edward Elgar, 1994.

10 See Bruce L. Benson, *The Enterprise of Law: Justice Without the State*. San Francisco, CA: Pacific Research Institute, 1990, for a discussion of private police and private court systems. Such a system can be seen firsthand in Guatemala, where government police protection is nearly nonexistent. Neighborhoods, restaurants, stores, hotels, and so forth hire their own armed security guards to protect themselves, and station those guards very visibly in front of their establishments.

11 See Hans-Hermann Hoppe, "The Private Production of Defense," *Journal of Libertarian Studies*, 14, No. 1 (Winter 1998/1999), pp. 27–52, and by the same author, *Democracy: The God that Failed: The Economics and Politics of Monarchy, Democracy, and Natural Order*. New Brunswick, NJ: Transaction Publishers, 2001.

12 See, for examples, Robert Nozick, *Anarchy, State, and Utopia*. New York: Basic Books, 1974; Daniel Sutter, "Asymmetric Power Relations and Cooperation in Anarchy," *Southern Economic Journal*, 61, No. 3 (January 1995), pp. 602–613; and Randall G. Holcombe, "Government: Unnecessary but Inevitable," *The Independent Review*, 8, No. 3 (Winter 2004), pp. 325–342.

13 Somalia has gone for more than a decade – beginning in the early 1990s – without a government, and is often cited as evidence that government is not inevitable and that anarchy is feasible. But because Somalia is poor, with a per capita income of about $200 per year, there is little incentive for opportunists to establish a government there. If it were wealthier, then much like in Russia, mafias would establish themselves to try to extract protection money from productive individuals, and those mafias would likely grow and consolidate over time until they established themselves as a government.

14 See Olson, *Power and Prosperity*. Olson's ideas are further developed in Omar Azfar and Charles A. Cadwell, eds, *Market-Augmenting Government: The Institutional Foundations for Prosperity*. Ann Arbor, MI: University of Michigan Press, 2003 and Stephen Knack, ed., *Democracy, Governance, and Growth*. Ann Arbor, MI: University of Michigan Press, 2003.

15 Landes, *The Wealth and Poverty of Nations*.

16 In an interesting bit of speculation, Martin L. Weitzman, "Hybridizing Growth Theory," *American Economic Review*, 86, No. 2 (May 1996), pp. 207–212, argues that the former Soviet Union took neoclassical growth theory as the foundation for economic policy, and when their continual efforts at increasing output by increasing inputs into their production functions failed, the Soviet economy and government collapsed. The prediction of collapse goes back to Ludwig von Mises, *Socialism*. New Haven, CT: Yale University Press, 1951 (orig. in German, 1922), but the underlying faulty model to which Weitzman refers was not developed until decades later. It is interesting to conjecture that the Soviet Union may have collapsed because its leaders took neoclassical growth theory too seriously.

17 Nobel laureate in economics Samuelson, *Economics*, p. 883, says that while per capita income in the United States was about double (in 1973) that of the Soviet Union, because of their more productive economic system, the Soviet Union would have higher economic growth, and would catch up to the United States in per capita income perhaps as soon as 1990, and almost surely by 2010. See also Krueger, *The Political Economy of Policy Reform in Developing Countries*, who documents the way that development economics has systematically recommended central planning over market systems as the way to create prosperity in less-developed economies, with poor results.

18 That does not stop people from calling for more government interference in the economy, however. At the beginning of the twenty-first century, it is common for people to ask for more government interference in health care markets, and for land use planning. For a discussion of some of these issues and for an analysis of market alternatives, see Randall G. Holcombe, *Public Policy and the Quality of Life*. Westport, CT: Greenwood, 1995.

19 This was not universally true. See, for example, P.T. Bauer, *Dissent on Development: Studies and Debates in Development Economics*. Cambridge, MA: Harvard University Press, 1972.

20 See Scully, "The Institutional Framework and Economic Development," pp. 652–662, and Gerald W. Scully, *Constitutional Environments and Economic Growth*. Princeton, NJ: Princeton University Press, 1992.

21 Scully used the Freedom House index of political rights and civil liberties. The index has been published for a number of years. See, for example, Raymond D. Gastil,

Freedom in the World: Political Rights and Civil Liberties, 1978. New York: Freedom House, 1978.

22 Robert J. Barro, "Democracy and Growth," *Journal of Economic Growth*, 1 (1996), pp. 1–27.

23 A discussion of the beginnings of this project can be found in Stephen T. Easton and Michael A. Walker, *Rating Global Economic Freedom*. Vancouver, BC: Fraser Institute, 1992. The first economic freedom index completed from the project is found in James Gwartney, Robert Lawson, and Walter Block, *Economic Freedom of the World: 1975–1995*. Vancouver, BC: Fraser Institute, 1996, and the index has been updated regularly since then.

24 The original index, in Gwartney, Lawson, and Block, *Economic Freedom of the World: 1975–1995*, had 17 components. The current index is described in James Gwartney and Robert Lawson, *Economic Freedom of the World: 2004 Report*. Vancouver, BC: Fraser Institute, 2004.

25 A review of this literature can be found in Niclas Berggren, "The Benefits of Economic Freedom: A Survey," *The Independent Review*, 8, No. 2 (Fall 2003), pp. 193–211.

26 See James Gwartney, Randall Holcombe, and Robert Lawson, "Economic Freedom, Institutional Quality, and Cross-Country Differences in Income and Growth," *Cato Journal*, 24, No. 3 (Fall 2004). For an earlier analysis using the original economic freedom index, see James Gwartney, Robert Lawson, and Randall Holcombe, "Economic Freedom and the Environment for Economic Growth," *Journal of Institutional and Theoretical Economics*, 155, No. 4 (1999), pp. 643–663.

27 Information on the Economic Freedom Index is taken from Gwartney and Lawson, *Economic Freedom of the World: 2004 Report*, cited earlier.

28 See Baumol, "Entrepreneurship," and *Entrepreneurship, Management, and the Structure of Payoffs*, both cited earlier.

29 This has been a theme of Friedrich Hayek's. See, for example, his "The Use of Knowledge in Society," pp. 519–530. Hayek further argues that business cycles can be caused by monetary fluctuations in *Monetary Theory and the Trade Cycle* and other works.

30 Smith, *The Wealth of Nations*.

31 Hernando de Soto, *The Mystery of Capital: Why Capitalism Triumphs in the West and Fails Everywhere Else*. New York: Basic Books, 2000, argues that this is a key reason why less-developed economies are unable to develop, and blames institutions for preventing well-developed financial markets in those countries.

32 Again, Hernando de Soto, *The Other Path: The Invisible Revolution in the Third World*. New York: Harper & Row, 1989, argues that costly and difficult government regulations in Third World countries stifle entrepreneurship and keep those countries from developing.

33 Krueger, "The Political Economy of the Rent-Seeking Society," pp. 291–303. This idea is earlier found in Tullock, "The Welfare Cost of Tariffs, Monopolies, and Theft," pp. 224–232.

34 See James M. Buchanan, "The Domain of Constitutional Economics," *Constitutional Political Economy*, 1, No. 1 (Winter 1990), pp. 1–18.

35 See, for example, Olson, *The Rise and Decline of Nations*. I have also contributed to this literature, for example in *An Economic Analysis of Democracy* (Carbondale: Southern Illinois University Press, 1985) and *From Liberty to Democracy: The Transformation of American Government* (Ann Arbor, MI: University of Michigan Press, 2002). Olson presents arguments consistent with this section in "Big Bills Left on the Sidewalk," pp. 3–24.

36 Keynes, *The General Theory of Employment, Interest, and Money*, p. 383.

37 Of course, one might think that the transition to socialism was a good idea, in which case the transition back to market institutions in the 1990s was a bad idea. Regardless of one's belief, this example shows that good ideas do not necessarily win in the short run.

38 Academic economists may have an incentive to overstate the importance of human capital because they receive their incomes from the production of education. If academics can convince the population at large of the importance of education, their incomes will rise. Thus, as Holcombe, "A Theory of the Theory of Public Goods," pp. 1–22, notes, one must be inherently suspicious of academics who argue the importance of education.

9 National income accounting and public policy

1 Even consumer surplus is not a perfect measure. One problem is that aggregation requires equating a dollar's worth of consumer surplus for one person with a dollar's worth for another person, raising the issue of interpersonal utility comparisons. Another problem is deciding whether total consumer surplus or per capita consumer surplus would be the goal. If one wanted to raise per capita consumer surplus, killing off less productive people would be a way to accomplish that goal. Maximizing total consumer surplus could point toward policies that would immiserate some in order to produce large consumer surplus gains for others. Thus, while a measure of consumer surplus, if it could be calculated, would be a better measure of national income than GDP, it would still leave much to be desired.

2 See Paul Studenski, *The Income of Nations – Theory, Measurement, and Analysis: Past and Present*. New York: New York University Press, 1958, for a comprehensive history of the development of national income accounting.

3 This theme is found in Robert Higgs, *Crisis and Leviathan: Critical Episodes in the Growth of American Government*. New York: Oxford University Press, 1987.

4 Stephen Skowronek, *Building a New American State: The Expansion of National Administrative Capacities, 1877–1920*. New York: Cambridge University Press, 1982.

5 Guy Alchon, *The Invisible Hand of Planning: Capitalism, Social Science, and the State in the 1920s*. Princeton, NJ: Princeton University Press, 1985.

6 Alchon, *The Invisible Hand of Planning*, p. 17.

7 J. Ronnie Davis, *The New Economics and the Old Economists* (Ames: Iowa State University Press, 1971).

8 See Studenski, *The Income of Nations*, for a good history of national income accounting.

9 Higgs, *Crisis and Leviathan*.

10 Alchon, *The Invisible Hand of Planning*, p. 26.

11 Alchon, *The Invisible Hand of Planning*, p. 61.

12 Alchon, *The Invisible Hand of Planning*, pp. 63–64.

13 Alchon, *The Invisible Hand of Planning*, p. 67.

14 Edgar Z. Palmer, *The Meaning and Measurement of the National Income*. Lincoln, NE: University of Nebraska Press, 1966, p. 31.

15 Francesco Forte and James M. Buchanan, "The Evaluation of Public Services," *Journal of Political Economy* 69, No. 2 (April 1961), pp. 107–121.

16 Even here, some issues arise. Because government often exercises monopoly power in its pricing, it may be that some prices are misstated relative to their market values, but this is a minor point compared to the larger points raised in this section.

17 To balance the national income accounts, taxes can be subtracted from income, because the constitute a transfer from taxpayers to recipients of government goods and services.

18 For evidence, see James Gwartney, Randall Holcombe, and Robert Lawson, "The Scope of Government and the Wealth of Nations," *Cato Journal*, 18, No. 2 (Fall 1998), pp. 163–190.

19 These figures from the *Statistical Abstract of the United States*, 1999 edition.

20 See Sam Peltzman, *Regulation of Pharmaceutical Innovation*. Washington, DC: American Enterprise Institute (1974), and Holcombe, *Public Policy and the Quality of Life*.

21 For an excellent analysis see Armentano, *The Myths of Antitrust, Antitrust and Monopoly*, and *Antitrust Policy*.

22 Smith, *The Wealth of Nations* and Ricardo, *The Principles of Political Economy*. Note that despite the contrasts in Smith's and Ricardo's approach to growth, they shared the policy conclusion that free trade would enhance prosperity. For examples of nineteenth centuries policies limiting regulation, in the United States, the Bank of the United States was abolished in 1836, reducing government's role in monetary affairs, and although government did get involved again to a limited degree as a by-product of financing the War Between the States, the nation remained on a gold standard through the end of the century. Ross Starr, *The Social Transformation of American Medicine* (New York: Basic Books, 1982) reports that while states regulated the medical profession early in the 1800s, this regulation disappeared (only to reappear again late in the century). These two examples are illustrative of a nineteenth century economic policy that was oriented toward fostering entrepreneurship rather than trying to engineer the economy to prosperity.

10 The political environment and entrepreneurship

1 The analysis that follows takes place mainly within the context of representative democracy, but this requirement that others must cooperate for successful political entrepreneurship is true in general. Dictators must have the support of underlings, and bureaucrats are subject to oversight and counterveiling actions, for example, by the courts. See Bruce Bueno de Mesquita *et al.*, *The Logic of Political Survival*. Cambridge, MA: MIT Press, 2003, for a discussion that encompasses the generation of political support in all types of regimes from democracies to dictatorships.

2 See Gary S. Becker, "A Theory of Competition Among Pressure Groups for Political Influence," *Quarterly Journal of Economics*, 98 (1983), pp. 371–400, Donald A. Wittman, "Why Democracies Produce Efficient Results," *Journal of Political Economy*, 97 (1989), pp. 1395–1424, and Donald A. Wittman, *The Myth of Democratic Failure*. Chicago, IL: University of Chicago Press, 1995 for some of the work that lays the foundation for this strand of literature.

3 Peter H. Aaronson, "Electoral Competition and Entrepreneurship," *Advances in Austrian Economics*, 5 (1996), pp. 183–215, notes that political entrepreneurs may have the incentive to create political instability to enhance their electoral opportunities.

4 This chapter sticks closely to the views of Kirzner, *Competition and Entrepreneurship* in its definition of entrepreneurship, as has most of the book up to this point, but includes acting on the entrepreneurial insight as a part of entrepreneurial activity.

5 Ronald H. Coase, "The Problem of Social Cost," *Journal of Law & Economics*, 3 (1960), pp. 1–44.

6 A review of some of this literature (related to ideological voting) is found in Bruce Bender and John R. Lott, Jr, "Legislator Voting and Shirking: A Critical Review of the Literature," *Public Choice*, 87 (1996), pp. 67–100. Bruce Bender, "The Influence of Ideology on Congressional Voting," *Economic Inquiry*, 39 (1991), pp. 416–428, and "A Reexamination of the Principal–Agent Relationship in Politics," *Journal of Public Economics*, 53 (1994), pp. 149–163, notes that there is a substantial opportunity for ideological voting in congress, implying a weak principal–agent link between elected representatives and their constituents. As Gordon Tullock, "Entry Barriers in Politics," *American Economic Review*, 55 (1965), pp. 458–466, W. Mark Crain, "On the Structure and Stability of Political Markets," *Journal of Political Economy*, 85 (1977), pp. 829–842, and W. Mark Crain, Randall G. Holcombe, and Robert D. Tollison, "Monopoly Aspects of Political Parties," *Atlantic Economic Journal*, 7 (1979), pp. 54–48, have noted, this weak link is due to a political market structure that creates barriers to entry into politics, giving elected officials considerable monopoly power.

7 Anthony Downs, *An Economic Theory of Democracy*. New York: Harper & Row, 1957.

8 Hayek, "The Use of Knowledge in Society," pp. 519–530.

9 See Becker, "A Theory of Competition Among Pressure Groups for Political Influence," and Wittman, *The Myth of Democratic Failure*, both cited earlier.

10 William A. Niskanen, "The Opportunities for Political Entrepreneurship," in William A. Niskanen, ed., *Policy Analysis and Public Choice*. Cheltenham, UK: Edward Elgar, 1998, pp. 321–328, analyzes political entrepreneurship within the context of Pareto-improving entrepreneurial opportunities.

11 See Usher, *The Welfare Economics of Markets, Voting, and Predation*, for an excellent discussion of predation by government, and ways that it might be controlled.

12 This predation is often referred to as rent-seeking when it occurs in the public sector. The seminal articles are Gordon Tullock, "The Welfare Costs of Tariffs, Monopolies and Theft," *Western Economic Journal*, 5 (June 1967), pp. 224–232, and Ann O. Krueger, "The Political Economy of the Rent-Seeking Society," *American Economic Review*, 64 (June 1974), pp. 291–303.

13 Governments may often conspire with private sector predators for the benefit of both, and often are lax in enforcing their laws against private sector predation, but this does not change the fact that governments universally view predation as exclusively their domain.

14 Richard A. Musgrave, *The Theory of Public Finance*. New York: McGraw-Hill, 1959.

15 This requires some qualification, as explained in Chapter 4. See also Randall G. Holcombe, "Equilibrium Versus the Invisible Hand," *Review of Austrian Economics*, 12, No. 2 (1999), pp. 227–243, for a discussion of concepts of equilibrium. It is true in the neoclassical setting, however, and is true following Kirzner, *Competition and Entrepreneurship*, cited earlier.

16 See Stanley L. Winer and Walter Hettich, "What is Missed If We Leave Out Collective Choice in the Analysis of Taxation?" *National Tax Journal*, 51 (1998), pp. 373–389, for an application of the approach advocated in Becker's and Wittman's work to the tax system cited in footnote 2. Randall G. Holcombe, "Tax Policy from a Public Choice Perspective," *National Tax Journal*, 51 (1998), pp. 359–371, presents an alternative point of view.

17 Fred S. McChesney, "Rent Extraction and Rent Creation in the Economic Theory of Regulation," *Journal of Legal Studies*, 16 (1987), and *Money for Nothing: Politicians, Rent Extraction, and Political Extortion*. Cambridge, MA: Harvard University Press, 1997.

18 Barry R. Weingast, Kenneth A. Shepsle, and Christopher Johnsen, "The Political Economy of Benefits and Costs: A Neoclassical Approach to Distributive Politics," *Journal of Political Economy*, 89 (1981), pp. 642–664.

19 Many other factors might lead to political instability and the lack of an equilibrium. Roberto Perroti, "Growth, Income Distribution, and Democracy: What the Data Say," *Journal of Economic Growth*, 1, No. 2 (June 1966), pp. 149–187, suggests that income inequality is a potential cause of political instability.

20 Becker, "A Theory of Competition Among Pressure Groups for Political Influence," cited earlier.

21 Some reasons are given by Arthur T. Denzau and Michael C. Munger, "Legislators and Interest Groups: How Unorganized Interests Get Represented," *American Political Science Review*, 80 (1986), pp. 89–106.

22 This argument is persuasively made by Donald Wittman, *The Myth of Democratic Failure*, cited earlier.

23 Anyone who argues that the market underproduces public goods, thus justifying government production, ought to be sympathetic to the idea that political outcomes that are public goods create the same incentives to underproduction.

24 See Gordon Tullock, "Why So Much Stability?" *Public Choice*, 37 (1982), pp. 189–202, for an insightful discussion of the issues. Peter Moser, *The Political Economy of Democratic Institutions*. Cheltenham, UK: Edward Elgar, 2000, especially chs 2 and 3, gives a good overview of the theoretical causes of political instability and the ways that political decision making is stabilized by different institutional arrangements.

25 This strategy is touted in William H. Riker, *The Theory of Political Coalitions*. New Haven, CT: Yale University Press, 1962.

26 Tim Groseclose and James M. Snyder, Jr, "Buying Supermajorities," *American Political Science Review*, 90 (1996), pp. 303–315.

27 Clifford J. Carrubba and Craig Volden, "Coalitional Politics and Logrolling in Legislative Institutions," *American Journal of Political Science*, 44 (2000), pp. 261–277.

28 This is discussed by Peter Kurrild-Klitgaard, *Rational Choice, Collective Action, and the Paradox of Rebellion*. Copenhagen: Institute of Political Science, University of Copenhagen, 1997 and Aaronson, "Electoral Competition and Entrepreneurship," pp. 183–215.

29 However, even if everyone is explicitly included in a political exchange, even the requirement of unanimous approval would not allocate resources the same way as market exchange, as Russell S. Sobel and Randall G. Holcombe, "The Unanimous Voting Rule Is Not the Political Equivalent to Market Exchange," *Public Choice*, 106 (2001), pp. 233–242, argue.

30 Weingast, Shepsle, and Johnsen, "The Political Economy of Benefits and Costs," pp. 642–664.

31 Crain, "On the Structure and Stability of Political Markets," pp. 829–842.

32 Randall G. Holcombe and Glenn R. Parker, "Committees in Legislatures: A Property Rights Perspective," *Public Choice*, 70 (1991), pp. 11–20.

33 Randall G. Holcombe, "Barriers to Entry and Political Competition," *Journal of Theoretical Politics*, 3 (1991), pp. 231–240.

34 Holcombe, *An Economic Analysis of Democracy*, analyzes the competition between incumbents and challengers in more detail.

35 For an elaboration of this idea, see Harold Demsetz, "Why Regulate Utilities?" *Journal of Law & Economics* 11 (1968), pp. 55–65, and Tullock, "Entry Barriers in Politics," pp. 458–466.

36 This is suggested by the well-known model of Downs, *An Economic Theory of Democracy*.

37 Hayek, "The Use of Knowledge in Society," cited earlier.

38 Hobbes, *Leviathan*.

39 Baumol, "Entrepreneurship," pp. 893–921, and *Entrepreneurship, Management, and the Structure of Payoffs*.

11 Conclusion

1 Whether too much equity funding might sometimes be available, causing booms and busts like the stock market boom and crash in the 1920s and the dot.com bubble in the 1990s is a question beyond the scope of this study, but the existence of those bubbles does reinforce the point that equity funding becomes more readily available in an entrepreneurial economy.

2 An interesting biography of Sutton can be found at www.fbi.gov/libref/historic/famcases/sutton/sutton.htm

3 Of course, government policy can thwart this type of progress. Government impediments to genetically engineered crops is an example. In this example, as in many cases,

existing producers have an incentive to use the political process to keep innovators from invading their markets.

4 See Baumol, "Entrepreneurship," pp. 893–921, and *Entrepreneurship, Management, and the Structure of Payoffs*.

5 See Richard Posner, "Taxation By Regulation," *Bell Journal of Economics and Management Science*, 2 (Spring 1971), pp. 22–50.

6 Schumpeter, *Capitalism, Socialism, and Democracy*.

7 See Holcombe, *Public Policy and the Quality of Life*, for a discussion.

8 See, for example, Robert H. Frank, *Luxury Fever: Why Money Fails to Satisfy in an Era of Excess*. New York: Free Press, 1999, who argues that once people's basic needs are taken care of, they judge their well-being by how well off they are relative to their peer group. On this basis, Frank argues for highly progressive taxation which would preserve people's relative income and wealth rankings, and so would make them feel no worse off.

9 A third alternative explanation, not directly discussed in this volume, is that economic progress is determined by geographical factors that may be largely out of a country's direct control. For examples, see Jeffrey D. Sachs, "Tropical Underdevelopment," NBER Working Paper No. w8119, February 2001, and by the same author, "Institutions Don't Rule: Direct Effects of Geography on Per Capita Income," NBER Working Paper No. 9490, February 2003. Jared Diamond, *Guns, Germs, and Steel*. New York: W.W. Norton & Company, 1997, also offers a geographic explanation for differences in development rates across countries. Some evidence weighing against this geographic explanation can be found in Gwartney, Holcombe, and Lawson, "Economic Freedom, Institutional Quality, and Cross-Country Differences in Income and Growth," pp. 205–233.

10 Oskar Lange and Fred M. Taylor, *On the Economic Theory of Socialism*. Minneapolis, MN: University of Minnesota Press, 1938, describe how socialist planners could recreate a market equilibrium and conclude that socialism would be capable of emulating the performance of a market economy, not recognizing that market economies are characterized by continual progress, not static equilibrium. In contrast, Schumpeter, *Capitalism, Socialism, and Democracy*, cited earlier, argues that economic progress is an integral feature of the normal operation of a market economy.

References

Aaronson, Peter H., "Electoral Competition and Entrepreneurship," *Advances in Austrian Economics*, 5 (1996) pp. 183–215.

Alchian, Armen A. and Harold Demsetz, "Production, Information Costs, and Economic Organization," *American Economic Review*, 62 (1972) pp. 777–795.

Alchon, Guy, *The Invisible Hand of Planning: Capitalism, Social Science, and the State in the 1920s*. Princeton, NJ: Princeton University Press, 1985.

Armentano, Dominick T., *The Myths of Antitrust: Economic Theory and Legal Cases*. New Rochelle, NY: Arlington House, 1972.

——, *Antitrust and Monopoly: Anatomy of a Policy Failure*. New York: Wiley, 1982.

——, *Antitrust Policy: The Case for Repeal*. Washington, DC: Cato Institute, 1986.

Arthur, W. Brian, "Competing Technologies, Increasing Returns, and Lock-In by Historical Events," *Economic Journal*, 99 (March 1989) pp. 116–131.

Audretsch, David B. and Maryann P. Feldman, "R&D Spillovers and the Geography of Innovation and Production," *American Economic Review*, 86, No. 3 (June 1996) pp. 630–640.

Azfar, Omar and Charles A. Cadwell, eds, *Market-Augmenting Government: The Institutional Foundations for Prosperity*. Ann Arbor, MI: University of Michigan Press, 2003.

Barro, Robert J., "Democracy and Growth," *Journal of Economic Growth*, 1 (1996) pp. 1–27.

Barro, Robert J. and Xavier Sala-i-Martin, *Economic Growth*. New York: McGraw-Hill, 1995.

Bator, Francis M., "The Simple Analytics of Welfare Maximization," *American Economic Review*, 67 (1957) pp. 22–59.

Bauer, Peter T., *Dissent on Development: Studies and Debates in Development Economics*. Cambridge, MA: Harvard University Press, 1972.

Baumol, William J., "Entrepreneurship: Productive, Unproductive, and Destructive," *Journal of Political Economy*, 98, No. 5, Part 1 (October 1990) pp. 893–921.

——, *Entrepreneurship, Management, and the Structure of Payoffs*. Cambridge, MA: MIT Press, 1993.

——, *The Free-Market Innovation Machine: Analyzing the Growth Miracle of Capitalism*. Princeton, NJ: Princeton University Press, 2002.

Becker, Gary S., "A Theory of Competition Among Pressure Groups for Political Influence," *Quarterly Journal of Economics*, 98 (1983) pp. 371–400.

Bender, Bruce, "The Influence of Ideology on Congressional Voting," *Economic Inquiry*, 39 (1991) pp. 416–428.

Bender, Bruce, "A Reexamination of the Principal–Agent Relationship in Politics," *Journal of Public Economics*, 53 (1994) pp. 149–163.

Bender, Bruce and John R. Lott, Jr, "Legislator Voting and Shirking: A Critical Review of the Literature," *Public Choice*, 87 (1996) pp. 67–100.

Benson, Bruce L., *The Enterprise of Law: Justice Without the State*. San Francisco, CA: Pacific Research Institute, 1990.

Berggren, Niclas, "The Benefits of Economic Freedom: A Survey," *The Independent Review*, 8, No. 2 (Fall 2003) pp. 193–211.

Besanko, David and Ronald R. Braeutigam, *Microeconomics*, 2nd ed. Hoboken, NJ: John Wiley & Sons, 2005.

Besanko, David, David Dranove, Mark Shanley, and Scott Schaefer, *Economics of Strategy*, 3rd ed. Hoboken, NJ: John Wiley & Sons, 2004.

Blanchard, Oliver Jean and Stanley Fischer, *Lectures on Macroeconomics*. Cambridge, MA: MIT Press, 1989.

Boettke, Peter J., "Information and Knowledge: Austrian Economics in Search of its Uniqueness," *Review of Austrian Economics*, 15, No. 4 (December 2002) pp. 263–274.

Bohm-Bawerk, Eugen von, *Capital and Interest*, 3 vols. Spring Hills, PA: Libertarian Press, 1959 (orig. 1884, 1889, 1909).

Boudreaux, Donald J. and Randall G. Holcombe, "The Coasian and Knightian Theories of the Firm," *Managerial and Decision Economics*, 10 (1989) pp. 147–154.

Buchanan, James M., *Cost and Choice: An Inquiry in Economic Theory*. Chicago, IL: Markham, 1969.

——, *The Limits of Liberty: Between Anarchy and Leviathan*. Chicago, IL: University of Chicago Press, 1975.

——, "The Domain of Constitutional Economics," *Constitutional Political Economy*, 1, No. 1 (Winter 1990) pp. 1–18.

Bygrave, William and Maria Minniti, "The Social Dynamics of Entrepreneurship," *Entrepreneurship: Theory and Practice*, 24, No. 3 (2000) pp. 25–36.

Carrubba, Clifford J. and Craig Volden, "Coalitional Politics and Logrolling in Legislative Institutions," *American Journal of Political Science*, 44 (2000) pp. 261–277.

Christensen, Clayton M., *The Innovator's Dilemma*. Boston, MA: Harvard Business School Press, 1997.

Coase, Ronald H., "The Nature of the Firm," *Economica*, 4 (1937) pp. 386–405.

——, "The Problem of Social Cost," *Journal of Law & Economics*, 3 (1960) pp. 1–44.

Collins, Richard L., "On Top," *Flying*, 129, No. 7 (July 2002) pp. 20–27.

Cox, W. Michael and Richard Alm, *The Right Stuff: America's Move to Mass Customization*. Annual Report, Federal Reserve Bank of Dallas, 1998.

——, *Myths of Rich and Poor: Why We're Better Off Than We Think*. New York: Basic Books, 1999.

Crain, W. Mark, "On the Structure and Stability of Political Markets," *Journal of Political Economy*, 85 (1977) pp. 829–842.

Crain, W. Mark, Rrandall G. Holcombe, and Robert D. Tollison, "Monopoly Aspects of Political Parties," *Atlantic Economic Journal*, 7 (1979) pp. 54–48.

Darby, Michael R. and Lynne G. Zucker, "Growing by Leaps and Inches: Creative Destruction, Real Cost Reduction, and Inching Up," *Economic Inquiry*, 41, No. 1 (January 2003) pp. 1–19.

David, Paul A., *Technical Choice, Innovation, and Economic Growth*. Cambridge: Cambridge University Press, 1975.

——, "Clio and the Economics of QWERTY," *American Economic Review*, 75, No. 2 (May 1985) pp. 332–337.

Davis, J. Ronnie, *The New Economics and the Old Economists*. Ames, IA: Iowa State University Press, 1971.

Demsetz, Harold, "Why Regulate Utilities?" *Journal of Law & Economics*, 11 (1968) pp. 55–65.

Denzau, Arthur T. and Michael C. Munger, "Legislators and Interest Groups: How Unorganized Interests Get Represented," *American Political Science Review*, 80 (1986) pp. 89–106.

de Soto, Hernando, *The Other Path: The Invisible Revolution in the Third World*. New York: Harper & Row, 1989.

——, *The Mystery of Capital: Why Capitalism Triumphs in the West and Fails Everywhere Else*. New York: Basic Books, 2000.

Desrochers, Pierre, "Geographical Proximity and the Transmission of Tacit Knowledge," *Review of Austrian Economics*, 14, No. 1 (2001) pp. 25–46.

Diamond, Jared, *Guns, Germs, and Steel*. New York: W.W. Norton & Company, 1997.

Downs, Anthony, *An Economic Theory of Democracy*. New York: Harper & Row, 1957.

Easton, Stephen T. and Michael A. Walker, *Rating Global Economic Freedom*. Vancouver, BC: The Fraser Institute, 1992.

Ferguson, C.E., *Microeconomic Theory*, rev. ed. Homewood, IL: Richard D. Irwin, 1969.

Foldvary, Fred, *Public Goods and Private Communities: The Market Provision of Social Services*. Brookfield, VT: Edward Elgar, 1994.

Forte, Francesco and James M. Buchanan, "The Evaluation of Public Services," *Journal of Political Economy*, 69, No. 2 (April 1961) pp. 107–121.

Frank, Robert H., *Luxury Fever: Why Money Fails to Satisfy in an Era of Excess*. New York: Free Press, 1999.

Friedman, David, *The Machinery of Freedom: A Guide to Radical Capitalism*, 2nd ed. La Salle, IL: Open Court Press, 1989.

Friedman, Milton, *Essays in Positive Economics*. Chicago, IL: University of Chicago Press, 1953.

Galor, Oded and David N. Weil, "Population, Technology, and Growth: From Malthusian Stagnation to the Demographic Transition and Beyond," *American Economic Review*, 90, No. 4 (September 2000) pp. 806–828.

Garrison, Roger W., *Time and Money: The Macroeconomics of Capital Structure*. London: Routledge, 2001.

Gastil, Raymond D., *Freedom in the World: Political Rights and Civil Liberties, 1978*. New York: Freedom House, 1978.

George, Henry, *Progress and Poverty: An Inquiry into the Cause of Industrial Depressions, and of Increase of Want with Increase of Wealth – The Remedy*. London: Kegan Paul, Trench, 1889.

Graaf, J. de V., *Theoretical Welfare Economics*. Cambridge: Cambridge University Press, 1957.

Groseclose, Tim and James M. Snyder, Jr, "Buying Supermajorities," *American Political Science Review*, 90 (1996) pp. 303–315.

Gwartney, James and Robert Lawson, *Economic Freedom of the World: 1997 Report*. Vancouver, BC: Faser Institute, 1997.

Gwartney, James and Robert Lawson, *Economic Freedom of the World: 2004 Report*. Vancouver, BC: Faser Institute, 2004.

Gwartney, James, Robert Lawson, and Walter Block, *Economic Freedom of the World: 1975–1995*. Vancouver, BC: Fraser Institute, 1996.

Gwartney, James, Randall Holcombe, and Robert Lawson, "The Scope of Government and the Wealth of Nations," *Cato Journal*, 18, No. 2 (Fall 1998) pp. 163–190.

Gwartney, James, Robert Lawson, and Randall Holcombe, "Economic Freedom and the Environment for Economic Growth," *Journal of Institutional and Theoretical Economics*, 155, No. 4 (1999) pp. 643–663.

Gwartney, James, Randall Holcombe, and Robert Lawson, "Economic Freedom, Institutional Quality, and Cross-Country Differences in Income and Growth," *Cato Journal*, 24, No. 3 (Fall 2004) pp. 205–233.

Hahn, Frank H., *Equilibrium and Macroeconomics*. Cambridge: Cambridge University Press, 1984.

Harper, David A., *Entrepreneurship and the Market Process: An Enquiry into the Growth of Knowledge*. London and New York: Routledge, 1996.

Hayek, Friedrich A., *Prices and Production*, 2nd ed. New York: Augustus M. Kelley, 1935.

——, "Economics and Knowledge," *Economica*, n.s. 4 (1937) pp. 33–54, reprinted in F.A. Hayek, *Individualism and Economic Order*. London: Routledge and Kegan Paul, 1949.

——, *The Pure Theory of Capital*. Chicago, IL: University of Chicago Press, 1941.

——, "The Use of Knowledge in Society," *American Economic Review*, 35 (1945) pp. 519–530.

——, *Monetary Theory and the Trade Cycle*. New York: Augustus M. Kelley, 1966 (orig. 1933).

Heilbroner, Robert L., *The Making of Economic Society*. New York: Prentice-Hall, 1962.

——, *The Economic Problem*, second edn. Englewood Cliffs, NJ: Prentice-Hall, 1970.

Higgs, Robert, *Crisis and Leviathan: Critical Episodes in the Growth of American Government*. New York: Oxford University Press, 1987.

Hobbes, Thomas, *Leviathan*. New York: E.P. Dutton, 1950 (orig. 1651).

Holcombe, Randall G., *An Economic Analysis of Democracy*. Carbondale, IL: Southern Illinois University Press, 1985.

——, *Economic Models and Methodology*. New York: Greenwood, 1989.

——, "Barriers to Entry and Political Competition," *Journal of Theoretical Politics*, 3 (1991) pp. 231–240.

——, *Public Policy and the Quality of Life*. Westport, CT: Greenwood, 1995.

——, "A Theory of the Theory of Public Goods," *Review of Austrian Economics*, 10, No. 1 (1997) pp. 1–22.

——, "Entrepreneurship and Economic Growth," *Quarterly Journal of Austrian Economics*, 1, No. 2 (Summer 1998) pp. 45–62.

——, "Tax Policy from a Public Choice Perspective," *National Tax Journal*, 51 (1998) pp. 359–371.

——, "Equilibrium Versus the Invisible Hand," *Review of Austrian Economics*, 12, No. 2 (1999) pp. 227–243.

——, *From Liberty to Democracy: The Transformation of American Government*. Ann Arbor, MI: University of Michigan Press, 2002.

——, "Political Entrepreneurship and the Democratic Allocation of Economic Resources," *Review of Austrian Economics*, 15, Nos. 2/3 (June 2002) pp. 143–159.

——, "Information, Entrepreneurship, and Economic Progress," in Roger Koppl, ed., *Advances in Austrian Economics: Austrian Economics and Entrepreneurial Studies*, 6 (2003) pp. 173–195, Amsterdam: JAI.

——, "The Origins of Entrepreneurial Opportunities," *Review of Austrian Economics*, 16, No. 1 (2003) pp. 25–43.

——, "Progress and Entrepreneurship," *Quarterly Journal of Austrian Economics*, 6, No. 3 (Fall 2003) pp. 3–26.

——, "Government: Unnecessary but Inevitable," *The Independent Review*, 8, No. 3 (Winter 2004) pp. 325–342.

Holcombe, Randall G. and Glenn R. Parker, "Committees in Legislatures: A Property Rights Perspective," *Public Choice*, 70 (1991) pp. 11–20.

Hoppe, Hans-Hermann, "The Private Production of Defense," *Journal of Libertarian Studies*, 14, No. 1 (Winter 1998/1999) pp. 27–52.

——, *Democracy: The God that Failed: The Economics and Politics of Monarchy, Democracy, and Natural Order*. New Brusnswick, NJ: Transaction Publishers, 2001.

Ikeda, Sanford, *Dynamics of the Mixed Economy: Toward a Theory of Interventionism*. London: Routledge, 1997.

Jevons, William Stanley, *The Theory of Political Economy*, 4th ed. London: Macmillan, 1931 (1st ed. 1871).

Johnson, D. Gale, "Population, Food, and Knowledge," *American Economic Review*, 90, No. 1 (March 2000) pp. 1–14.

Jones, Larry E. and Rodolfo Manuelli, "A Convex Model of Equilibrium Growth: Theory and Policy Implications," *Journal of Political Economy*, 98, No. 5, Part 1 (October 1990) pp. 1008–1038.

Kaldor, N., "The Irrelevance of Equilibrium Economics," *Economic Journal*, 82 (1972) pp. 1237–1255.

Keynes, John Maynard, *The General Theory of Employment, Interest, and Money*. New York: Harcourt Brace and Company, 1936.

Kirzner, Israel M., *Market Theory and the Price System*. Princeton, NJ: Van Nostrand, 1963.

——, *Competition and Entrepreneurship*. Chicago, IL: University of Chicago Press, 1973.

——, *Perception, Opportunity, and Profit: Studies in the Theory of Entrepreneurship*. Chicago, IL: University of Chicago Press, 1979.

——, *Discovery and the Capitalist Process*. Chicago, IL: University of Chicago Press, 1985.

——, "Roundaboutness, Opportunity, and Austrian Economics," in Martin J. Anderson, ed., *The Unfinished Agenda*. London: Institute of Economic Affairs, 1986, pp. 93–103.

——, *The Meaning of Market Process*. London and New York: Routledge, 1992.

——, "Creativity and/or Alertness: A Reconsideration of the Schumpeterian Entrepreneur," *Review of Austrian Economics*, 11 (1999) pp. 5–17.

Knack, Stephen, "Institutions and the Convergence Hypothesis: The Cross-National Evidence," *Public Choice*, 87, Nos. 3–4 (June 1996) pp. 207–228.

——, ed., *Democracy, Governance, and Growth*. Ann Arbor, MI: University of Michigan Press, 2003.

Knight, Frank H., *Risk, Uncertainty, and Profit*. New York: Harper & Row, 1965 (orig. 1921).

Krueger, Anne O., "The Political Economy of the Rent-Seeking Society," *American Economic Review*, 64 (June 1974) pp. 291–303.

Krueger, Anne O., *The Political Economy of Policy Reform in Developing Countries.* Cambridge, MA: MIT Press, 1993.

Krugman, Paul, "Increasing Returns and Economic Geography," *Journal of Political Economy*, 99, No. 3 (June 1991) pp. 483–499.

Kurrild-Klitgaard, Peter, *Rational Choice, Collective Action, and the Paradox of Rebellion.* Copenhagen: Institute of Political Science, University of Copenhagen, 1997.

Landes, David S., *The Wealth and Poverty of Nations: Why Some Are So Rich and Some So Poor.* New York: W.W. Norton, 1998.

Lange, Oskar and Fred M. Taylor, *On the Economic Theory of Socialism.* Minneapolis, MN: University of Minnesota Press, 1938.

Lewin, Peter, "Hayekian Equilibrium and Change," *Journal of Economic Methodology*, 4 (1997) pp. 245–266.

Lucas, Robert E., Jr, "An Equilibrium Model of the Business Cycle," *Journal of Political Economy*, 83, No. 6 (December 1975) pp. 1113–1144.

——, "On the Mechanics of Economic Development," *Journal of Monetary Economics*, 22 (1988) pp. 3–42.

McChesney, Fred S., "Rent Extraction and Rent Creation in the Economic Theory of Regulation," *Journal of Legal Studies*, 16 (1987) pp. 101–118.

——, *Money for Nothing: Politicians, Rent Extraction, and Political Extortion.* Cambridge, MA: Harvard University Press, 1997.

Malthus, Thomas Robert, *An Essay on Population.* New York: E.P. Dutton, 1914 (orig. 1798).

Marshall, Alfred, *Principles of Economics.* London: Macmillan, 1890.

Menger, Carl, *Principles of Economics.* New York: New York University Press, 1976 (orig. 1871).

Mesquita, Bruce Bueno de, Alastair Smith, Randolph M. Siverson, and James D. Morrow, *The Logic of Political Survival.* Cambridge: MIT Press, 2003.

Minniti, Maria, "Entrepreneurship and Economic Growth," *Global Business and Economic Review*, 11, No. 1 (1999) pp. 31–42.

Mises, Ludwig von, *Socialism.* New Haven, CT: Yale University Press, 1951 (orig. in German, 1922).

——, *The Theory of Money and Credit.* New Haven, CT: Yale University Press, 1953 (orig. in German, 1912).

——, *Human Action*, 3rd rev. ed. Chicago, IL: Henry Regnery Company, 1966.

——, "Monopoly Prices," *Quarterly Journal of Austrian Economics*, 1 (1998) pp. 1–28.

Mitchell, Wesley C., *Business Cycles.* Berkeley, CA: University of California Press, 1913.

Mokyr, Joel, *The Lever of Riches.* Oxford: Oxford University Press, 1990.

——, *The Gifts of Athena: Historical Origins of the Market Economy.* Princeton, NJ: Princeton University Press, 2002.

Moore, Stephen and Julian L. Simon, "The Greatest Century That Ever Was: 25 Miraculous Trends of the Past 100 Years," Cato Institute Policy Analysis No. 364 (December 15, 1999).

Moser, Peter, *The Political Economy of Democratic Institutions.* Cheltenham, UK: Edward Elgar, 2000.

Musgrave, Richard A., *The Theory of Public Finance.* New York: McGraw-Hill, 1959.

Niskanen, William A., "The Opportunities for Political Entrepreneurship," in William A. Niskanen, ed., *Policy Analysis and Public Choice.* Cheltenham, UK: Edward Elgar, 1998, pp. 321–328.

Nozick, Robert, *Anarchy, State, and Utopia*. New York: Basic Books, 1974.

Olson, Mancur, Jr, *The Rise and Decline of Nations*. New Haven, CT: Yale University Press, 1982.

——, "Big Bills Left on the Sidewalk: Why Some Nations are Rich, Others Poor," *Journal of Economic Perspectives*, 10, No. 2 (Spring 1996) pp. 3–24.

——, *Power and Prosperity: Outgrowing Communist and Capitalist Dictatorships*. New York: Basic Books, 2000.

Palmer, Edgar Z., *The Meaning and Measurement of the National Income*. Lincoln, NE: University of Nebraska Press, 1966.

Peltzman, Sam, *Regulation of Pharmaceutical Innovation*. Washington, DC: American Enterprise Institute, 1974.

Perotti, Roberto, "Growth, Income Distribution, and Democracy: What the Data Say," *Journal of Economic Growth*, 1, No. 2 (June 1996) pp. 149–187.

Posner, Richard, "Taxation by Regulation," *Bell Journal of Economics and Management Science*, 2 (Spring 1971) pp. 22–50.

Quah, Danny T., "Convergence Empirics Across Economies with (Some) Capital Mobility," *Journal of Economic Growth*, 1, No. 1 (March 1996) pp. 95–124.

Ricardo, David, *The Principles of Political Economy*, 3rd ed. London: J.M. Dent, 1912 (orig. 1821).

Richardson, G.B., "Adam Smith on Competition and Increasing Returns," in Andrew S. Skinner and Thomas Wilson, eds, *Essays on Adam Smith*. Oxford: Clarendon Press, 1975, pp. 350–360.

Riker, William H., *The Theory of Political Coalitions*. New Haven, CT: Yale University Press, 1962.

Romer, Paul M., "Increasing Returns and Long-Run Growth," *Journal of Political Economy*, 94 (1986) pp. 1002–1037.

——, "Endogenous Technological Change," *Journal of Political Economy*, 98, No. 5, Part 2 (October 1990) pp. S71–S102.

Rothbard, Murray N., "Toward a Reconstruction of Utility and Welfare Economics," in Mary Sennholz, ed., *On Freedom and Free Enterprise: Essays in Honor of Ludwig von Mises*. Princeton, NJ: Van Nostrand, 1956, pp. 224–262.

——, *Man, Economy, and State*. Los Angeles, CA: Nash, 1962.

——, *For a New Liberty*. New York: Macmillan, 1973.

Sachs, Jeffrey D., "Tropical Underdevelopment," NBER Working Paper No. w8119, February 2001.

——, "Institutions Don't Rule: Direct Effects of Geography on Per Capita Income," NBER Working Paper No. 9490, February 2003.

Samuelson, Paul A., *Economics*, 9th ed. New York: McGraw-Hill, 1973.

Samuelson, Paul A. and Robert M. Solow "Analytical Aspects of Antiinflation Policy," *American Economic Review*, 50 (1960) pp. 177–194.

Schiller, Bradley R. and P.E. Crewson, "Entrepreneurial Origins: A Longitudinal Inquiry," *Economic Inquiry*, 35, No. 3 (1997) pp. 523–531.

Schumpeter, Joseph A., *The Theory of Economic Development*. Cambridge, MA: Harvard University Press, 1934.

——, *Business Cycles: A Theoretical, Historical, and Statistical Analysis of the Capitalist Process*. New York: McGraw-Hill, 1939.

——, *Capitalism, Socialism, and Democracy*, 2nd ed. London: George Allen & Unwin, 1947.

Scully, Gerald W., "The Institutional Framework and Economic Development," *Journal of Political Economy*, 96 (1988) pp. 652–662.

——, *Constitutional Environments and Economic Growth*. Princeton, NJ: Princeton University Press, 1992.

Shapiro, Carl and Hal R. Varian. *Information Rules: A Strategic Guide to the Network Economy*. Boston, MA: Harvard Business School Press, 1999.

Skowronek, Stephen, *Building a New American State: The Expansion of National Administrative Capacities, 1877–1920*. New York: Cambridge University Press, 1982.

Smith, Adam, *An Inquiry Into the Nature and Causes of the Wealth of Nations*. New York: Modern Library, 1937 (orig. 1776).

Sobel, Russell S. and Randall G. Holcombe, "The Unanimous Voting Rule Is Not the Political Equivalent to Market Exchange," *Public Choice*, 106 (2001) pp. 233–242.

Solow, Robert M., "A Contribution to the Theory of Economic Growth," *Quarterly Journal of Economics*, 70 (1956) pp. 65–94.

Starr, Paul, *The Social Transformation of American Medicine*. New York: Basic Books, 1982.

Stigler, George J. and Gary S. Becker, "De Gustibus Non Est Desputandum," *American Economic Review*, 67, No. 2 (1977): 76–90.

Stiglitz, Joseph E., "The Causes and Consequences of the Dependence of Quality on Price," *Journal of Economic Literature*, 25 (1987) pp. 1–48.

——, *Whither Socialism?* Cambridge, MA: MIT Press, 1994.

Studenski, Paul, *The Income of Nations – Theory, Measurement, and Analysis: Past and Present*. New York: New York University Press, 1958.

Sutter, Daniel, "Asymmetric Power Relations and Cooperation in Anarchy," *Southern Economic Journal*, 61, No. 3 (January 1995) pp. 602–613.

Tullock, Gordon, "Entry Barriers in Politics," *American Economic Review*, 55 (1965) pp. 458–466.

——, "The Welfare Cost of Tariffs, Monopolies, and Theft," *Western Economic Journal*, 5 (June 1967) pp. 224–232.

——, "Why So Much Stability?" *Public Choice*, 37 (1982) pp. 189–202.

Usher, Dan, *The Welfare Economics of Markets, Voting, and Predation*. Ann Arbor, MI: University of Michigan Press, 1992.

Varian, Hal R. *Intermediate Microeconomics: A Modern Approach*, 6th ed. New York: W.W. Norton, 2003.

Wallace, Lane, "December 18, 1903: The Morning and Era After," *Flying*, 130, No. 12 (December 2003) pp. 64–68.

Walras, Leon, *Elements of Pure Economics; or The Theory of Social Wealth*. Translated by William Jaffe. Homewood, IL: R.D. Irwin, 1954 (orig. 1874).

Weingast, Barry R., Kenneth A. Shepsle, and Christopher Johnsen, "The Political Economy of Benefits and Costs: A Neoclassical Approach to Distributive Politics," *Journal of Political Economy*, 89 (1981) pp. 642–664.

Weitzman, Martin L., "Hybridizing Growth Theory," *American Economic Review*, 86, No. 2 (May 1996) pp. 207–212.

Williamson, Oliver E., "A Comparison of Alternative Approaches to Economic Methodology," *Journal of Institutional and Theoretical Economics*, 146, No. 1 (1990) pp. 61–71.

Winer, Stanley L. and Walter Hettich, "What is Missed If We Leave Out Collective Choice in the Analysis of Taxation?" *National Tax Journal*, 51 (1998) pp. 373–389.

Wittman, Donald A., "Why Democracies Produce Efficient Results," *Journal of Political Economy*, 97 (1989) pp. 1395–1424.

——, *The Myth of Democratic Failure*. Chicago, IL: University of Chicago Press, 1995.

Young, Allyn, "Increasing Returns and Economic Progress," *Economic Journal*, 38 (December 1928) pp. 527–542.

Young, Alwyn, "Invention and Bounded Learning by Doing," *Journal of Political Economy*, 101, No. 3 (June 1993) pp. 443–472.

Index